AMERICAN PRINCE(SS), AMERICAN PAUPER
THE CONTEMPORARY VICE PRESIDENCY AND PRESIDENTIAL RELATIONS, 3D. ED.

MARIE D. NATOLI

outskirts
press

TO MY TWO SETS OF PARENTS:
Carmela and Frank Natoli, my mother and father
and
Mary and Ferro Mingardi, my aunt and uncle
and to
My son, Jonathan Alexander Natoli, whom I hope
will grow into a caring young man with fond
memories of his parents, aunts, and uncles

TABLE OF CONTENTS

Acknowledgements   i

Preface   iii

Introduction: "His Superfluous Excellency"   ix

1   The Vice President's Constitutional Functions: An Overview   1

2   Vice Presidential Selection: Choosing The Heir Apparent   18

3   The Vice Presidency As A Stepping Stone   92

4   The Vice President As Heir Apparent   134

5   The Role Of The Modern Vice Presidency:
    Growth Of The Alter Ego   171

6   The Vice Presidency:
    The Impact of Events and Personalities   235

Appendix A "Civil Rights And Rioting"   263

Appendix B   265

Chapter Notes   267

ACKNOWLEDGEMENTS

Any successful work has a great variety of people behind its author. Some of my early influences are among the most important and deserve considerable thanks: The late Dr. Nancy Dean, Professor Emeritus, of Hunter College's English Department, who not only taught me how to write (even though I still use more dashes than she would probably like) but who was and always will be a role model and friend; the late Professor Robert S. Hirschfield of Hunter College's Political Science Department, with whom I first studied the American Presidency and who is responsible for instilling in me my continuing excitement about the subject; and the late Professor Robert R. Robbins of Tufts University, who guided my early studies of the Vice Presidency and was one of the most loving and genuinely caring individuals anyone could know.

Supportive friends are essential in both the highs and lows of the many stages of research and writing, and I am fortunate in having more than my fair share of them. Especially important to the first edition of this work were (in no order other than alphabetical): Bill Adams; Peter Cohen; Jean Cummiskey; Curt Martin; Lenore G. Martin; Elizabeth Moesel; Janet Morahan; Page Morahan; Nancy Sandman; Michael St. Clair; Jennifer Tebbe; and Rosemary Tobin.

For the second and third editions of this work, I am especially appreciative of these friends (again, in alphabetical order): Edward Bernald; Catherine S. Bueker; Joyce Caruso; Jean Cummiskey; Florencia Gabriele; Joy Graw; Louise Hogan; Rita Kalil; William Leonard; Javier Marion; Lenore G, Martin; Elizabeth Moesel; Melanie Murphy; Jonathan Alexander Natoli; the Joseph and Vincent Natoli families; Patricia Packard; Patricia Rosen; Lynne Rosenburg; Kathryn M. Severson; Trish Tower; Ashley Tyler; Petros Vamvakas and Fr. James Woods, SJ.

For the third edition of this work, very special thanks go to my immediate family: Kathryn M. Severson and Jonathan A. Natoli, who put up with all of the time and energy I put into this work and who love me despite that fact.

I shall always be grateful for the help provided by the archivists at the presidential libraries I had the opportunity to visit, especially Jo August and Donna Smerlas of the John F. Kennedy Library and Mike Gillette of the Lyndon B. Johnson Library.

Many colleagues at the Center for the Study of the Presidency and on the Editorial Board of the Center's publication *The Presidential Studies Quarterly* encouraged my work on the Vice Presidency. Special thanks go to the late Dr. R. Gordon Hoxie, former President of the Center; the late Ambassador Ruth Farkas (ret.), former Chair of the Board of Trustees of the Center, and Dr. Ken Davison, former Book Review Editor of the Quarterly.

Colleagues, administrators and staff at Emmanuel College have been of immeasurable support. Special thanks go to Sr. Janet Eisner, SND, Ph.D., President of Emmanuel College and to Sr. Anne Mary Donovan, SND, Treasurer of Emmanuel College for their continuing efforts to support faculty research.

Last, but not least, a special thanks to several student assistants at Emmanuel College: Andrew Ammon, Carlo Faccini, Douglas Gillum, Mia Steupert. Their assistance and moral support were invaluable.

PREFACE

The Vice Presidency is a unique institution and has long been a focal point of constitutional concern. Its functions are unclear and ill-defined; yet as the institution "a heartbeat away" from the Presidency, it is pivotal in maintaining continuity and stability. Since World War II, the power of the United States has expanded rapidly, and its government has been buffeted by many grave challenges, both foreign and domestic. Presidential continuity and stability have been seriously challenged on more than one occasion, and political turmoil has heightened controversy regarding the second highest office in the land.

Political scientists and historians generally acknowledge that the Roosevelt years mark the beginning of the "modern" Presidency and Vice Presidency. As proof, they point to the enormous social and political changes emanating from that period:

- The abandonment of an isolationist foreign policy that contributed to the growth of the Presidency inasmuch as the President has the inherent power to deal with the heads of other nations and to suggest the agenda for relations with those nations;
- The technological advances within the mass media – particularly broadcasting during President Franklin D. Roosevelt's incumbency and his astute use of radio, with subsequent

Presidents using increasingly evolving media technology including television, the internet, exponentially expanding forms of social media -- which marked the development and continued growth of the "personal" Presidency;

- The secret development of atomic weapons during the Roosevelt years, which made the Presidency the advocate of weapons use and control and the ultimate decision-maker;
- The shift in federal-state relations as a result of the Great Depression, with a growth in the demand for federal involvement in problem-solving and program development and an increased role of the federal government as a whole;
- The Congress's "abdication" to the Presidency of the initiative in problem-solving and program development as a result of the Depression, beginning the growth of the "institutionalized" Presidency.

It is logical that, as the Presidency grew, that growth would extend to the Vice Presidency.

It must be stressed at the outset of this work what this book is about and what it is not about.

This study probes the nature and development of the modern Vice Presidency by focusing on the period from the end of World War II to the present and following a *thematic rather than a chronological or biographical approach.* Among the areas examined are the selection of vice presidential candidates; the development of the Vice Presidency as a stepping stone to the Presidency; the contemporary usages of the Vice Presidency and the double-edged sword of disability and succession to the Presidency; the role of presidential and vice presidential backgrounds and personalities in shaping the Vice President's role; the importance of White House staff and circumstances -- political, domestic, and international -- in the workings of a particular Vice Presidency. So, for those readers expecting that every Vice President since John Adams will be included here, stop reading now. Recall that the time frame of this work begins with the end of the FDR Presidency and the Truman succession following Roosevelt's death. Occasionally, reference will be made to earlier incumbents of the office, but they are not the focus of this work. Relatedly, biographical works on Vice Presidents abound. Indeed, this is the very reason for the thematic approach in this work. Readers need a *generic* statement about the nature of the office, and the way to achieve this is through the exploration of themes contributing to the essence of the office. This work places the functioning of the Vice Presidency as a constitutional institution within the framework of all of the above as well as structural development.

A salient characteristic of the Vice Presidency is that, while it is the only nationally elected office besides the Presidency itself, it is simultaneously void of any significant ongoing constitutional functions and is almost entirely subject to presidential whim for its activity and growth. Certainly, circumstances have from time to time focused renewed attention on the second office, as has been true in the three instances of succession since World War II: Harry S. Truman in 1945; Lyndon B. Johnson in 1963; and Gerald R. Ford in 1974. And the office received attention during the controversy surrounding the Monica Lewinsky scandal during the Clinton Administration, with impeachment potentially in the President's future and again, received attention very early during the Trump Administration, with cries for impeachment of the controversial 45th President and the potential succession of his Vice President, Mike Pence.

Delving into each instance of actual succession, this study reveals the particular patterns which these Vice Presidents followed in succeeding to the Presidency, both in terms of problems encountered and policies followed. It also serves as a guide of sorts in terms of what might be expected should future successions from the second to the first office occur. Because the approach in this study is thematic rather than biographical or chronological, occasional repetition of points and issues may occur. Similarly, selective case studies are used in greater depth and material of related interest is introduced as appropriate.

Attention has also been focused on the Vice Presidency as a source of presidential aspiration. Beginning with the development of the second office during Richard Nixon's incumbency, the Vice Presidency has consistently been in the national limelight of presidential politics. Each Vice President since that time has either become a presidential candidate or been the object of speculation for such a candidacy, except for Vice President Richard ("Dick") Cheney under President George W. Bush. Cheney's unusual circumstances of age and especially poor health opened the field to would-be Republican presidential candidates who would most likely have otherwise been deterred to compete with the "heir apparent." But the very fact that circumstances speaks to the prominence of the Vice Presidency as a stepping stone to the nomination. Similarly, the Vice Presidency of Joe Biden would have been a stepping stone to the presidential nomination in 2016 but for two factors – the prominence of Hillary Clinton who emerged as the frontrunner following her 2008 nomination defeat to Barack Obama combined with the tragic death of Vice President Biden's beloved son, Beau, following which the Vice President announced that he would not seek the presidency while he and his family were in mourning. Even so, the name Joe Biden is prominently spoken of as a potential challenger to a Trump re-election in 2020.

A peculiar dilemma yet understandable has become associated with the phenomenon of the Vice Presidency as a stepping stone to the presidential nomination. Two incumbent Vice Presidents (Nixon in 1960 and Humphrey in 1968) who served as their party's standard bearer suffered defeat primarily because of their association with the programs of the President under whom they served. And in the 1984 presidential election, former Vice President Walter Mondale – despite a four-year hiatus since he was a member of the Carter Administration – found it almost impossible to dissociate himself from negative images of that Presidency. And Vice President Al Gore, while having won the popular vote in the 2000 presidential election, suffered a defeat in the Electoral College. Problems of the Clinton Administration, many observers felt, contributed to Gore's not being able to conduct a campaign that would have given him a decisive victory, although he did win a majority of the popular vote.

As more prominent individuals have accepted nomination to the second office and as more and more duties, especially within the areas of foreign affairs and domestic campaigning, have been assigned to the Vice President, a new role has emerged: the Vice President as "administration spokesperson." This role reached its zenith with Vice President Spiro Agnew, but all modern Vice Presidents have had to fulfill it to varying degrees. Richard Nixon provided such a service for President Eisenhower, and Hubert Humphrey, in his defense of President Johnson's Vietnam War policies, served the function well. Interestingly, during the controversy concerning who rightfully won Florida's electoral votes in the 2000 election, it was running mate Dick Cheney who was typically in the forefront of the debate, with the presidential candidate taking a back seat. And Vice President Mike Pence has had to put aside his own views as he supports and defends President Trump's actions and policies.

The office, then, has evolved in terms of both statutory (for example, the Vice President is a member of the Cabinet and the National Security Council, thanks to President Harry S. Truman) and contemporary events and exigencies. Until the middle of the twentieth century, the office offered little more than ceremonial responsibilities, and the President determined what duties what Vice President had. The twentieth century was kinder to Vice Presidents, and yet whatever duties a Vice President assumes remain up to the President; the 21st century Vice Presidency – even Dick Cheney's – remains the province of presidential need and willingness to assign roles.

Nonetheless, nine Vice Presidents have succeeded to the Presidency upon the death or resignation of a President, and several others have come close to succeeding. George Herbert Walker Bush might very well have become President in the wake of the assassination attempt on President Ronald Reagan in March of 1981. In these respects, the Vice Presidency is both a prince and a pauper; the heir apparent and yet a person who often goes "begging" for a role. Subsequent chapters explore the paradox of these roles and concentrate on the modern Vice Presidency since 1945.

INTRODUCTION
"HIS SUPERFLUOUS EXCELLENCY"

"You're not going to take it, are you?" —
    Grace Coolidge to her husband, Calvin, after he was
    nominated for vice president in 1920.

"I suppose I'll have to." — Coolidge's reply. He became
president upon Warren Harding's death in 1923.

Our first Vice Presidents were actually runners-up for the Presidency. From 1788 until the adoption of the Twelfth in 1804, the Electors or each state cast *two* votes for the office of President and none for the office of Vice President, since the Framers of the Constitution had provided that the second highest vote getter would serve as Vice President. A Vice President was necessary, they felt, in the event of the President's death, disability, resignation, or impeachment.

In a sense, then the Electors ignored the office of Vice President -- and the qualifications necessary to hold it. Each Elector voting for his candidates was unable to designate which he preferred to be President, although the method insured that a person of high caliber and renown would be selected for the second office. But a negative outcome was also possible, and this occurred with the election of 1800, which marked a crucial turning-point for the Vice Presidency.

In that election, Thomas Jefferson and Aaron Burr, both of the Republican Party, received an equal number of electoral votes for the Presidency. This, according to the Constitution, sent the election to the House of Representatives. The Federalists attempted, but failed, to have Burr or a Federalist elected to the Presidency by soliciting a few Republican votes. Jefferson, however, was chosen President, and Burr, as provided by the Constitution, became his Vice President.1

Even though Jefferson and Burr had received the same number of electoral votes, members of the Republican Party did not consider Burr a desirable choice for the Presidency; in fact, he was considered dangerous. Thus, what was perceived as a narrow escape revived interest in separate votes for each office, and my May 1802 an amendment had been passed in the House of Representatives to this effect.2 By no means were opinions unanimous for either the necessity or the virtue of the change, and the opinions of the opponents contained a good deal of prophecy. The two major arguments in opposition were that, first, contrary to the intention of the Framers of the Constitution that the Vice Presidency go to someone qualified for the Presidency, the Twelfth Amendment did no such thing, but merely gave it to someone specifically chosen for the inferior spot. Clearly, the argument ran, this would not ensure the election of "fit men" and would "degrade the Vice Presidency.3

The second objection was based on fears that residents of the smaller states would be discriminated against in seeking the office of the Presidency. The debate became so heated that at one point an amendment was introduced (but defeated) for the abolition of the Vice Presidency. When the opposing sides finally lined up, fears for the stature of the Vice Presidency and for the influence of the smaller states were fare outweighed by fears of a repetition of the crisis and near calamity of the initial results of the election of 1800.4 The vice presidential election was thus established.

To a far larger extent, the fears of those who opposed the Twelfth

Amendment were realized, and the caliber of the individuals holding the Vice Presidency changed considerably. phenomenon would not change until the period of the modern Vice Presidency. And additional impact of the electoral change was the subjection of the Vice Presidency to the bartering of the political marketplace.

The early (pre-Twelfth Amendment) Vice Presidents possessed much more independent energy than did many of their obscure successors. As the next highest vote-getter for President, the Vice President was obviously a rival of the top vote-getter. As Vice President, this rivalry continued, and the Vice President often assumed the leadership of the President's opposition.

It is little wonder, then, that President George Washington chose to exclude his Vice President, John Adams, a highly, prestigious, eminent figure, from Cabinet deliberations. Both despite and because of the Vice President's role as an opposition party leader and administration critic, the executive role of the Vice President was insignificant, even when performed by the likes of Adams.

The Vice Presidency was regarded as so insignificant that Adams once dubbed the incumbent of the office "His Superfluous Excellency" and Daniel Webster refused to accept the nomination as Zachary Taylor's running mate, saying "I do not choose to be buried until I am really dead."**5** Henry Clay, resenting having been chose for second place, twice turned down offers of the nomination, first on the William Henry Harrison ticket and later with Taylor. Ironically, both Harrison and Taylor died in office. And once Vice President, John C.Calhoun, resigned the office in favor of a Senate seat.**6**

In one respect, little changed after the adoption of the Twelfth Amendment. Although the Vice President was not voted for as Vice President, it usually happened that the position, as the Framers had feared, was parceled out to a member of a competing faction with the presidential nominee's party. But one important element must be noted. Unlike pre-Twelfth Amendment elections, the vice presidential nominee, chosen for second place (and with the development of the political party system, running in "partnership" with the presidential nominee) was more bound up with and indebted to the number one on the ticket. And he/she was subject as ever to presidential whim in terms of the jobs assigned.

The Framers' view the Vice Presidency as the solution to numerous controversies at the Constitutional Convention: namely the need to provide someone fit to take over for a deceased, disabled, impeached or resigned President; to alleviate the smaller states' fears that they might be discriminated against in the election of a President (the solution of Electors cast two ballots, one of which *had* to be for a candidate from a state other than their own, was a compromise); and, lastly, to have an objective presiding officer of the Senate who would decide a question in the event of a tie. With this consideration uppermost, little thought was given to what the Vice President's day-to-day functions would be. This latter function nonetheless created constitutional controversy at the Convention, for many delegates feared that the executive branch would thereby gain a foothold in the legislature. Judging from some of their strong misgivings about the Vice President's role in the Senate, it is evident that they had expected him to be quite active in it. On the contrary, the history of the office has revealed that the Vice President as President of the Senate has never presented any serious threat of executive infiltration of the legislature.

One function of the Vice Presidency that the Framers undoubtedly did not foresee was its used as a graveyard to which competitors or troublesome creatures might be relegated. Probably the most blatant instance of this use was in the selection of Theodore Roosevelt as William McKinley's running mate. McKinley, as far as the party bosses were concerned, was to see to it that Roosevelt behave himself. They might have tried it on a less dynamic individual. Needless to add, Teddy Roosevelt succeeded to the Presidency upon McKinley's assassination. There is some speculation (as Chapter 1 explains) that Lyndon Johnson was chosen as John F. Kennedy's running mate for precisely this reason -- that Johnson as Vice President might have been far less dangerous to Kennedy than as Majority Leader. As with the Roosevelt succession following McKinley, the irony is that Lyndon Johnson, too, became President.

Chapter 1

THE VICE PRESIDENT'S
CONSTITUTIONAL FUNCTIONS:
AN OVERVIEW

*"It's an awkward office. You've got two left feet, most of
the time trying to walk a straight line – not getting into
the President's hair, or getting into the business of the
Senate, and yet you are in both of these."*
Hubert H. Humphrey

"TWO LEFT FEET... ON A TIGHT ROPE"

MOST OBSERVERS WOULD suggest that the most crucial function of the
office of Vice President is to succeed to the Presidency. While increased
awareness of the Vice President as "a heartbeat away" from the Presidency
has occurred as a result of the nine instances of vice presidential succession, the Founding Fathers were actually more concerned that there be

a presiding office of the Senate who would serve to break a tie vote. The Framers did not want to vest this power in a member of the Senate, since that would give that senator two votes. Thus, since the Vice President seemed to be "without employment," that office was available.

The first Vice President, John Adams, apparently became far more involved in Senate debates than would most of his successors. Adams saw his role as an activist one, and he often "played the schoolmaster."[1] Later Vice Presidents tended to limit their involvement to parliamentary questions, although John C. Calhoun occasionally sent correspondence to senators regarding his point of view.[2]

Few incumbents of the early Vice Presidency were the likes of Adams and Calhoun, and this was particularly so following the enactment of the Twelfth Amendment. Incumbents of the second office soon learned that a Vice President must conform to the nature and personality of the U.S. Senate. Few statements capture this fact as well as that made by Vice President Calvin Coolidge.

> Presiding over the Senate was fascinating to me. That branch of the Congress has its own methods and traditions, which may strike the outsiders as peculiar, but more familiarity with them would disclose that they are only what long experience has demonstrated to be the best methods of conducting its business. It may seem that debate is endless, but there is scarcely a time when it is not informing, and… the power to compel due consideration is the distinguishing mark of a deliberative body. If the Senate is anything it is a great deliberative body.[3]

The unanticipated development of the Vice President's role as Presiding Officer of the Senate has produced an anachronism. Very little of any Vice President's time is spent in the Senate. Although he or she is entitled to preside over the Senate without vote "unless they be equally divided," the President Pro Tempore of the Senate is the usual

presiding office. Furthermore, it might well be regarded as an imperti-
nence should a Vice President attempt to utilize influence on and off
the Senate floor, especially within the confines of his or her own party.
In recent decades, Presidents and Vice Presidents have come increasingly from the legislative branch rather than from the governors' mansions, the earlier source. This might suggest that the flow of influence
between a Vice President and his or her former colleagues in the Senate
is significant- but quite to the contrary, for the environment in which
the Vice President moves militates against such operations.

In recent years, as the Vice President has received more and more
assignments from the President, the second office has moved more fully
into the executive branch. The original constitutional job of the office
has atrophied and has little significance today. There may, for example,
be an occasional tie vote or a parliamentary ruling advantageous to the
administration. Business of this sort makes very little demand on the
Vice President to spend time on Capitol Hill.

Vice Presidents suffer from being subject to both the nature of the
institution over which they are intended to preside and to the exigencies of the Presidency and its staff. Straddling the executive and legislative branches, the Vice President is regarded as an outsider in the
Senate, which has had no choice in his selection as presiding officer.[4]
And even if the Vice President is a former member of the upper house,
it matters little how strong or lengthy a legislative background he has
had or how well liked he has been as a legislator. A "once you're out,
you're out" rule is long established and pervades the Senate's attitude
toward the Vice President, a reflection in part of the institutional conflict between Congress and the White House.[5]

At the other end of Pennsylvania Avenue, the Vice President who
attempts to arm twist on behalf of the administration's legislative program finds himself dealt with sternly by a legislative body that prides
itself on its independence. Spiro Agnew, the first Vice President in recent years without legislative experience, had to discover this and never
recovered from the blow.

Agnew knew little of the Senate - its style, its customs, its view of acceptable behavior. In his early days in the Vice Presidency, he attempted to compensate for his legislative ignorance by spending a good deal of time on Capitol Hill, mingling and talking with senators, eating with them in their dining room.**6** Early on, however, he made a critical mistake. At the request of the White House in July 1969, Agnew attempted to solidify what was feared to be waning Republican support of the administration's surtax extension. His timing was faulty; ignorant of Senate custom, he tried to buttonhole potentially recalcitrant senators just as a roll call was about to be taken. This prompted one senator, Len Jordan of Idaho, to formulate the notorious "Jordan Rule." He told Agnew he has planned to vote for the extension but that the Vice President's behavior had convinced him to vote in the opposite direction. At the next Republican senators' weekly meeting, Jordan postulated a rule: always vote the other way if the Vice President dares to lobby a senator on the floor.**7** Jordan later remarked, "It worked, too."**8**

The Jordan incident marked the end of Agnew's attempt to have a positive role in the legislature, and thereafter he spent considerably less time on Capitol Hill.**9** As Agnew became increasingly vocal in lashing out at administration critics, he again ran up against Senate form, especially in his attempt to purge the Senate of liberals in both parties. His success in ridding the administration of Senator Charles Goodell during the campaign of 1970 continued to evoke hostility from even his fellow Republicans in the Senate.**10** The November 1969 *Economist* quoted Republican senators as saying, following Agnew's New Orleans speech in which he had lashed out against "an effete corps of impudent snobs," that "effete is what Spiro puts in his mouth."**11** Agnew did not have the long-standing relationships that former Senator Hubert Humphrey had had. Moreover, he had trampled on established codes of behavior.

Lyndon Johnson, in moving from the legislative to the executive branch, might well have appreciated how strongly his former colleagues in the Senate felt about executive intrusion into the legislature when the "clubbishness" of which he had been such a vital part in the past was about to backfire on him. Johnson, it seems, had fully expected to continue to play a significant role in the inner workings of the Senate Democratic Party.12 In January 1961, as the Democratic senators caucused in order to set up the machinery of government, Johnson expected to participate, and possibly preside, as was suggested by the new Majority Leader, Mike Mansfield. The senators, much to Johnson's surprise, reacted hostilely: Johnson would be permitted to sit in on the caucuses, but by no means would he be allowed to run the show with the new Majority Leader as merely titular leader.13 Johnson thus experienced the application of the "once you're out, you're out" rule, and this hostility on the part of fellow Democrats came as a blow to him.14 "He could no longer snap his fingers," remarked one senator.15 Although he "got some things done, he wasn't able to crack the whip. ... He didn't have as much to trade as Vice President as he had had as Majority Leader,"16 and he found himself "walking an awful [sic] thin tightrope."

Following his "defeat" in the Democratic caucus, Lyndon Johnson did not attempt very much legislative work. A very sensitive man, despite outward appearances, he preferred not to attempt an active legislative role. LBJ aide Walter Jenkins commented that everyone had expected Johnson to be errand boy, but Johnson shied away from a liaison role with Congress. Johnson, reported Jenkins, would probably never have refused a Kennedy request, but he did not really want to be liaison man.18 Arthur Schlesinger, Jr., in discussing Johnson's rejection by the Democratic caucus, has maintained that "the incident reduced his usefulness on the Hill. Once the necromancer had left his senatorial seat, the old black magic evidently lost some of its power."19

Kennedy's own predisposition worked against a legislative role for a Vice President who had been the most powerful man in Congress shortly before assuming the Vice Presidency. Kennedy viewed the relationship between Congress and the White House differently than

President Johnson would. Kennedy took much more of a "separation of powers" attitude than Johnson who, as Jenkins has said, believed in a "hit'em over the head" approach. Other observers close to the scene have pointed to other motivations on Kennedy's part. To have given Johnson a major legislative role would have meant losing "control over his own program...something no sensible President would do."[20]

Johnson attended legislative breakfast meetings[21] and would occasionally but quietly offer advice on legislative matters, especially on the question of civil rights legislation and the best approach toward the likely recalcitrant senators involved,[22] but he did relatively little in the way of pushing the administration's legislative program. Instead he took on as much travel as possible as well as other administrative duties assigned to him both statutorily and by the President. Hubert Humphrey reports that Johnson once told him that President Kennedy had made a mistake in choosing him as his vice-presidential running mate; he would have been more effective in the Senate. Added Humphrey, "He was really a trapped animal in terms of all of his energy, all of his ego, everything else being sublimated."[23]

In a 1974 interview with this author, six years following his defeat for the presidency, the much respected and well-liked former Vice President Hubert H. Humphrey (who had by now been reelected to his former Senate seat) described the uncertain role of the Vice President in the Senate and the straddling position anyone in that office must maintain because of his or her constitutionally assigned role.

> The Vice Presidency can work to strain the relationship between old friends-even with the old friends in the Congress because you're no longer a member of the Club, and you're not quite out.... And you're the President's man, but you know just by the nature of the office that the President is looking over his shoulder at you, wondering, "What's he up to?"
>
> So you live in the forest of suspicion and doubt-that is

your cultural environment. You really do.

You walk a very-not fearsome-but a rather uncertain course all the time. You're never quite sure what's going to happen.**24**

Humphrey did not deny that a Vice President can and does play a role in pushing the administration's legislative program. Depending on legislative expertise and rapport with the legislators, the Vice President may be very successful. Truman, Vice President for only three months before assuming the Presidency, had similar recollections.

The Vice President…may have considerable status as a party member. He is considered as the No. 2 man in the party setup, and this may-or may not-give him influence in the Senate. It depends upon the man. If the senators find him likeable, he has considerable influence, and this was true of Garner and Barkley, both of who were outstanding vice-presidents. If he is not liked or is not familiar with politics of with the Senate approach to things, he is left on the outside…. Barkley, as Vice-President, was in a class by himself. He had the complete confidence of both the President and the Senate. He had been majority leader longer than any other senator in the history of the Senate.**25**

Alben Barkley himself pointed out, "Many times I have been asked what influence the Vice President may have over legislation pending in the Senate or even in the House of Representatives. The answer depends considerably upon the man himself. If he has been a member of both, he may undoubtedly within proper limits exercise some influence in the guiding principle of legislation…"**26**

Undoubtedly a Vice President who is well liked by members of the Senate and by the corresponding members of the House in charge of legislation can exercise considerable power in the shaping of the program of legislation, which every administration seeks to enact. The "proper limits" Barkley mentions include the very nature of the legislature itself - its sense of pride and independence as well as its suspiciousness of executive interference.

In this context, the "sense of the Senate" and of the average senator's self-image which Donald Matthews has described in his popular study, U.S. Senators and Their World (1960), is apt: "The greatest deliberative body in the world"27 frame of mind which pervades the Senate takes its toll on what an outsider, in this case the Vice President, can do, and the traditional suspiciousness of the executive branch, of course, extends to the Vice President. The senators' first and foremost loyalty is to their own "aristocratic" legislative body.

These and other "rules" of behavior form what have come to be known as the "folkways," "the clubbishness," of the Senate.28 They affect the Senate's relationship with its "competitor," the executive branch. Former Senator Herman Talmadge of Georgia has pointed out that the Vice President technically belongs between two branches.29 While he suffers from association with the legislative branch, the senators view him as an alter ego of the President. When asked whether there was any inevitability to the Vice President's relationship with the Senate, Hubert Humphrey responded,

> Inevitable - because of the separation of powers. First of all, who are you? You're not the President, and yet you preside over the Senate. You're not a Senator; you don't have a vote. What are you doing abound here? I *know* what you're doing-you're spying. And even your best friends, while they'll be very sociable with you and they like to have you around, they never really confide in you like they did as a Senator. You never feel quite as free to walk back in the cloakroom or the reading room as you did as a Senator. And also they know it's a little different office. The fact is, while the pundits have downgraded it, it's the second highest elective office in the history of the American people. And the Senators who are elected know that. And yet it's a peculiar [office]-it's an

awkward office. You've got two left feet, most of the time trying to walk a straight line-not getting into the President's hair, or getting into the business of the Senate, and yet you are in both of these. On the one hand-I was over here trying to get legislation through without looking too obvious, reporting back to department heads and the President what was going on-the problems we had. If I became too popular or too effective, whoever the Vice President, the President says, "What's he up to?" Not so much the President, but his staff....This office is filled with all the uncertainties of human emotion-unbelievable.**30**

The success any Vice President has in the legislature will be spotty, at best; there is little guarantee or regularity to it. He must know how and when to act, Johnson had an excellent sense of timing. He reportedly told Humphrey, following their 1964 landslide, "Hubert, I figure we have got about nine months to get our way in Congress, no more." And Johnson was right.**31** A former Humphrey aide has pointed out that a Vice President must decide when to use up his credibility, "because he is a political animal and wants to preserve that and develop whatever his known ambitions are."**32** Humphrey grasped the sense of the Senate and of his feasible legislative role as Vice President. He knew when and how to persuade and that the art of persuasion was critical.**33** Because he had this understanding, he had a measure of success in the legislative arena enjoyed by few Vice Presidents, notably in his efforts for the Great Society programs to which he had been committed for years and which he could work for as part of his continuing personal goals. In the same manner, he contributed his legislative skills and relationships toward the passage of the Model Cities Program, the Youth Opportunity Program, Medicare, the 1965 Voting Rights Act, the development of the Department of Housing and Urban Development, housing and rent supplement bills, increased aid to education-all of which were consistent with his past legislative interests and record.**34** As noted elsewhere in this work, Johnson in selecting Humphrey as a running mate in 1964 was well aware of Humphrey's major assets, notably his legislative record and expertise. Moreover, the two men worked well together on legislative matters.**35** Humphrey also knew and understood his President and was very careful in his legislative efforts to let it be known that is was *LBJ's* legislative program he was pushing.**36** Again, Humphrey knew where he could act, when he could act, and, above all, how to do so quietly. Humphrey recalled,

> I also was many times able to mediate between the times when the President had a difficult assignment-for example, one time when the President just could not permit a postal wage bill, for the postal workers, to go through as high as they wanted it-yet the President did not want to be on record as having to veto that bill. So he put me to work with the postal workers because I was supposed to be able, and he got me to negotiate it out so that he wouldn't have the difficulty of a veto or having the President have to express a "no"-a negative. It worked out-because I had the contacts, and I was able to carefully, quietly, work it out.**37**

Other Vice Presidents have not been as fortunate, skilled, or inclined to devote much time to the Senate. Apart from Alben Barkley this has been generally true of the modern Vice Presidency. Relatively little can be undertaken by the Vice President in the Senate because of so many demands that time be spent elsewhere. Even so able a legislative expert as Hubert Humphrey spent more of his time as Vice President on non-legislative chores. As former Senator Gale McGee observed, while Humphrey was "good at buttonholing Senators," the larger portion of his time was spent in the international theater, especially as Vietnam began to dominate the Johnson Administration.**38**

Although fully loyal to administration policies,39 Richard Nixon, as Vice President, spent very little time in the legislature, either in presiding over the Senate or in working for administration programs. By his own account, less than 5 percent of his time was spent on legislative matters.**40**

In addition to his short tenure as a senator himself, Nixon did not possess the personal requisites to be a useful liaison with the legislative body over which he was supposed to preside. Besides, as has been increasingly true of all Vice Presidents during the modern Vice Presidency, he had weighty tasks in other areas. The growth of the Presidency and its burdens have made this inevitable, as Vice President Walter Mondale's assumption of extraneous presidential activity during the Iranian crisis in 1979 indicated.

The Vice President's decreased presence in the Senate is a positive sign of the office's increased functioning in administrative areas. For example, in his early days in the Vice Presidency Nelson A. Rockefeller received few assignments from President Gerald Ford, with the exception of heading the blue-ribbon commission to investigate the Central Intelligence Agency. Ford's promise of a very active role for Rockefeller began to be fulfilled in February 1975 when the Vice President was given full supervisory powers over the Domestic Council, the executive body in charge of all domestic legislation and programs.**41** Despite the protest of some of Ford's aides, the President also allowed Rockefeller to appoint his own men to fill senior staff positions on the council.**42** As Rockefeller spent more and more time and exerted more influence in this and other areas in which he had expertise, the time he spent in the Senate diminished accordingly.

The Mondale role in the Senate revealed the Vice President's potential role in an administration. As the Republicans began to look ahead to the 1978 congressional campaign, the Carter Administration came under attack for its "ineptness." President Carter seemed to be in trouble, particularly with Congress. One of the President's legislative problems revolved around the administration's energy problems. But this was a critical problem, not only because the President himself places so much emphasis on it, but also because certain facets of the increasing storm over an energy plan were beginning to take on far-reaching dimensions in areas beyond energy.

One facet that emerged was the battle over deregulation of natural gas, with the administration favoring continued regulations of natural gas prices. During late September and early October 1977, the battle took on filibuster proportions in the U.S. Senate, with the traditionally anti-filibuster liberal members of the Senate leading in the use of the device in support of the administration's position.43 Much to the dismay and, sometimes, anger of their colleagues, the liberals seemed willing to persist for as long as necessary. Among those most angered was the Senate Majority Leader, Robert C. Byrd. But then the liberal plan was broken. With the indispensable assistance of Vice President Mondale, constitutionally the presiding officer of the Senate, Byrd was able to manipulate an end to the protracted debates.

Historically, Vice Presidents, particularly recently, have tended to avoid the frustrating job of being *in* the legislature but not *of* the legislature - having the "two left feet" of which Humphrey spoke. This has been true of all Vice Presidents, regardless of legislative experience. Those with a legislative background generally find that their departure from the Senate for the executive branch places them outside the trusted entourage of the Senate; those without such experience find themselves ignorant of Senate mores. Both the experienced and inexperienced discover that their time can be better-spent elsewhere - except when a tie vote may need to be broken or when parliamentary rulings can be strategically used to determine the outcome of a controversial issue.

Early October 1977 was precisely one of those exceptions to the rule that Vice Presidents avoid the Senate. Ignoring the Senate customs with which he was so familiar, Walter Mondale allied himself with Byrd to break the filibuster and, in effect, to allow a vote to take place which was contrary to the administration's position. The liberal plan, silently supported by the Carter Administration, was to introduce some 500 amendments and to vote on each of them. Mondale's rulings aborted this plan. He simply declared, as presiding officer, that amendments to the natural gas bill were "dilatory," and therefore out of order. In a 50-46 vote, the Senate voted to deregulate the natural gas industry.44

The questions that loomed large were, why did Mondale act in this manner? Why, if the liberal filibuster had the support, indeed, the blessings, of the White House, was an attempt not made to push the President's position? Why would the President's Vice President do this when he had the parliamentary power to allow the filibuster to continue? The questions were especially compelling since Mondale's own political leanings were compatible with the liberal filibuster leaders and that, had *he* still been in the Senate, he too undoubtedly would have been filibustering on the issue in support of the President.

In order to understand Mondale's seemingly strange move, one must be familiar with the larger context in which it took place-to perceive the finest subtleties of the administration's *overall* relationship with Congress as well as its struggle in the specific instance of the gas deregulation controversy.

Most assuredly, the administration preferred to maintain controls. But as the filibuster to that end continued, it appeared increasingly obvious that, despite the stamina of its leaders, the filibuster would not force Senate conservatives to change their position. Only a frustrating stalemate seemed likely.

It was also increasingly apparent to the administration that it had incurred the displeasure of the Democratic Majority Leader, whose good graces were critical to both the part in the Senate and to the president. To continue in a futile filibuster that was evidently very annoying to Byrd, who prided himself on the smooth workings of the Senate under his leadership, would have probably meant not only losing the battle, but also alienating a vital future ally.

Nonetheless, the President remained relatively consistent in his public stand. He had no choice. In fact, the President cried out against the Senate vote as "an injustice" to the people.45 It was the

Vice President who stuck his neck out. The development of the Vice Presidency over the years demonstrates that Vice Presidents can and must very often do things Presidents are unable to do.

In addition, the Vice President was aware of the White House's knowledge that the House of Representatives - which had dealt with the issue in August and had maintained price controls on natural gas- would not under any circumstances change its mind.**46** In essence, then, no matter how the Senate voted, the administration could always fall back on the House once the disagreeing chambers of congress met in conference committee, the vehicle that had been designed to iron out the differences between the House and the Senate versions of legislation.

So while it appeared as if Mondale were working contrary to the administration's best interests, he was actually serving them. Forcing a Senate vote ended the futile measure that was delaying the Senate's business at the same time that the administration had the House of Representatives' firm position as a backup.

But what effect would all of this have on Walter Mondale? In a television interview early in his incumbency, the Vice President had stated what all Vice Presidents sooner or later come to realize: that his future was dependent on the success of the President's administration.**47**

Vice Presidents in the past have found themselves in a position where they have very few alternatives: their future is tied to their President, the person responsible for their nomination and for their continuing functioning, for better or for worse. For those like Hubert Humphrey, making the decision to link their fate with that of the administration ultimately meant defeat. Through his action during the natural gas filibuster, Mondale was sticking the vice presidential neck out by being the administration spokesman in an area where the administration itself had to remain silent. Walter Mondale was not fully out of the Senate and in the executive branch.**48**

Mondale keenly perceived the view Congress held of the President, and it was less than flattering. Mondale's advice to Carter was to veto something -anything - to demonstrate to the first branch of government that the second branch was indeed in control in many respects. It was Mondale, too, who selected the bill to be the example: a defense authorization bill of some $37 billion. Although Carter's advisers argued against this move, Mondale prevailed. Not only did the President veto the legislation, but the veto stuck. Congress's inability to override it was an even greater victory for the President because defense authorization bills are usually considered untouchable by presidential veto.**49** Clearly, the Vice President's finely tuned understanding of the legislative frame of mind and presidential power vis-à-vis that frame of mind contributed to many of the Carter successes in Congress.

In summary, then, the Vice President *can* be an effective congressional liaison, but he often finds himself walking a tightrope between the two ends of Pennsylvania Avenue. Hubert Humphrey's observation best captures the position of the Vice President, when he observed, "The Vice Presidency ... is what the man that you work with is willing to let you make of it, because the President can put the damper on you. First of all, you don't have any real staff. Your staff ... is from the legislative budget over here, and the Senate guards it very jealously; they don't give the Vice President much, whoever he is. I had been Majority Whip over here-a very popular fellow around here-but when I became Vice President, that was different.**50**

"A Heartbeat Away"

The second constitutional function of the Vice President is to succeed to the Presidency if need be. The Constitution fails, however, to provide a prescription for training the Vice President for this possibility. Nonetheless, in the pre-modern Vice Presidency, six Vice Presidents succeeded the President; three others have done so in the modern period (see Table 1).

As the first Vice President to move up to the Presidency, John Tyler set the crucial precedent for the Vice President's actions under such circumstances. The constitutional provision, vague and ambiguous, states: "In Case of the Removal of the President from Office, or at his Death, Resignation, or Inability to discharge the Powers and Duties of the said Office, the same shall devolve on the Vice President."

Tyler chose the clause to mean that a Vice President does not *act* as President but *becomes* President, an interpretation that is symbolically underscored by his decision to that the presidential oath of office. All subsequent Vice Presidents who have succeeded have followed this precedent to the Presidency, but nowhere does the Constitution state this is necessary. Interestingly, a great deal of gravity and ceremony have become attached to the symbolic swearing-in ceremony of the unscheduled transfer of the Presidency.

While the Tyler precedent determined the course of events in the case of the death of a President, his decision had subtler ramifications. The decision set off a great controversy, which, while it did not alter the impact of Tyler's precedent – setting action, set the stage for confusion regarding the other half of a dual problem, presidential disability.**51**

TABLE 1 - VICE PRESIDENTIAL SUCCESSION

President	Vice President	Date of Succession
William Henry Harrison	John Tyler	April 6, 1841
Zachary Taylor	Millard Fillmore	July 10, 1850
Abraham Lincoln	Andrew Johnson	April 15, 1865
James A. Garfield	Chester A. Arthur	September 20, 1881
William McKinley	Theodore Roosevelt	September 14, 1901
Warren G. Harding	Calvin Coolidge	August 3, 1923
Franklin D. Roosevelt	Harry S Truman	April 13, 1945
John F. Kennedy	Lyndon B. Johnson	November 22, 1963
Richard M. Nixon	Gerald R. Ford	August 9, 1974

If, as Secretary of State Daniel Webster argued at the time of the Tyler succession, the *powers* and *duties* of the Presidency could not be separated from the *office* of the Presidency, it became questionable whether a Vice President could ever *temporarily* assume the office of Presidency upon the disability of a President. Unlike "removal," "death," or "resignation," disability need not be permanent. After the Tyler precedent, was it constitutionally possible for a disabled President, once recovered, to regain not merely his powers and duties, but the office as well? No Vice President seemed willing to test the question, and during periods of presidential disability the problem lingered. The problem was not solved until the passage of the Twenty-fifth Amendment in the second half of the twentieth century.

The succession of Millard Fillmore in 1850, following the death of President Zachary Taylor, resulted in an administration that "struck about an average in its virtues and faults."[52]

Andrew Johnson inherited not only the Presidency from the assassinated Abraham Lincoln in April 1865, but also the scars of a nation that had been split apart in a bitter civil war. The executive could not deal with the problems that had to be solved, as Johnson attempted to do, but his tenure as President ended in a narrow escape from impeachment. Of the three remaining accidental Presidents during this earlier time frame, only Theodore Roosevelt headed an administration that would be ranked among the greatest in the history of the Presidency. Both Chester A. Arthur and Calvin Coolidge had mediocre administrations at best. overall, then, the early record set by Vice Presidents succeeding to the Presidency is not an illustrative one, and it remained for the post-World War II Vice Presidency to demonstrate that the success of the Roosevelt succession was not a unique event in the history of vice presidential succession. Those instances are traced in a separate chapter.

Chapter 2

VICE PRESIDENTIAL SELECTION: CHOOSING THE HEIR APPARENT

"Have you ever heard of anyone running
for the Vice Presidency?"

Nelson A. Rockefeller

EVERY FOUR YEARS since the birth of this Republic, the American electorate has journeyed to the polls to designate its only nationally elected leaders, the President and the Vice President. Only recently, however, has the electorate begun to appreciate the importance of the second of these leaders. This new development requires a fresh understanding of the vice presidential selection process, particularly its evolution during the modern period. The analysis provided in this chapter is thematic rather than chronological, and it views the selection process via the categories of criteria that have emerged. Therefore, not all vice presidential candidates during this period are examined. Table 2 provides a chronological perspective as well as an overview of the "source" of running mates during this period.

TABLE 2 - PRESIDENTIAL AND VICE PRESIDENTIAL CANDIDATES (1944-2016)

Democrats		Republicans	
1944			
<u>Presidential Candidate</u>			
Franklin D. Roosevelt	President	Thomas E. Dewey	Governor
<u>Vice Presidential Candidate</u>			
Harry S. Truman	U.S. Senate	John Bricker	Senate
1948			
<u>Presidential Candidate</u>			
Harry S. Truman	President	Thomas E. Dewey	Governor
<u>Vice Presidential Candidate</u>			
Alben Barkley	Senate	Earl Warren	Governor
1952			
<u>Presidential Candidate</u>			
Adlai E. Stevenson	Governor	Dwight D. Eisenhower	Military
<u>Vice Presidential Candidate</u>			
John Sparkman	Senate	Richard M. Nixon	Senate
1956			
<u>Presidential Candidate</u>			
Adlai E. Stevenson	Governor	Dwight D. Eisenhower	President
<u>Vice Presidential Candidate</u>			
Estes Kefauver	Senate	Richard M. Nixon	Vice President
1960			
<u>Presidential Candidate</u>			
John F. Kennedy	Senate	Richard M. Nixon	Vice President
<u>Vice Presidential Candidate</u>			
Lyndon B. Johnson	Senate	Henry Cabot Lodge	Senate
1964			
<u>Presidential Candidate</u>			
Lyndon B. Johnson	President	Barry M. Goldwater	Senate
<u>Vice Presidential Candidate</u>			
Hubert H. Humphrey	Senate	William Miller	House
1968			
<u>Presidential Candidate</u>			
Hubert H. Humphrey	Vice President	Richard M. Nixon	Vice President
<u>Vice Presidential Candidate</u>			
Edward M Muskie	U.S. Senate	Spiro Agnew	Governor
1972			
<u>Presidential Candidate</u>			
George McGovern	Senate	Richard M. Nixon	President
<u>Vice Presidential Candidate</u>			
Sargent Shriver	Diplomacy	Spiro Agnew	Vice President
1976			
<u>Presidential Candidate</u>			
Jimmy Carter	Governor	Gerald R. Ford	President
<u>Vice Presidential Candidate</u>			
Walter F. Mondale	Senate	Robert Dole	Senate

	Democrats		Republicans	
1980				
Presidential Candidate				
	Jimmy Carter	President	Ronald Reagan	Governor
Vice Presidential Candidate				
	Walter F. Mondale	Vice President	George H. W. Bush	Diplomacy
1984				
Presidential Candidate				
	Walter F. Mondale		Ronald Reagan	President
Vice Presidential Candidate				
	Geraldine Ferraro	U.S. House	George H. W. Bush	Vice President
1988				
Presidential Candidate				
	Michael Dukakis	Governor	George H.W. Bush	Vice President
Vice Presidential Candidate				
	Lloyd Bentsen	U. S. Senate	Dan Quayle	U. S. Senate
1992				
Presidential Candidate				
	William Clinton	Governor	George H.W. Bush	President
Vice Presidential Candidate				
	Al Gore	U. S. Senate	Dan Quayle	Vice President
1996				
Presidential Candidate				
	William Clinton	President	Robert Dole	U.S. Senate
Vice Presidential Candidate				
	Al Gore	Vice President	Jack Kemp	Cabinet
2000				
Presidential Candidate				
	Al Gore	Vice President	George W. Bush	Governor
Vice Presidential Candidate				
	Joseph Lieberman	U. S. Senate	Richard Cheney	Cabinet
2004				
Presidential Candidate				
	John Kerry	U. S. Senate	George W. Bush	President
Vice Presidential Candidate				
	John Edwards	U. S. Senate	Richard Cheney	Vice President
2008				
Presidential Candidate				
	Barack Obama	U. S. Senate	John McCain	U.S. Senate
Vice Presidential Candidate				
	Joseph Biden	U. S. Senate	Sarah Palin	Governor
2012				
Presidential Candidate				
	Barack Obama	President	Mitt Romney	Governor
Vice Presidential Candidate				
	Joseph Biden	Vice President	Paul Ryan	U.S. House

Democrats		Republicans	
2016			
Presidential Candidate			
Hillary Clinton	Cabinet	Donald Trump	Businessman
Vice Presidential Candidate			
Tim Kaine	U. S. Senate	Michael Pence	Governor
2020			
Joseph Biden	Vice President		

An examination of a series of vice presidential nominations indicates that a number of selection criteria have emerged. In each case, the presidential nominee is seeking to attract more votes for the ticket.[1] Vice Presidential candidates are chosen for a diversity of reasons (and many a running mate selection falls within more than one of these):

1. As a "safety valve" for a party that feels the presidential nomination is "predetermined" because an incumbent President is virtually reassured of re-nomination or, as in more recent development, because the proliferation of party primaries across the states "sews up" the presidential nomination for a candidate well in advance of the convention and the only thing left is the vice presidential spot on the ticket, for example, Harry S Truman (1944); Alben Barkley (1948); and George Bush (1980).

2. To emphasize a particular issue that is popular with the people, for example, Richard Nixon (1952; communism); Spiro Agnew (1968; law and order).

3. To serve as an internal party unifier: the struggle to achieve party unity often requires the conciliation of a particular party faction of a defeated nominee's followers, for example, Lyndon Johnson (1960); Hubert Humphrey (1964); Robert Dole (1976); George H.W. Bush (1980); Dan Quayle (1988).

4. To ensure broader electoral appeal by balancing the geographical or personal characteristics of a presidential candidate: state size, region of the country, age, profession, and, as a newer

trend, religion and ethnic background. Virtually all tickets are balanced geographically; a particularly popular combination pairs candidates from large states (with more electoral votes) in different regions. Some examples of balancing personal characteristics include John Bricker (1944; profession-senator) John Sparkman (1952: profession: Senator); Estes Kefauver (1956; profession-senator); Richard Nixon (1952;age); Spiro Agnew (1968; profession-governor); Edmund Muskie (1968; ethnic background and religion); Thomas Eagleton/Sargent Shriver (1972; religion); Walter Mondale (1976; profession-senator); Geraldine Ferraro (1984; gender);Joseph Lieberman (2000; religion); Sarah Palin (2008; gender)

5. To balance what may be lacking in a presidential nominee's political background and expertise, for example, Walter Mondale (1976); George H. W. Bush (1980); Lloyd Bentsen (1988); Al Gore (1992); Richard ("Dick") Cheney (2000); Joseph Biden (2008); Mike Pence (2016).

Any one or any combination of these criteria have been and can be used in selecting a running mate for the national ticket. Indeed, the vice presidential, candidate who manages to satisfy several of these criteria, especially if he or she does not seriously negate any of the other, negate any of the others, is well sought after. Obviously, these criteria are overlapping, and the selection process becomes a composite of as many of them as possible. Which particular criterion(ia) will prevail in a given election is largely dependent on the environmental factors of that years: the issues, a presidential candidate's assets and liabilities, the state of the party, the state of the other party. Ultimately, a "framework of acceptability" emerges that is unique to that time and place.

Pervading all of the criteria is a very critical elimination process. The selection of a suitable running mate frequently involves screening out individuals who do not meet a satisfactory combination of criteria for circumstances of the moment or who do not satisfy the presidential candidate's personal predilections. Until relatively recent times and the increasing ideological polarization of the two major political parties, the very nature of U. S. political parties as more "umbrella" parties made it seem that the convention itself had to "forfeit" the selection of the vice presidential nominee to unify the party so as to be able to appeal to a wide breadth of voters. If the characteristics of contemporary parties continue to widen the impact on both presidential and vice presidential selection will inevitably be impacted. Until now, with the exception of the open Democratic National Convention of 1956, the trend has been increasingly toward rubber-stamping the choice of the presidential nominee.2

THE ROLE OF THE PRESIDENTIAL NOMINEE

Although the ultimate choice of a running mate belongs to the presidential nominee, it would be a mistake to assume that his choice is an entirely autonomous one. The presidential candidate has *restricted* free choice: s/he must work within the framework of acceptability, both of the party and of the times at hand. Forces that are largely beyond his/her control shape the criteria important to the election.

It follows that the presidential nominee's freedom will vary from one candidate to another and will take in the full range of possibilities, from the nominee who is able to "handpick" a running mate to one who is virtually backed into an inescapable corner. The history of the office repeatedly demonstrates that the necessity of working within a framework of acceptability frequently requires that personal intimacy or even compatibility be abandoned. This in turn may seriously affect the role the Vice President will play in the administration. Among recent incumbents, Lyndon Johnson's own nomination and Vice Presidency are probably the most striking example of this possibility. Kennedy and Johnson, while cordial and friendly toward each other, were not intimates, either personally or professionally. The Johnson nomination had unforeseen ramifications for the Kennedy Administration. Kennedy accepted Johnson as a running mate in an effort to unify a fractured party. As far as the Kennedy staff was concerned, however, the memories of the pre-convention fight were bitter ones, and Lyndon Johnson was an unwanted outsider.3

One consequence of the central role played by the presidential nominee is that little attention centers on the vice presidential slot until a presidential nominee has been chosen. Add this to the rather negative image the office has had, and it is little wonder that its choice is oftentimes anticlimactic.

Crucial, too, is the fact that so much focus is placed on capturing the party's presidential nomination that the competing candidates themselves frequently give little thought to the selection of a running mate. Indeed, they are sometimes caught unaware. This was the case with the McGovern nomination victory in 1972 and the resulting scramble for a vice presidential running mate ending with the hasty and ill-fated choice of Senator Thomas Eagleton. McGovern obstinately held on to his belief that his first choice for Vice President, Senator Edward M. Kennedy, would eventually relent and agree to run on the McGovern ticket. Despite repeated telephone calls and pleadings by the presidential candidate, however, Kennedy remained steadfast in his refusal to run. What impact a Kennedy acceptance and victory would have had on the Vice Presidency is a matter of speculation. Could any President who had virtually pleaded for his vice presidential running mate have refused him a significant, and possibly a dominant, role in the administration? Or would his Vice President have suffered the usual fate and gone the route of other Vice Presidents?4

An electoral system that forces all attention to be placed on the number one spot creates another necessity. Only after a contender for the presidential nomination has run the gamut and seen the lineup of the opposition, only when s/he has seen the issues and divisions as they develop (and the frequently develop right there on the convention floor in his attempt to persuade delegations to cast their ballots for him), can s/he begin to see what type of running mate might best satisfy the rigors of the forthcoming general election. Only then can the presidential candidate envisage and assess what deals may have to be struck and which of the criteria may weigh most heavily in his/her selection of a running mate. This grave responsibility is most often handled within the space of a few hours.

An entirely different situation emerges when an incumbent President is up for re-nomination. S/he is virtually assured of his party's label, and s/he can think of her/his running mate long in advance. Two possible situations are apparent. The first-term Vice President might command such a segment of the electorate's loyalty, as was the case with Spiro T. Agnew in 1972, that dropping him/her from the ticket would be politically dangerous, if not impossible. As in the Agnew case, the Vice President may also represent a wing of the party that would feel trop upon if he were to be replaced. This doubtless was the case regarding Lyndon Johnson's Vice Presidency and the speculation in 1963 regarding whether he would be dropped from the 1964 ticket.[5] A similar situation existed in 1944 with regard to the Henry Wallace Vice Presidency under FDR, although in that case there were considerable forces against Wallace as well that ultimately prevailed. FDR, however, avoided alienating the staunchest Wallace supporters (especially labor) by nominating Harry S. Truman, a candidate well respected by Wallace supporters.[6]

Thus, even an incumbent President may be operating within a framework of acceptability as far as running mate selection is concerned. Indeed, if the only alternative left is to stick with the first-term Vice President, the framework of operation has narrowed and is much *more* restricted than in the case of a first-term presidential candidate.

President Eisenhower found this to be his situation in 1956. Despite denials from his associates to the contrary,[7] Eisenhower's actions seem to point to an attempt to edge Nixon off the second-term ticket. Eisenhower did not go so far as to ask Nixon to leave the Vice Presidency; he did suggest, however, that perhaps a Cabinet post would give Nixon the executive experience needed if he were to contemplate the Presidency. In addition, although the President announced his intention to seek reelection on February 29, he steadfastly declined to commit himself on Nixon's future, preferring to take refuge in talk about an "open" convention. Meanwhile, a "Dump Nixon" movement, led by Harold Stassen, had begun to roll. The President said little to discourage Stassen's efforts. Eisenhower found, however, that, although opinions within the Republican ranks were divided, one thing was clear: dumping Nixon from the 1956 ticket would take its toll within the right wing - the Taft wing - of the party, unless Nixon were replaced by a candidate more pleasing to the right (which would have meant someone with even more conservative views).**8** In this case, it was considerably less detrimental to let the status quo prevail than it would have been to engineer Nixon's exit. Eisenhower's personality itself was crucial to this episode. Preferring not to fight, the President gave in to the desires of the Republican National Committee and kept Nixon on the ticket.**9**

In this connection, an incumbent President who is reluctant to "dump" his/her Vice President may sometimes appear to be the victim of irresistible forces. In 1944 Roosevelt did not wish to see Henry Wallace re-nominated, but he did not want to remove him openly since he had backed Wallace so strongly only four years earlier. But as Vice President, Wallace was outspoken, advocating extreme liberal policies that were not in keeping with the times. This had caused considerable dissension within the party and even produced the threat of a Southern revolt.**10** Clearly, Wallace had to be dropped, and the most pragmatic solution was to have the President's decision made by "uncontrollable forces." Finesse was required to regiment the forces which Roosevelt called upon and utilized to his advantage in the "consultations" then taking place regarding the next vice presidential nominee. Meanwhile, the President gave lukewarm support to Wallace- a far cry from the position he had taken in 1940 – while the Vice President was out of sight and circulation, having been sent on a mission to China.**11**

Former President George W. Bush's 2010 book, <u>Decision Points,</u> revealed that he considered removing Vice President Cheney for the 2004 re-election campaign. Actually, Bush wrote, the Vice President himself suggested such a move because of the controversy his incumbency in the second office brought to the Bush Administration. As Bush wrote, "While Dick helped with important parts of our base, he had become a lightning rod for criticism from the media and the left. He was seen as dark and heartless -- the Darth Vader of the administration. Moreover, the frequently depicted view that Cheney was the one "in charge," not Bush, added fuel to the fire. And Bush himself wrote, "Accepting Dick's offer would be one way to demonstrate that I was in charge," but ultimately determined that Cheney's expertise was an asset. An interest parenthesis is that, as one observer noted, "Mr. Bush's consideration of replacing Mr. Cheney on the ticket has an interesting anecdote. During his father's ultimately unsuccessful reelection bid in 1992, Mr. Bush says he urged him to dump Vice President Dan Quayle and put Mr. Cheney, then the defense secretary, on the ticket. His father declined, but 'I never completely gave up on my idea of a Bush-Cheney ticket."**12**

THE VICE PRESIDENTIAL NOMINATION
AS A SAFETY VALVE

When FDR's advisors so skillfully engineered the removal of Vice President Wallace from the 1944 ticket and in his place vested Harry Truman, they did so with an understanding that the next Vice President of the United States - should the Roosevelt ticket move on to its expected victory in the general election - would probably succeed to the Presidency. Wallace was far too controversial a figure to permit him to remain a heartbeat away from the most powerful institution in the world. Some observers have maintained that because of fatigue and failing health or perhaps other reasons, the President himself did not really much care who was Vice President. Even if FDR might have wished things to remain as they were, he could neither ignore the handwriting on the wall nor push in any direction. In this regard, the 1944 Democratic vice presidential choice also came to serve as a safety valve for the party.

In 1940, the controversial third-term nomination of FDR had caused internal dissension within Democratic ranks, and the vehement opposition to liberal Henry Wallace was, in part, a venting of resentment against the President himself.[13] By 1944, the fourth-term candidacy was not the issue, but by that time the opposition to Wallace had come full circle. Now, the President would let "forces" take their course, and he would ultimately acquiesce "reluctantly."[14] The nomination appeared to have been "taken" from the President's hands; the myth of party control made it impossible to blame FDR for Wallace's rejection. The vice presidential issue in 1944 supplanted any questioning of FDR's nomination for a fourth term and served to pacify the convention as well as to enhance its self-esteem as a body with the capacity to make decisions.

The ability of the party to "let off steam" through the vice presidential nomination was also demonstrated in the 1948 Democratic nomination of Senator Alben Barkley - the one moment of exhilaration for a party (mistakenly) resigned to impending disaster at the polls with the incumbent President, Truman.

The safety valve may operate in another direction. The 1976 "dumping" of Vice President Nelson Rockefeller by President Gerald Ford is a clear-cut example of an incumbent President, facing opposition to his own re-nomination, seeking ways to appease recalcitrant segments of his party. Rockefeller had to be sacrificed to maximize the security of the number one spot for the President. In this regard, too, the early fall 1979 (prior to President Carter's announcement that Vice President Walter Mondale would indeed be his running mate again) White House staff criticism of Mondale perhaps sought to have the

Vice Presidency serve as a safety valve, thus reducing pressure on the presidential nomination.

ISSUE EMPHASIS:
THE NIXON SELECTION OF 1952 AND
THE AGNEW SELECTION OF 1968

Issue emphasis- the selection of a running mate who is identified with an issue which the presidential nominee wants to or must focus on-has become a major criterion for selecting the vice presidential running mate. The issue, if any, is determined by the broader social and economic contexts in which the selection and campaign are taking place. The selection of Richard Nixon as Dwight Eisenhower's running mate in 1952, Hubert Humphrey as Lyndon Johnson's in 1964, and Spiro Agnew as Richard Nixon's in 1968 all bear this in common. The Humphrey selection included other criteria as well and will be treated in a separate section of this chapter.

Both Nixon in 1952 and Agnew in 1968 were chosen as vice presidential running mates in order to conciliate potentially troublesome segments of the Republican Party as well as to emphasize particular issues in the upcoming campaign.

The political climate of the 1950s has been well documented. Fraught with the renewed fear of communism at home and abroad following the end of the world war, this climate provided the arena for the 1952 campaign. Richard Nixon, former Representative from California's Twelfth Congressional District, had clearly emerged as a beneficiary of this national paranoia. By 1952, Nixon's meteoric public career was inextricably linked to search for the enemy within.

In 1946, Nixon had waged a successful congressional campaign against an incumbent Democrat of many years. Once elected, he had served as a member of the much-publicized House Un-American Activities Committee. Nixon was perhaps the most influential agent in the actively followed Alger Hiss-Whitaker Chambers case; the young congressman's name rapidly became well-known. In 1950, Nixon grasped the opportunity to win a seat in the U.S. Senate and waged a successful campaign against Helen Gahagan Douglas using a campaign technique that had been so effective in 1946: the innuendo. Through this technique, Nixon had very cleverly placed his opponents on the defensive, largely in terms of the issue of the day, communism. The technique and the issue fit the climate of the times, and by the time the Republican Party met to select its 1952 presidential and vice presidential candidates, Richard Nixon's name was prominent.

Once General Dwight D. Eisenhower had secured the nomination as the party standard-bearer, the task remained to select a suitable running mate. Eisenhower, who prided himself on not being particularly political, consulted with his advisers and drew up a list of some half-dozen "younger men, that I admired that seemed to me to have made a name for themselves."[15]

In addition to Nixon's youth, Eisenhower was impressed by the Californian's nationwide reputation on the issue of communism as well as by his political maturity.[16] Nixon might be useful to Eisenhower in the event Joe McCarthy, the crusading senator from Wisconsin, might have to be dealt with.

In retrospect, it is not surprising that Eisenhower placed Richard Nixon at the head of the list of eligible running mates. To counterbalance his own candidacy, Eisenhower virtually *had* to have a young, energetic, and political running mate. What better choice than a candidate who had rallied all of these characteristics in a fight against the major issue of the day?[17]

Years later, in 1968, an unpopular war 6,000 miles away hit home at its hardest; Lyndon Johnson, who had been very popular in 1964, was forced not to seek reelection; the nation's foremost civil rights leader, the Reverend Martin Luther King, Jr., was assassinated in Memphis; and a young, vibrant, popular presidential candidate bearing the Kennedy name was shot down moments after a victorious primary battle in California. In short, this country seemed to be in a tailspin.

While thee critical events were occurring, another storm was brewing that ultimately relegated the war in Vietnam to second place in the voters' minds. Issues of law and order: crime in the streets, ghetto riots, burning cities, especially following the assassination of King, all hit white American hard and produced an outcry for solutions. The "Social Issues" were in "full flower," as the noted observers of American elections, Richard Scammon and Ben Wattenberg, have suggested.18

Richard Nixon was the centrist candidate in 1968-the position of power in American politics-and won because he had a profound understanding of what the real issues in that campaign were. His selection of Spiro Agnew as his running mate was, in large measure, a product of that understanding.

The Spiro Agnew of 1968 was just what Nixon had in mind: a candidate who was strong on domestic issues and who had struck a chord on the critical question of law and order. Nixon, meanwhile, planned to devote the major portion of his own time to the foreign arena.

As governor of Maryland, Agnew had had occasion to demonstrate his position on what would come to be the critical issue of the 1968 campaign. A year prior to that campaign, in July 1967, following riots in Cambridge, Maryland, Governor Agnew issues a statement entitled "Civil Rights and Rioting," which demonstrated his reaction to immoderate black leaders. The occasion was Agnew's response to H. Rap Brown, who had delivered a scathing antiwhite speech in Cambridge, which contributed to the later riots.19

In March 1968, trouble was building up on Maryland's predominantly black Bowie State Campus. Dr. Samuel Myers, president of the college, had pleaded with Agnew to make a personal appearance so that the students could air their grievances. Agnew declined, choosing instead to send a representative. Unfortunately, the representative chosen, Charles Bresler, was not especially noted for tact or diplomacy. Meanwhile, Agnew, believing that militants were inciting the students, began to grow more and more rigid, refusing to give in under pressure.**20** Instead, state police were sent to the campus, and Governor Agnew threatened the students with forcible removal if necessary. Myers, however, was able to come to an agreement with the students, but several days later Agnew made the mistake of choosing to make a personal appearance at Towson State College for the purpose of hearing student (predominantly white) grievances. The Bowie State students were incensed; when they decided to go en masse to the State Capitol, Bowie State was closed, and they were arrested.**21**

To make matters worse, this incident occurred on the same night as the assassination of Martin Luther King, Jr. On April 7, in declaring a state of emergency in Baltimore, Agnew once again proclaimed his firm commitment to law and order: "To all those who have been victimized, I pledge to you that all possible power will be exerted to restore order and security to your lives, and to assist those made homeless by the fire. To those few who loot and burn we shall have no sympathy, nor will we tolerate those few who would take the law into their own hands.**22** Agnew's message was clear: above and beyond all else, law and order must reign supreme.

In a confrontation with black leaders following the Baltimore riots and the looting and pillaging in response to the King assassination, Agnew had yet another opportunity to demonstrate his firm position. In a speech on April 11 which would cause approximately seventy out of one hundred of the leaders to walk out while he was speaking, Agnew lashed out against militant leaders (none of whom was present) and criticized those nonmilitants present for giving in to the demands of those leaders.**23**

Agnew had made his point. For him there was no room for softness when it came to law and order. He, as well as the bulk of white American, had had enough. Furthermore, he would not be silent while the Kerner Commission blamed white racism for American's problems. Agnew blasted the commission and its findings just several days before the opening of the 1968 Republican National Convention.

Prior to the convention, Agnew had been an avowed Rockefeller man and had actively engaged in a draft Rockefeller movement, only to suffer the humiliation of hearing, in the company of a roomful of reporters, his candidate declare his noncandidacy (on the very day Agnew had expected Rockefeller to declare himself in the running). The Nixon camp began to court Agnew's support by playing to Agnew's vanity, seeking his advice and ideas. Following Lyndon Johnson's withdrawal from the race at the end of March, and again after Robert Kennedy's assassination in early June, Rockefeller reconsidered his own plans and made efforts to win Agnew back. But Agnew had found his man in Richard Nixon. As for his own future, Agnew typically behaved like the office-seeking politician, engaging in conflicting actions and statements: on the one hand, he disavowed any interest in national politics, and on the other, he sent out clear indications of his position on the crucial issue of the upcoming campaign.

Agnew's speech on the convention floor on August 7 placing the name of Richard Nixon in nomination hinted at what Agnew's role in the campaign and the administration would ultimately be. Again, he vigorously voiced the law and order theme:

- A nation plagued with disorder wants a renewal of order.
- A nation haunted by crime wants respect for law.
- A nation wrenched by division wants a rebirth of unity.[24]

Richard Nixon was eminently successful in convincing the leadership of his party that his time had come. The delegates to the convention agreed on him as their presidential choice on the first ballot, moving the choice of a running mate to the fore.

Spiro Agnew more than fulfilled the requirements Nixon sought in a vice-presidential candidate. In addition to his experience and his ability to achieve, he had other appealing characteristics. He was a self-made man, the son of a poor Greek immigrant; he epitomized the Great American Dream. Agnew seemed very much akin to what Nixon viewed himself as being and what would strike a note of empathy among that segment of voters soon to become known as "the vast majority of silent Americans." Nixon's acceptance speech in 1968 itself dwelled on both law and order and the Great American Dream and gave voice to the silent majority; it masterfully captured the heart of the social issue.

CONCILIATION:
THE SELECTION OF LYNDON B. JOHNSON

As amalgams of a diversity of groups and interests, the political parties have the burden of emerging from the national convention with a presidential ticket that alienates as few, if any, of these factions. The period of the modern Vice Presidency has witnessed the utilization of the second office as a key resource to achieve party harmony at the convention. The 1960 nomination of Lyndon B. Johnson as the Democratic vice presidential running mate to John F. Kennedy represents such an attempt at party conciliation.

Kennedy's position in 1960 was a particularly vulnerable one. He was young, rich, Catholic, and running for the Presidency against an incumbent Vice President who had served under an immensely popular President. Faced with such handicaps, it was imperative for him to muster all the resources at his disposal.

Having waged a hard and bitter preconvention fight against Senator Lyndon Johnson of Texas, Kennedy had created animosities that would last throughout his administration and well into Johnson's. The young presidential candidate from Massachusetts had to mend fences if the party was to achieve victory in November. Kennedy's most ardent opponent for the nomination, Johnson was not only "a Protestant with a capital P,"[25] but commanded a wealth of prestige and votes as well. Yet the scars of the nomination fight were deep. Johnson and his followers had to be conciliated; if not, Kennedy's nomination victory would be a shallow one.

Kennedy's position was not enviable. Somehow, he had to pacify the South without alienating his own liberal supporters. Kennedy was further hemmed in by the strong civil rights plank his team had indicated it would support. Moreover, both Bobby Kennedy and Kenneth O'Donnell had been affirming that the vice presidential candidate would have an ideological position akin to Kennedy's and would probably hail from the Midwest.

There are numerous versions of what lay behind the Johnson nomination for the Vice President, but a definitive scenario is still lacking. One account (denied by all three Kennedy brothers and their lieutenants)[26] reports that John Kennedy, aware that he had no alternative to making a conciliatory move toward Johnson, decided to do so under the assumption that Johnson would be unwilling to give up the power of the Majority Leadership of the Senate for the relative impotence of the Vice Presidency and would, therefore, refuse the offer. In his memoirs, Johnson recalls that, "When John Kennedy offered me the Vice Presidential nomination, I asked him to be candid with me. If it was only a courteous gesture, I said, I wanted him to say so. He replied that he needed me to run with him if the ticket was to be successful."[27]

Johnson's comments in the preconvention campaign seemed to indicate that he would not be a candidate for the second office. In a Chicago press conference on July 7, for example, Johnson responded to a question that he was only interested in the Presidency and that he would most assuredly not trade a vote (as a senator) for a gavel (as Vice President and thus presiding officer of the Senate, who only casts a vote in the case of a tie).[28] He echoed this sentiment three days later in a "Meet the Press" television interview and added: "I have the assignment of Majority Leader of the Senate, and I think every person should seriously consider where he can be most effective and what job he can do best, and bear that in mind."[29]

As this version has it, Kennedy thought he could have his cake and eat it too. Since neither Kennedy nor anyone in his camp had expected an acceptance from Johnson, Kennedy could appear as both a conciliator by making a generous offer as well as a healer of party wounds. Author Hugh Sidey has related a preconvention conversation with Kennedy, which underscores Kennedy's perception of where Johnson stood. "I remember once Chalmers Roberts and I were talking with him on the *Caroline* about Johnson," said Sidey, "and we put the question right straight to him...: 'Would you accept Lyndon?' Kennedy said he would accept Johnson 'in a minute.' And went on to say Johnson would 'carry the South and that's where we need the strength, and he's a good man. But...he [Johnson] won't accept it.'" From this conversation, Sidey speculated that following Johnson's refusal, Kennedy would be able to choose his own nominee, probably Stuart Symington.**30**

Another version of the Johnson nomination holds that the Johnson camp itself, with the aid of Speaker of the House Sam Rayburn, manipulated the vice presidential nomination and that Johnson had actually forced himself onto the ticket.**31** Johnson discusses this allegation at length and denies it in his memoirs.**32**

The role played by Robert Kennedy remains unclear. The presidential candidate's younger brother had not forgiven Johnson for the disparaging remarks which he and his aides had made about the Kennedy family during the campaign. Once his brother's nomination had been achieved and the name of Lyndon Johnson began to emerge in talks which the two brothers had with their father, Joseph Kennedy, it is reported that Robert Kennedy attached little credibility to a Johnson nomination because it was "so inconceivable."**33**

How Johnson finally made it onto the ticket is beclouded by indistinct events and conflicting versions of what took place. Unclear, too, are the reasons for Johnson's turnabout on his availability for the second spot. It seems that when Kennedy (whether as a gesture toward reconciliation or out of the pragmatic belief that Johnson was necessary for victory in the general election) initially offered Johnson the nomination, as Johnson had expected him to do, the Texan planned in advance to decline it or at least to be very "hesitant to accept."**34**

Perhaps the clearest fact that emerges about the Johnson nomination is that Rayburn's advice was critical to Johnson's ultimate acceptance. The Speaker, skeptical about the possibility of a Catholic being elected to the Presidency, was initially hostile to the thought of a Johnson candidacy for the Vice Presidency. He also had misgivings about Kennedy's age. Johnson, despite the urgings of some, would not accept the nomination without his mentor's approval. Rayburn had been like a father to Johnson. Theirs was a relationship nurtured by the years; Johnson respected his judgment and wisdom. Furthermore, Johnson loved and was satisfied with his work in the Senate. So, when he reported that he might be offered the vice presidential nomination, Rayburn initially told him not to accept; with this Johnson agreed. However, when Kennedy ultimately made his approach, Johnson at first wavered and then, much to Kennedy's surprise, accepted.**35**

Other observers believe that Johnson very much wanted the Vice Presidency, and, in fact, that he "was angling for the Vice Presidential nomination."**36** According to this thesis, he was aware that no Southerner at that time could be nominated for the Presidency. The second office could provide an entrance for a Southerner onto the stage of nationwide politics,**37** so that even if he himself could not be President, at least "a Southerner might be President one day."**38** Perhaps too, Johnson was concerned that the role of Majority Leader under a new President might change markedly from what it had been under President Eisenhower. One of Johnson's top aides speculates that Johnson could have had some concern about the strain of continued Majority Leadership on his already weakened heart.**39**

While still undecided, Johnson suggested that Kennedy confer with Rayburn. Thus, Kennedy had to pursue what he had begun. Despite Rayburn's skepticism about Kennedy's chances, as well as his reluctance to have Johnson leave the legislature, one factor loomed large: the prospect of Richard Nixon in the White House.**40** Rayburn's hatred for Nixon was deeply embedded. The Speaker believed, correctly or incorrectly, that Nixon had once deemed him a traitor. And for this he had not forgiven him.**41**

By the time Kennedy made his appeal promising the Speaker that Johnson would enjoy an expanded Vice Presidency, particularly in the area of foreign affairs, Rayburn acquiesced. According to George Christian, LBJ's press secretary, he did so especially "to save the country from Nixon."**42** Liz Carpenter (Mrs. Johnson's press secretary) told this writer that President Johnson always said that "Kennedy walked down two flights of steps"**43** to invite him to contract what another insider has described as a "marriage of convenience."**44**

The unexpected Johnson acceptance produced a flurry of reactions. The Kennedy staff, already divided in their opinion over the vice presidential nomination, was stunned - as was Robert Kennedy.**45** It was at this juncture that the younger Kennedy allegedly paid his visit to Johnson in an attempt to get him to change his mind in exchange for the chairmanship of the Democratic National Committee. It was also at this point that the nomination, intended to produce party reconciliation, caused an uproar among liberals and Southerners alike. Liberals felt betrayed; Southerners thought Johnson a turncoat.

In the face of so much adverse reaction, especially the threat of a liberal revolt, Kennedy undertook to reassess his decision and to consider what, if anything, could be done about it. The two brothers, Jack and Bobby, weighed the pros and cons of getting out of the commitment. On the negative side, besides the threat of a liberal revolt, Kennedy was disturbed about what it might be like to work with the temperamental Texan, "a proud and testy man, well known for his sensitivity and his egotism, unlikely to defer to a backbencher nine years his junior."**46** In addition, Robert Kennedy had apparently assured labor that the choice would definitely not be Johnson.

The arguments in favor of keeping Johnson weighed heavily as well. First, Johnson and his backers were too powerful to alienate. Second, Johnson would bring the ticket strength in the South. Kennedy felt the liberal storm could be ridden out and that the benefits of having

Johnson on the ticket would far outweigh the disadvantage. Third, the vice presidential spot would not only heal the party wounds; it would also place Johnson in a position where he could be of greater legislative use to the Kennedy Administration.

CONCILIATION:
THE SELECTION OF HUBERT H. HUMPHREY

Although many of the criteria involved in LBJ's consideration of his own vice-presidential running mate in 1964 were of the traditional variety (a candidate who would complement him geographically, "even out" his views and political record, and, at worst, not lose any votes for the ticket), less emphasis had to be placed on these because of the political circumstances of the moment. With one exception, Johnson had virtually the freest hand possible in his vice-presidential options. Ironically, the Kennedy assassination that had given Johnson the Presidency set the scene for his choice of running mate: Johnson had to conciliate the Kennedy and liberal forces in the Democratic Party who suddenly found a southern conservative as the party standard-bearer.

With only one year in office behind him, Johnson was immensely popular. He had pulled a grief-stricken nation through a crisis and had demonstrated the workability of the American political system. Although he enjoyed immense flexibility in his choice of a running mate-far more than most presidential nominees-he nonetheless had to operate within a prevailing framework of circumstances, events, and personalities.

Johnson's main problem from the moment he succeeded to the Presidency was that of overcoming his ideological image, of bridging the gap to the liberals. On November 23, 1963, just one day follow-ing the tragic assassination of the President, Johnson's aide and adviser Walter Jenkins transmitted a message from Secretary Orville Freeman stating that "the liberal movement needs badly a good clear impact from the President's speech."[47] Freeman accurately believed that Johnson had to win the confidence of the liberal community in his forthcoming address to a Joint Session of Congress. The November 27, 1963 speech indicated that Johnson was well along in creating a liberal image, but time was short, and the new President needed to reinforce that image as the presidential election neared. His insistence on the immediate passage of civil rights legislation had served as one more building block in closing the ideological gap. He had done all he could to remake his own image; the vice-presidential nomination would provide added strength. He had taken the plunge that had clearly separated him from Southern conservatives. Earlier in his career, as Majority Leader of the Senate, he had found himself with a different constituency and had moved towards a position of greater consensus, especially on civil rights. Indeed, in his home state, he had been viewed as a liberal.**48** As Vice President, his constituency had changed again but in the direction of a more consensual position. While the plunge towards a civil rights position separated him from the conservatives, it was not enough to bring confidence to the liberals. During his tenure as Vice President, Johnson had worked as chairman of the President's Commission on Equal Employment Opportunity, and his performance in that role led some observers to believe that Johnson was much more dedicated to civil rights than was Kennedy himself.**49** He had traveled about the country in an effort to achieve business compliance. He had made speech after speech in which he spoke of the distressing conditions in the employment field. He tried desperately to impart his understanding of the South and of Congress to President Kennedy in an effort to deal with the racial crisis during the summer of 1963. He knew that no President in the summer and fall of 1963, especially following the Birmingham bombings, could have done anything else but press for civil rights legislation. Johnson had urged Kennedy, however, to lay the groundwork for this legislation cautiously. The events in Dallas on November 22 thrust responsibility for this crucial legislative leadership on a President with a Southern background who had less than one year in which to prove himself before the next election.

Above and beyond the moral prerequisites of the civil rights bill were the political necessities. The new President was cognizant of the delicate situation in which he found himself confronting the burdens of the Presidency and the selection of a running mate with solid liberal credentials.**50**

In the months following John Kennedy's death, Lyndon Johnson, aided by Hubert Humphrey and others, worked feverishly for the passage of the 1964 civil rights civil rights legislation. As he approached the summer and fall of 1964 and the forthcoming election campaign, he had done all he could to establish and burnish a liberal image of himself. Someone else now had to lend a hand, someone who would not be accused of changing ideological courses midstream for political reasons, someone who was clearly identified as a liberal yet who would not alienate the conservatives.

Other factors affected the necessity of balancing. An incumbent President is lucky: there is the opportunity to see what cards the opposition holds before placing a bet on a running mate. The nomination of Senator Barry Goldwater as Johnson's Republican opponent further shaped the environment in which Johnson selected his running mate. Goldwater refused to compromise himself by ideologically balancing his choice of a running mate, so he selected Congressman William Miller of New York, also a conservative. This dictated that Johnson place greater store on the liberal than on the conservative vote.

Besides conciliating the liberals of his party, Johnson had another problem as he moved toward the 1964 campaign. The major obstacle to Johnson's free hand in 1964 was the position of the Attorney General, Robert Kennedy, who had been de facto the second most powerful individual in the government under his brother.

Johnson had suffered all the frustration inherent in the office of the Vice Presidency and more. He had been Vice President in and administration that had no room for him; he had simply never fit in. Despite President Kennedy's orders to the contrary, he was the odd man out of the administration. He was out of their element, and they were out of his. And he suffered most severely of all in his relationship with Robert Kennedy, a relationship going back to the bitter days of the 1960 convention in Los Angeles.

In the months before the 1964 convention, a groundswell of support arose for Robert Kennedy as a vice presidential candidate. This presented a dilemma for Johnson because of the emotional and political forces that existed in the aftermath of the assassination. Johnson was a President who had not been elected to that office. To some he seemed a sorry replacement for a young, vibrant leader who was also a handsome, polished, well-spoken man with a Harvard education. In contrast, Lyndon Johnson appeared to many as elderly, somewhat crude - a Southwest Texas State Teachers College graduate and former high school teacher who was not very impressive before an audience. As Vice President, Johnson had had great difficulty living in Kennedy's shadow and image; trying to follow him in the Presidency was even tougher. To have Bobby Kennedy and his supporters potentially trying to "reclaim" the White House was anathema to him. He was determined to win the White House on his own, to get out from under the Kennedy image. But because of circumstances-because Bobby Kennedy was extremely popular, because so much of the nation's heart longed for a Kennedy in the White House-Johnson had to act gingerly, and the vice presidential candidate he ultimately selected would have to sooth ruffled feathers. Lyndon Johnson was engaging in a politically volatile process of elimination: solving the "Bobby problem" but emerging with the support of Robert Kennedy's followers.

Eliminating Kennedy from vice presidential consideration was done with a master stroke: Johnson announced that *no* member of the Cabinet would be eligible for the nomination. Conciliating the Kennedy forces would be more difficult.

Johnson needed not just a liberal but a *particular* liberal: one who would be embraced by the Kennedy forces. Johnson thus considered placing a Catholic on the Democratic ticket, and Eugene McCarthy, Hubert Humphrey's Minnesota competitor for the nomination, appeared to be a likely possibility. Johnson liked McCarthy; they were close personal friends. However, when Johnson tossed out the suggestion of McCarthy for Vice President in a meeting with his advisers soon after his decision regarding the ineligibility of Cabinet members, all but Walter Jenkins were opposed to the idea.**51**

Linked to the desire for a running mate who would support the aims Jonson hoped to achieve in his "Great Society" programs were additional considerations that mad more to do with Jonson's personality and convictions than anything else. Johnson had strong, well-defined views of what the Vice Presidency should be and what he wanted in a Vice President. He wanted someone with whom he could work, someone who could work well with Congress, and above all, someone who would be loyal, almost to the point to the point of subservience at times, and who would avoid public disagreements. Johnson sought someone willing to enter into a relationship that would be comparable to an "insoluble marriage."

Hubert Humphrey seemed to be more than satisfactory on all counts. He was very well-liked within the legislative chamber. His person and professional relationship with Johnson extended back many years, and Johnson had rapport with, as well as affection with, Humphrey. Both men shared similar backgrounds with not "much of a gap socially." They had worked closely as Majority Leader and Majority Whip, respectively, in the Senate. Indeed, in the Senate Humphrey had worked subordinately to Johnson, as he would be doing in the Vice Presidency. This situation was in sharp contrast to that in Kennedy's 1960 selection of Johnson as his running mate, wherein Johnson found it difficult to become subordinate to a man much his junior, not only in age, but especially in political experience. More importantly, Humphrey *understood* the loyalty Johnson demanded and was willing to accept all the requirements placed on the second spot. Humphrey aspired to win the vice presidential nomination and hoped to succeed by demonstrating his helpfulness to Johnson. That Humphrey had been appreciative of the requirements for a vice-presidential aspirant is implicit in the comment of one of his aides who pointed out that when Humphrey looked to Senator Edmund in 1968 as *his* running, he perceived Muskie as a man in whom he "could have complete confidence."

With the aid of James Rowe, Humphrey's West Virginia campaign manager in 1960 as well as long-time Johnson friend, Humphrey set out to prove himself. Humphrey did his by praising Johnson in television interviews (as did his competitor, Senator Eugene McCarthy); by courting the business community (especially via his publication of The Cause Is Mankind*)*; and by demonstrating his talents as the "master of compromise," as he had done as floor manager of the 1964 civil rights legislation. It was Jim Rowe who had transmitted Johnson's demands to Humphrey. It was he who had carefully screened Humphrey's background for Johnson, to ensure that there was nothing in Humphrey's past that might jeopardize the ticket (in sharp contrast to the lack of investigation that would later occur in the 1972 vice presidential selection process.)

So, Humphrey emerged as the quintessential asset. Following his elimination of all Cabinet members, the President found himself faced with the possibility of a party split. Humphrey, however, was a suitable second choice of those who had wanted Robert Kennedy nominated, and Kennedy himself came out in support of Humphrey. Humphrey carried great weight with important liberal segments of the Democratic Party and the electorate-labor, civil rights advocates, and party leaders. Humphrey's identification as a champion of urban area problems as well as the floor manager of the 1964 civil rights bill clinched his liberal credentials, and those credentials were exactly what Johnson needed to emerge from the 1964 Democratic Convention with a united party behind him.

CONCILIATION AND AN UNEPECTED SET OF CIRCUMSTANCES:
THE SELECTION OF SPIRO T. AGNEW

In 1968, Nixon, too, wanted to find a candidate who would conform to his view of the Vice Presidency, someone who would not lose any votes for the Republican ticket and, moreover, someone who was not a superstar. The party superstars were out. They would not be subordinate enough, and clearly, this was how Nixon envisioned the Vice Presidency in his administrations.

Despite the protests of his aides who supported a candidate who would be ideologically different from Nixon, who was viewed as a centrist, Nixon wanted a vice presidential running who would encompass and be acceptable to all wings of the party. Agnew, a "conservative liberal, met
all these criteria. Moreover, Agnew had proven that he could appeal to Democrats, critical to a Republican candidate because Democrats far outnumbered Republicans in voter registration.

The circumstances surrounding Nixon's own nomination as the presidential candidate as well as the anticipated circumstances of the forthcoming presidential campaign need to be recalled. First, Nixon had to rely heavily on the support of Southern and Border state delegations, and he was not their favorite candidate. Second, the specter of the third-party candidate George Wallace had to be offset. Thus, while he hoped to avoid leaning either left or right, Nixon had grace concerns that made it difficult to remain in the center.

The so-called "Southern Strategy" was beginning to take shape. The dictates of circumstance had again meshed with the personality of the presidential nominee to form the criteria for the selection of the 1968 Republican vice presidential candidate. Governor Spiro T. Agnew was the product of that strategy.

CONCILIATION AND CAUTIOUSNESS: THE SELECTION OF WALTER F. MONDALE

Although Jimmy Carter did not enjoy the full luxury that LBJ had had in selecting a vice-presidential running mate, Carter's early capture of the 1976 Democratic Party nomination allowed him considerably greater flexibility than is usually afforded presidential candidates.[52]

Earlier candidates set the stage for the Carter victory, Lyndon Johnson's in particular, since it removed the long-standing taboo surrounding a Southern candidacy. Nonetheless, Carter's candidacy had to be carefully balanced, and the former Georgia governor was up against some of the same constraints that Johnson had faced in choosing a running mate. Carter, too, was considered "conservative" by factions in his party and the country, although Carter was perceived as far more liberal than LBJ had been. While not entirely having to overcome the conservative label, Governor Carter still had to counteract his "Southernness" and the ideological orientation it implied. And so began the search for a liberal who would bring with him that wing of the party.

Comfortable primary victories behind him and assured of the nomination significantly prior to the opening of the convention, Carter paraded vice presidential hopeful after vice presidential hopeful before him and, more importantly, before the national news media. Carter took full advantage of the leverage the early nomination victory had given him and used the vice presidential search to the media hilt. He did this for two reasons: to guarantee the soundness of his ultimate choice and to benefit from continuous media coverage of the selection process itself.

Mondale, the Carter people increasingly felt, was the clear-cut choice. The Minnesotan's long affiliation with Senator Hubert Humphrey set the stage for the remaining litany of advantages on his side. As Humphrey's protégé, long-time associate, Senate successor, and later colleague in the same body, Mondale enjoyed a positive record and image as a liberal champion of many of the causes with which Humphrey had long been associated—civil rights, poverty, minority programs, and labor, whose support Carter needed to solidify. As one commentary noted at the time of the Mondale nomination, "If there is one characteristic that has dominated Mr. Mondale's political life, it is his genuine compassion for the underdog."[53] Indeed, if Hubert Humphrey's qualification for the Vice Presidency in 1964 had included a long arm extended into the liberal camp, Walter Mondale's arm was equally extended in 1976. Jimmy Carter needed this arm to overcome what Democratic polls were telling him: the liberals were wary.**54**

It was Humphrey who placed Mondale's name in nomination, symbolizing the passing of the torch to the younger Minnesotan, and Senator Humphrey's remarks underscored the essential qualities of the "new generation of leadership" and its political significance. Senator Mondale, said Humphrey, was "a truly good and great American…a man who will give of himself for the common good—mind, body, and soul." Humphrey added, "The Carter-Mondale ticket means a significant turning point in the political and social history of this Republic… It represents the final reunification of the North and South…from Canadian border to the Rio Grande, from the Golden Gate to the Potomac."**55** This reunification also represented a blending of ideologies. In an overall nominating atmosphere of party unity and congeniality that seemed uncharacteristic of the Democratic Party in relatively recent times, Jimmy Carter's acceptance speech stressed the need for "a time for healing," "a time for great national deeds." The nomination of Walter Mondale, reconciling the inevitable fears of some liberals within the party in response to the Carter nomination, brought full circle the harmonious aura surrounding this party convention.

The Republican side, equally uncharacteristic, was not quite as compatible. The incumbent President faced a serious ideological challenge for the nomination. As the Mondale nomination unfolded, both President Gerald Ford and conservative challenger Ronald Reagan assessed their positions and shaped their strategies: turn around and emphasize what Jimmy Carter perceived as the ideological benefits of the Mondale nomination: the vice presidential candidate's extremely liberal record. Ford himself, it will be recalled, had been forced by ideological circumstances to rid himself of a liberal running mate, Vice President Nelson A. Rockefeller. His assessment now was that a liberal running mate was not only anathema within the Republican Party, but would also be so across a country that seemed to be in a conservative frame of mind.

As they prepared to do their own internal battle, both Ford and Reagan, acting independently, determined to portray *both* Democratic candidates as liberals; but the Mondale nomination solidified this determination. Ford, who ultimately won the Republican nomination, found his choice of a running mate shaped by the prevailing framework of acceptability, a framework shaped principally by party and ideological circumstances as well as by the campaign strategy predicated by Mondale's candidacy. As Ford sought to pacify the conservative wing of his party, Senator Robert Dole of Kansas thus became the beneficiary of this framework. Dole, a Midwesterner from the conservative wing of the party and a strong party man, rounded out the Ford ticket. Those Republicans who saw Ford as too close to the center rallied around Dole's vice presidential nomination. Ironically, Dole's candidacy may have cost the Republicans the campaign, for as the campaign unfolded and Dole assumed a "hatchet man" pose, Mondale's temperament and well-spokenness—particularly during the nationally televised debate in which both running mates squared off—seemed to sway the decision of many an undecided voter in what was ultimately a razor-thin victory by the Carter-Mondale team.56

CONCILIATION: GERALD FORD AS HEALER?
GEORGE H. W. BUSH AS SECOND BEST?

After leaving the Presidency, Gerald Ford wrote poignantly of "A Time to Heal," a time in which he had been critical of Ronald Reagan's "penchant for offering simplistic solutions to hideously complex problems."57 During the 1980 Republican National Convention, Reagan would turn to Ford himself as perhaps the one individual who could so dramatically and most effectively "heal" and unify the party by agreeing to serve as Reagan's running mate. There were unprecedented discussions and negotiations regarding a former President as "the second man." Both because of the unusual circumstances surrounding this event and because of what it tells us about the Presidency and

Vice Presidency, the Reagan-Ford-ticket-that-never-materialized merits examination.

As the Democratic party seemed to be torn asunder by internal dissatisfaction and divisions, by a nomination challenge to the incumbent President, and by a threat of a convention upheaval that might result in an "open convention," the time was ripe for Republican presidential candidate Ronald Reagan—the nomination was clearly his—to solidify his prospects of electoral victory. Perhaps it can be aptly said that conditions were so ripe for a Republican victory that only a serious mishap could have lost the election for Ronald Reagan. Just four years earlier, this same Republican Party had narrowly lost the Presidency to Jimmy Carter following a challenge by Reagan himself to the incumbent President Ford. Now the tables were turned in more ways than one. The Democrats were even more divided than the Republicans had been in 1976. Now, too, Gerald Ford perhaps stood between victory and defeat, just as Reagan had in 1976. What better way to salve the wounds inflicted on Ford and his wing of the party four years earlier than to offer the still very popular former President the second spot on the Reagan ticket? What better way to appease the more moderate segment of the Republican Party, a segment already disgruntled by an extremely conservative platform? What better way to appeal to disgruntled Democrats across the country—many of whom no doubt often regretted having voted for Carter rather than Ford in 1976?

The analysts all said no; no former President would even consider the second spot. But there had never been a former President like Gerald Ford. Always true to his political and personal character, Ford placed party loyalty above all else. Moreover, he had never suffered from false pride, and his behavior during the 1980 Republican Convention demonstrated just how unassuming and direct he could be.

Approached by Reagan just hours before the presidential candidate's own nomination, Ford did not dismiss the possibility of joining the Reagan ticket. He knew such a conciliation would help his party. But the former President made clear that his role as Vice President would have to be forged in advance; he would be no figurehead. In his usual forthright manner, Ford stated, "If I go to Washington, and I'm not saying that I'm accepting, I have to go there with the belief that I would play a meaningful role, across the board, in the basic, crucial, tough decisions that have to be made in the four-year period."**58**

Ford was equally forthright in stating his hesitation about accepting Reagan's offer—a hesitation that highlights, incidentally, the basic nature of the presidential-vice-presidential relationship, especially in terms of the inevitable staff tensions. As Ford said, "I don't have any hang-up on pride," but he realized that staff tensions might set up an "unworkable, unhealthy situation," exacerbated by the fact that the Vice President had once been President himself.**59**

As speculation mounted and the convention progressed, it became readily apparent that the Reagan forces were hard at work trying to convince Ford to take the second spot. It was equally apparent that the Ford forces were not as resistant as they might have been expected to be. Determined not to settle for a figurehead Vice Presidency, Ford repeatedly sought many concessions from the Reagan camp. Perhaps the magnitude of these concessions is what led to speculation that Reagan was considering a "co-Presidency," a move that was clearly out of keeping with the essence of presidential leadership. Indeed, this notion of a "co-Presidency" would lead to serious criticism of Governor Reagan and to charges that he was naïve in his understanding of presidential power. In fact, former Reagan campaign manager John Sears observed, "It doesn't sit well with people who are looking for a leader…The people want to see one man in charge."**60** Reagan's naiveté about Washington politics seemed about to undo the edge he had achieved over President Jimmy Carter, who himself had so often been criticized on the same grounds. Contrary to this kind of criticism were the commentaries praising Reagan's "flexibility," his "openness," his willingness to broaden his ideological base in his attempt to achieve electoral victory.**61**

AMERICAN PRINCE(SS), AMERICAN PAUPER

It was ironic that, unlike their interaction four years earlier, when Reagan had perhaps been too lukewarm in his efforts toward the Ford reelection, Ford was now in the driver's seat. If the Ford forces had succeeded in their negotiations, the results would have been an unprecedented dismantling of presidential power. As Reagan's Vice President, Ford would indeed have been a "co-President," sharing in Cabinet, National Security Council, and other important appointments, and having the White House staff report to the President through him. In essence, the Vice President would have served as the "Chief Operating Officer," with the President in the position of a chairman of the board.**62**

Perhaps nothing more than a twist of fate aborted such a "constitutional coup," as Anthony Lewis of the *New York Times* termed it. Perhaps the television coverage of the convention, which seemed to reach the dimensions of the absurd in this rather unsurprising year, will be credited for so publicizing the negotiations over the Vice Presidency that the unwanted publicity and mounting speculation forced both Ford's and Reagan's hands. So little was happening at the convention that the media seemed desperate for "news" or anything that might pass as news. This led television reporters to spend an inordinate amount of time and energy on this one issue of a prospective Ford candidacy and its implications: the powers Reagan would give up in the bargain; its unprecedented nature; and, critically the potential role of former Secretary of State Henry Kissinger in a Reagan-Ford Administration. Ford was seen as the nice guy, as the unwitting victim of the devious Kissinger who was looking toward his own return to power, undoubtedly as Secretary of State. As the Ford forces dragged their heels, Reagan realized the speculation had to be ended. A decision had to be rendered and rendered immediately, both because "there was a major danger that they [the delegates] were going to draft Ford,"**63** according to a participant in the negotiations, and because allowing the speculation to continue was making Reagan look indecisive and like a poor leader. Ironically, the move that had been geared to solidify Reagan's electoral prospects emerged as a potential handle that the Democrats might grasp. Reagan was therefore prompted to refuse Ford the chance to have one more night to "think on it," and he decided to make an unscheduled appearance at the convention hall a day prior to his own official acceptance of the presidential nomination. Perhaps the essential nature of the Vice Presidency doomed the Ford negotiations from the outset. After all, no matter who the individual involved, no matter what level of popularity or influence of that individual, the *second* spot is dispensable. So, in his appearance before the Republican delegates, Ronald Reagan announced that George H. W. Bush would be his running mate.

Bush, the candidate who had taken an early lead in the 1980 presidential competition when he had "separated himself from the pack" with his victory in the Republican Iowa caucus, had initially threatened the prospects of an easy Reagan nomination victory. But the California governor made his comeback, and Bush eventually withdrew from the Republican primaries. Once the Reagan-Ford talks began, Bush seemed to lose hope of winning the second spot on the ticket.**64** But now, with those talks abandoned, Bush was exactly what Ronald Reagan needed to keep the Republican Party united as it left the convention site and moved into the electoral arena. Bush's most crucial credentials were his appeal to the more moderate wing of the party, whose support was vital, and his previously held position of Republican National Chairman, to which he had been appointed by Nixon in 1972 as Watergate began to emerge and which had earned him a reputation for helping the party stay together during troubled times.**65** Thus, despite the unhappiness among the party conservatives who had hoped for a clean sweep and a "pure" ideological ticket, Reagan saw the pragmatism in the Bush nomination.

Once nominated, George H.W. Bush studiously played down the differences between himself and the presidential candidate: "I'm not going to say I haven't had differences at some point with Governor Reagan…But what I will be doing is emphasizing common ground. I will be enthusiastically supporting this Republican platform."**66** He preferred instead to emphasize what united them. Bush was also studious in squelching a would-be issue: George H.W. Bush as second best to Gerald Ford. Clearly, Reagan's choice was principally geared toward party conciliation; either the Ford or Bush candidacy would have met his party's needs.

VICE PRESIDENTIAL SELECTION:
BALANCING PERSONAL CHARACTERISTICS

In a particular election, although one criterion might stand out as most important in the selection of a vice presidential running mate, in reality a composite of factors needs to be balanced. So, for example, although issue emphasis was the most important criterion Eisenhower had to consider in 1952, Nixon balanced Eisenhower's "Eastern Establishment" identification and could also be an asset with the California delegation over which the Eisenhower camp was troubled, and Nixon was very legitimately a solid Republican.**67**

Lyndon Johnson, following his abrupt succession to the Presidency, was aware that the circumstances that had propelled him into the Presidency drew attention to at least one criterion in the selection of a running mate, namely, the Vice President's ability to perform in the Presidency—"in case I fall out an airplane tomorrow," Johnson reportedly told his staff.**68** A major strategy of the Humphrey people, therefore, involved presenting the Minnesota senator as a fully qualified successor. In the wake of the Kennedy assassination, this was a strong selling point.

Humphrey had certain assets that were extraordinarily compatible with Johnson's hopes for his administration. The President's plan for a Great Society was, to a large extent the embodiment of the issues to which Hubert Humphrey had committed himself two decades earlier. If his advocacy of the civil rights bill in 1964, a performance testified to by Johnson in his memoirs,**69** was any indication of his abilities, he would be quite an asset.

Linked to the desire for a running mate who would support the aims Johnson hoped to achieve in his Great Society programs were additional considerations that had more to do with Johnson's personality and convictions than anything else. Johnson had strong, well-defined views of what the office of the Vice Presidency should be and what he wanted in a Vice President; namely, he wanted someone with whom he could work, someone who could work well with Congress, and, above all, someone who would be loyal, almost to the point of subservience at times, and who would avoid public disagreements. Johnson sought someone willing to enter into a relationship that would be an "insoluble marriage."**70**

Hubert Humphrey seemed to be more than satisfactory on all counts. He was very well liked within the legislative chamber. His personal and professional relationship with Johnson extended back many years, and Johnson had rapport with, as well as affection for, Humphrey. Both men shared similar backgrounds with not "much of a gap socially."**71** They had worked closely as Majority Leader and Majority Whip, respectively, in the Senate; indeed, in the Senate, Humphrey had worked subordinately to Johnson, as he would be doing in the Vice Presidency. This situation was in sharp contrast to that in Kennedy's 1960 selection of Johnson as his running mate, wherein Johnson found it difficult to become subservient to a man much his junior, not only in age, but especially in experience. More importantly, Humphrey *understood* the loyalty Johnson demanded and was willing to accept all the requirements placed on the second spot. Humphrey aspired to win the Vice Presidency, and he could hope to succeed by demonstrating his helpfulness to Johnson. That Humphrey had been appreciative of the requirements for a vice presidential aspirant is implicit in the comment of one of his aides who pointed out that when Humphrey looked to Edmund Muskie in 1968 as *his* running mate, her perceived Muskie as a man in whom he "could have complete confidence."**72**

With the aid of James Rowe, Humphrey's West Virginia campaign manager in 1960 as well as long-time Johnson friend, Humphrey had set out to prove himself. Humphrey did this by praising Johnson in television interviews (as did his competitor, Senator Eugene McCarthy); by courting the business community (especially via his publication of The Cause Is Mankind); and by demonstrating his talents as the "master of compromise," as he had done as floor manager of the 1964 civil rights legislation.73 It was Jim Rowe who had transmitted Johnson's demands to Humphrey. It was he who had carefully screened Humphrey's background for Johnson to ensure that there was nothing in Humphrey's past that might jeopardize the ticket (in sharp contrast to the lack of investigation that would later occur in the 1972 Democratic vice presidential selection process).

Nixon, too, wanted to find a candidate who would conform to his view of the Vice Presidency, someone who would not lose any votes for the 1968 Republican ticket and, moreover, someone who was not a superstar.74 The party superstars were out. They would not be subordinate enough, and, clearly, this was how Nixon envisioned the Vice Presidency in his administration.

Despite the protests of his aides who supported a candidate who would be ideologically different from Nixon (who was viewed as a centrist), Nixon wanted a vice presidential running mate who would encompass and be acceptable to all wings of the party. Agnew, a "conservative liberal," met all of these criteria. Moreover, Agnew had proven that he could appeal to Democrats, which is critical to a Republican candidacy because the Democrats far outnumber the Republicans in voter registration.

The circumstances surrounding Nixon's own nomination as the presidential candidate as well as the anticipated circumstances of the forthcoming presidential campaign need to be recalled. First, Nixon had to rely heavily on the support of Southern and Border state delegations, and he was not their favorite candidate. Second the specter of the third-party candidate George Wallace posed a large threat. South Carolina Senator Strom Thurmond and the South had to be placated;

George Wallace had to be offset. Thus, while he hoped to avoid leaning either left or right, Nixon had grave concerns that made it difficult to remain in the center.

The so-called Southern Strategy was beginning to take shape. The dictates of circumstance had again meshed with the personality of the presidential nominee to form the criteria for the selection of the 1968 Republican vice presidential candidate. Governor Spiro T. Agnew of Maryland was the product of that strategy.

As with many a presidential candidate, Nixon's search for a running mate was very much a process of elimination that restricted his freedom of choice. Nixon wanted desperately to avoid many of the names that had been speculated on—the Lindsays, Percys, and Rockefellers of the party. Nixon's efforts not to be out-starred led him on a search for a candidate who would be grateful to be on the ticket. Besides, the polls indicated that Nixon ran better alone than with any name with which he had been paired.[75] Therefore, the selection of a vice presidential running mate who would not *lose* any votes was critical. "The Vice President can't help you," Nixon told close aides. "He can only hurt you."[76] Moreover, the vice presidential candidate had to conform to Nixon's view of the second office. Nixon's criteria and Agnew's credentials were well matched. Agnew was no superstar, and he was in agreement regarding the subordination of the Vice Presidency.

When Jimmy Carter approached the vice presidential selection process in 1976, he had to conciliate the party liberals. In addition, as with all previous presidential candidates, Carter's choice of a running mate was also conditioned by the framework of acceptability prevailing at the time.

Ironically, one key liability in need of balancing was a characteristic of the Carter candidacy itself which provided much appeal in the post-Watergate campaign: Carter's lack of association and familiarity with Washington politics. Thus, it was no accident that the parade of vice-presidential hopefuls was limited to members of Congress. In addition to Mondale, consideration went to Senators Frank Church of Idaho, who emerged in the polls as the most popular potential running mate; John H. Glenn of Ohio, allegedly daughter Amy Carter's first choice for the spot; Adlai E. Stevenson of Illinois; and Representative Peter W. Rodino, Jr., of New Jersey, who had gained widespread praise as chairman of the House Judiciary Committee during the Nixon impeachment hearings.**77**

Carter spoke candidly of his need for an insider in his July 12, 1976, news conference in New York City. "I feel a need to know more about the Washington political procedure. This is an aspect of my own experience that is missing," he admitted.**78** (Four years later, Ronald Reagan, also an outsider to Washington politics, would also find his vice presidential choice conditioned by this necessity.)

In 1976, a second liability was indicated by polls taken among Democratic and independent voters prior to the convention. These polls showed concern for Carter's possible lack of understanding of regions outside the South.**79** Thus, the need for regional balance on the ticket emerged.

Following the Eagleton debacle of 1972 and the Agnew resignation of 1973 it seemed that no presidential candidate would ever be able to settle on a running mate haphazardly. While this proved to not be the case in the 2008 selection of Alaska Governor Sarah Palin (to be discussed below) by presidential candidate John McCain, Carter's team carefully vetted running mate options. The thorough investigation of background necessary was facilitated by Carter's early primary victories, affording him a comfortable three-month period in which to scrutinize candidates. Thus, not only did Carter benefit from the publicity of his vice presidential search: he had no choice *but* to focus attention on the thoroughness of his efforts to avoid a mistake.

No stone was left unturned to uncover "the best," as Carter himself put it. For Carter this person meant someone whose competence to assume the Presidency would be obvious, someone with whom he could be politically and personally compatible, and, of course, someone who could balance the ticket for the Democratic Party.

In announcing the choice he had made, Carter characterized Senator Mondale as "an uncommon man, terribly gifted, committed, skilled, experienced, ready, but above all a good man." Carter went on to say that he had selected Mondale not only because the Minnesotan was the "best equipped available" but also because this choice would result in "the best politics."**80** Two immediate problems, however, had to be dealt with, and Carter did so with dispatch.

Referring candidly to the fact that Walter Mondale suffered from hypertension, the presidential candidate felt that this relatively minor medical problem did not warrant the elimination of one so highly qualified. The second problem stemmed from statements Mondale had made regarding his dislike of and incompatibility with presidential campaigning. Mondale's book, The Accountability of Power, spends a good deal of time on the rigors of presidential politics.

In a November 21, 1975, news conference, following his withdrawal from the race for the 1976 Democratic presidential nomination, Mondale had bluntly stated: "I do not have the overwhelming desire to be President, which is essential for the kind of campaign that is required. I admire those with the determination to do what is required to seek the Presidency, but I have found that I am not among them."

Mondale's perspectives on presidential politicking would thus provide some initial controversy over Carter's choice for the number two spot. But this, too, Carter handled squarely and adeptly. "It was one of the major doubts that I had about him at the beginning," admitted Carter, but he added that his talks with Mondale prior to the decision to nominate him had allayed the presidential candidate's fears.**81** Once these considerations were out of the way, Mondale's credentials readily made themselves apparent.

Four years later, candidate Reagan would also have to turn to a running mate whose background and experience would fill in "gaps" in his own credentials. In addition to being able to conciliate the moderates and liberals of the Republican Party, George H.W. Bush was experienced in foreign affairs. Bush had served as U.S. delegate to the United Nations under the Nixon Administration, as head of the U.S. liaison office in Peking, and later as the director of the Central Intelligence Agency under President Ford. Thus, he would provide and expertise which Reagan lacked. Moreover, as a former two-term congressman, Bush was in a position somewhat parallel to Walter Mondale's in 1976: a "Washingtonian" paired with a candidate who held a disdain for and an unfamiliarity with Washington politics.

Clearly, the Reagan choice was geared principally toward party conciliation, but his framework was likewise conditioned by several other necessities, necessities met by George H.W. Bush: a candidate qualified to succeed to the Presidency; one who balanced Reagan's personal characteristics, particularly his advanced age; and one who could appeal to voters in the Northeast. Thus was the Reagan-Bush team ready for its "coast-to-coast, border-to-border campaign."**82**

While presidential candidates have traditionally sought to maximize their electoral strength by selecting vice presidential running mates who will unify the national party, the more recent trend has been away from an out-and-out, diametrically opposed balancing of political ideologies. This trend demonstrates the growing realization that the Vice Presidency is more than just a political plum to be passed around—a fear of the Founding Fathers—and the office has increased in importance as a positive, functioning institution.

Nonetheless, degrees of ideological balancing or ideological sameness remain. The candidate, while perhaps sharing views similar to those of the presidential candidate, simultaneously is either more appealing or at least more acceptable to a potentially troublesome wing of the party or the electorate. So, Nixon was seen as *more* conservative than Eisenhower but still within reach of Eisenhower's views; Humphrey already had the liberalism for which Johnson had been struggling and would not contribute to factionalism; the "New Nixon" of 1968, the centrist candidate, could simultaneously play the Southern Strategy with a non-offensive "conservative liberal," Spiro Agnew. John Kennedy could woo Southern votes while not bringing in a candidate of the extreme opposite but turning, instead, to Senate Majority Leader Lyndon Johnson, who had received the bulk of the Southern delegate votes as the convention. As a Southerner and a less liberal politician than Kennedy, Johnson had nevertheless been moving toward the center, especially on civil rights.

Nixon's choice of Lodge in 1960 avoided a candidate of opposing views while adding a candidate who appealed to the North. This became especially important once Kennedy had selected Johnson for the Democratic second spot since Johnson would probably take a major part of the Southern vote with him.

In 1968, Humphrey's choice of Maine Senator Edmund Muskie rounded out a moderate liberal ticket. Muskie was a stark contrast to Nixon's selection of Spiro Agnew, who soon became an embarrassment to the presidential nominee, a subject to be discussed below.

And in the subsequent presidential campaign of 1972, George McGovern had been confident that Senator Edward M. Kennedy would agree to be his running. But Kennedy was persistent in his refusal. So George McGovern had to cast about for an alternative, virtually at the last minute. He choice was Democratic Senator Thomas Eagleton of Missouri and, then following Eagleton's departure from the ticket due to aspects of his past that proved to be problematic, a subject to be discussed below, McGovern selected Sargent Shriver, a Kennedy brother-in-law. Shriver represented the selection of a running mate who would balance the ticket ideologically, since neither Eagleton nor Shriver was associated with McGovern's "extreme" views. The divergence from this trend, as noted earlier, was Senator Barry Goldwater's refusal in 1964 to strike a balance ideologically; instead, Goldwater selected the conservative Republican Congressman William Miller. The particular degree of ideological balancing within this trend toward an acceptable range of views hinges on the total political environment in which the balancing takes place; although patterns do emerge, each situation is unique.

When former Arkansas Governor William ("Bill") Clinton clinched the 1992 Democratic presidential nomination he broke a significant tradition of not selecting a running mate from the same geographical region of the country as his own. Clinton understood the political shift to the south. His selection of Tennessee Senator Albert Gore reflected that understanding as well as Clinton's need to bring Washingtonian and legislative experience to the ticket.

THE POLITICS OF TIMING: THE FERRARO SELECTION AND EXTERNAL INFLUENCES

Walter Mondale's former incumbency as Vice President had given him a head start as he sought the 1984 Democratic presidential nomination. Although Mondale was ultimately victorious in the primaries and amassed sufficient delegate support to claim the nomination, the challenges of Colorado Senator Gary Hart and civil rights figure the Reverend Jesse Jackson helped shaped Mondale's "framework of acceptability" in his choice of a running mate.

Had Mondale remained true to what many perceived as his traditionally cautious style, he might very well have selected Hart, since Hart had emerged as his major opponent in the primaries. Indeed, the Hart forces might have been able to back Mondale into a convention corner by playing to Mondale's hopes of achieving party unity. But the Jackson candidacy had brought other considerations to the forefront. Not only was Jackson the first serious black contender for the presidential nomination; early in his campaign he had also promised to name a woman as his running mate, if nominated himself. Thus, in addition to all of the traditional considerations that go into the choice of a vice presidential candidate, no presidential candidate in the 1984 season was able to ignore the added consideration of gender. Beyond this, Mondale's considerations were also shaped by the growing "gender gap" seemingly being suffered by the Reagan Administration and the increasingly vocalized demands of women's groups, particularly N.O.W., that the Democratic Party take a significant stance in support of women by actually naming a woman to the national ticket. In short, the time was ripe for just such a selection. Indeed, with the dismal Democratic prospects in 1984—Mondale trailed considerably behind the enormously popular incumbent Ronald Reagan—the vice presidential selection served as a "safety valve" through which the Democratic party, much as it had in 1948, was able to add a moment of hope and excitement to its electoral efforts.

As had Carter in 1976, Mondale used the time between securing enough delegate votes in the primaries and the opening of the convention to have the vice presidential selection become a media event. Ironically, perhaps, Mondale's "public" selection of his running mate, while engendering visibility and media coverage, further limited his freedom of choice. The astute Speaker of the House Tip O'Neill remarked during Mondale's interviews, "It's going to be Hart or a woman."**83**

Besides Hart, among the more "traditional" candidates under consideration were such prominent Democrats as Ohio Senator John Glenn, Texas Senator Lloyd Bentsen, Jr., Arkansas Senator Dale Bumpers, and New York Governor Mario Cuomo. Glenn certainly would have balanced the ticket ideologically; Bentsen would had added strength in the Southwest; Bumpers, generally considered a "liberal Southerner," could have been within the Mondale range of issues at the same time he offered geographical diversity; Cuomo could have attracted the important New York and ethnic votes.**84** But Mondale had to go beyond tradition if he hoped to have a fighting chance against the President. Perhaps if the race had been a closer one, presidential candidate Mondale would have taken a "safer" route and balanced his ticket within the traditional criteria. But circumstances mandated bold and courageous action. His candidacy needed an "energizer" and the hope was that the vice-presidential nomination would be just that.

Mondale's search extended the list of potential vice presidential characteristics and scored at least symbolic chords of the Democratic

Party's image as the party of diversity. Mondale's interviewees included Philadelphia Mayor Wilson Goode and Los Angeles Mayor Tom Bradley, both black, and San Antonio Mayor Henry Cisneros, the first Hispanic to ever be considered for a national ticket. Mondale also met with San Francisco Mayor Diane Feinstein, who would have added both a change of gender and religion to a national ticket; Martha Layne Collins, governor of Kentucky; and Congresswoman Geraldine Ferraro of New York.**85**

Mondale desperately needed to give his candidacy a flair that he himself seemed unable to bring to it. Beyond this, Mondale, himself still very much associated with the negativism of the Carter Administration, needed to redirect media and public attention elsewhere. The Ferraro nomination, announced prior to the convention, seemed to give the Mondale candidacy momentum and redirection.

Ferraro, a fast-talking, quick-witted forty-eight year old Congresswoman from Queens, was ideologically very much like Mondale; indeed, had Ferraro not been a woman, she might very well have been eliminated because she and Mondale were so ideologically similar. In addition to gender, Ferraro brought other attributes to the ticket. She added strength in the Northeast and Midwestern industrial states. As an Italian-American and also a Catholic, Ferraro, it was hoped, would lure back those two demographics of voters that the Democrats had slowly been losing over the previous several presidential elections. Beyond this, her immigrant and working-class roots and her personification of the "American success story" fit in well with the prevailing issues Mondale wanted to develop during the campaign: America as the land of opportunity in which the underdog could rise to prominence and the Democratic Party as the party which cared about, and represented, them. Moreover, Ferraro's congressional career had proven she could survive in the "man's world" of politics; early on she had won the respect of her colleagues and her "boss," House Speaker Tip O'Neill. In fact, O'Neill had pushed for Ferraro's candidacy.

The Mondale-Ferraro theme of caring extended into international issues, with Ferraro vociferously speaking of arms control as the "pre-eminent issue."**86** Ferraro, who was also a wife and mother, was able to incorporate those roles to underscore her concern for the issues. During one rally, for example, Ferraro said, "I see little children held up by mothers and fathers. You can't help but wonder what is going to happen to them unless we do something about arms control right now."**87** And she wondered aloud what would happen to her son and to the sons of those in her audience.**88**

Perhaps Ferraro's greatest asset to Mondale was that, as the first woman on a ticket, her candidacy was an unknown, an untested quantity; only the campaign would reveal its effect. Indeed, the Reagan-Bush team initially seemed stymied about how to deal with her as an opponent, since attacking her directly might be perceived as an attack on a woman's candidacy per se. The Republican strategy to a great extent, at least initially, was to ignore Ferraro. But various Ferraro remarks, especially one in which she bluntly questioned President Reagan's "Christianity" considering some of the consequences for the poor resulting from the administration's economic policies, pitted Mondale's running mate in direct confrontation with the Republican team.

The momentum of Ferraro's candidacy was slowed when controversy began to surround the finances of her husband, John Zaccaro. Ferraro herself proved her mettle under fire as she adeptly and candidly took on a barrage of media scrutiny in this area. Similarly, her candidacy took on controversy when differences of views on the abortion question found Ferraro in confrontation with New York Archbishop John J. O'Connor.**89** Despite these controversies and the fact that the Mondale-Ferraro ticket could not overcome the significant lead of the popular Reagan, Geraldine Ferraro's place on the 1984 Democratic ticket continued the evolution of acceptable criteria in the vice-presidential selection process. Much as John F. Kennedy's 1960 presidential candidacy once and for all laid to rest the unacceptability of a Catholic on a national ticket, so too did

Ferraro's presence eliminate the total unacceptability of a woman in a national leadership role.

Timing may very well have been the major force behind the McCain team in the selection of Alaska Governor Sarah Palin as McCain's 2008 running mate. At the time, bets regarding the Democratic frontrunner were on Hillary Clinton, and perhaps the thinking was to draw off some of the "women's vote." The Palin selection, which turned out to be an embarrassment, will be discussed below.

INHERITING EXPERIENCE? : THE CHENEY SELECTION

George W. Bush's selection of Richard ("Dick") Cheney as his running mate in both 2000 and 2004 also reflects the necessity of balancing personal characteristics. Cheney, Bush's senior in age, also brought with him an extraordinary record in national government. Indeed, he had served in several administrations as well as in the legislature, which warrants discussion of an additional category of consideration, that of "inheriting" from previous administrations. Perhaps no vice presidential selection better exemplifies this than the Cheney selection.

Initially in charge of vetting potential running mates for presidential candidate George W. Bush, Dick Cheney continued to impress the younger Bush. As Bush noted "As he came and gave me briefings on his vice presidential searching, I was really in my own mind interviewing him – he just didn't know it."[90]

While pursuing his assigned task of vetting potential vice presidential running mates, Cheney observed something that Richard M. Nixon had said many years before in different words. Said Cheney, "My experience over the years has been that you usually end up with the least worst (sic) option. . . . It's hard to find many examples in history where the vice presidential candidate has really made much difference in the final outcome. People don't vote for vice president. They vote for president."[91]

Interesting to note are the observations made by Pulitzer Prize winning author Barton Gellman, who wrote of Cheney's initial role at vice presidential running mate and finally Cheney's own anointment for the position.**92** Gellman describes Cheney's process of vetting numerous potential vice presidential nominees from the ranks of prominent Republicans, noting that "Secrecy was part of the bargain Cheney struck . . . when he agreed to run Bush's vice-presidential search. . . . For Cheney, the low profile was a means to an end, the way to get things done without obstruction. . . . Not even Bush's closest aides were allowed inside the machine that Cheney built to sift the vice-presidential contenders."**93**

Gellman notes that Cheney developed an elaborate an unusually expansive questionnaire for all of the potential nominees. Following many weeks and the influx of numerous contender questionnaires, it was Dick Cheney who emerged as the vice presidential nominee, and, as Gellman notes, without having to complete the very questionnaire he had distributed to others.**94** Gellman offers the interesting observation that "No one but Cheney can say for sure when he began to see a vice president in the mirror. By agreeing to manage the search, however Cheney did something he does as well as anyone in Washington. He placed himself in the only vantage point that could show him how much time he had left to decide. Had Bush displayed signs of settling on someone else, Cheney would be the first to know."**95**

While Cheney was vetting potential running mates, Bush often hinted to Cheney that he wanted *him* as a running mate. has a running mate. Finally, it came to the point, after a July 2000 lunch. after Cheney's extensive vetting of other potentials, when the presidential nominee decided once and for all that it was Cheney he wanted on the ticket, saying to Cheney, "You're the solution to my problem," the problem being whom to select.**96** Beyond this, the presidential nominee's father, former President George W. Bush advocated for Cheney's selection. As George W. Bush recalled, in talking with his father about the selection process, the elder Bush advised, "Dick would be a great choice. He would give you candid and solid advice. And you'd never have to worry about him going behind your back."**97** So following the Bush-Cheney July lunch, Cheney reconsidered Bush's offer, and as one observer noted, "It was an abrupt change of heart, influenced by two factors: a sense of duty and a growing believe that he was the least worst option. In his own work, <u>Decision Points,</u> George W. Bush observed that "By the time [Cheney] came to see me at the ranch in July, we had narrowed the list to nine people. But in my mind, there was always a tenth."**98**

Perhaps of utmost importance is that Bush knew Cheney had no presidential ambitions of his own. Cheney's health and age argued against such ambitions; thus, the presidential nominee could be sure that, if elected, his Vice President would not attempt to upstage him for his own political advantage.**100** NOTE: Cheney discusses at length his full disclosures to presidential nominee George W. Bush in his work, <u>In My Time.</u>**99** But as will be discussed below, extraordinary events served to change the reality of those stated ambitions that might had led to a de facto co-Presidency.

VICE PRESIDENTIAL SELECTION EMBARRASSMENTS

Unfortunately for some presidential nominees, the choice for the second spot may turn out to be an embarrassment. This was what Nixon in 1968, McGovern in 1972; George Herbert Walker Bush in 1980, and John McCain in 2000 experienced. So much for a "learning curve."

In 1968, Richard Nixon thought he had found the perfect running mate in Maryland Governor Spiro T. Agnew. This was also a classic moment when the overall political environment dramatically affected the Agnew selection. Once third party candidate, former Governor George C. Wallace, an ardent segregationist, introduced what became the theme of the 1968 presidential campaign. Ironically, the Vietnam War took a backstage position to the Wallace theme of "law and order." The Wallace theme was clearly racist, and reflect a great deal of the resentment in many parts of the U. S. Humphrey's own strong background on civil rights put him under far less pressure than what Nixon felt. Nixon sought a running who was both strong on "law and order" AND civil rights, a very odd and difficult background to have earned. So Agnew it was. But no sooner had the general election campaign begun than Agnew's frequent gaffes served to embarrass the Republican ticket, as noted earlier in this work.

1972 initially proved to be a very good year for the would-be Democratic presidential candidate Senator George McGovern, whose direction of the post-1968 Democratic Party delegate reforms certainly helped him gain the presidential nomination. But what was to follow dramatically harmed his general election chances of success.

Several factors seemed to be at work as McGovern selected Missouri Senator Thomas Eagleton. McGovern seemed certain that Massachusetts Senator Edward M. Kennedy would accept the second spot. But Kennedy declined. Reports are that McGovern actually telephoned Kennedy several times throughout the night. By morning, it became quite clear that Kennedy's answer was still "no." McGovern turned to Eagleton.

When McGovern spoke with Eagleton, he asked the Missouri Senator if there was anything in Eagleton's background that might embarrass or be harmful to the ticket. Eagleton said "no," and McGovern presented Eagleton's name to the convention delegates. But after the convention recessed, it became abundantly clear that McGovern had not done an adequate vetting process. The story broke; not only had Eagleton undergone psychiatric treatment – taboo in that era – but had also undergone electric shock therapy. Both disclosures were overwhelming for that period of time. McGovern made matters worse with his initial statement that he was behind Eagleton "1,000%" – only to drop him from the ticket days later.

So it was back to the drawing board for the Democratic presidential nominee. Recognizing the value of having a Catholic on the ticket, McGovern compiled a list of Kennedy alternatives (all of whom were of Catholic faith but one – Connecticut Senator Abraham Ribicoff, of

Jewish faith). All declined. Finally, Kennedy in-law Sargent Shriver, former Peace Corps Director, agreed to be on the McGovern ticket. By this time, however, an already popular incumbent President Nixon (for whom "Watergate" had barely surfaced) was travelling a safe road to re-election.

Neither party seems immune from potential embarrassment, and in 1988 and again in 2008, it was the Republicans who suffered from the selection of running mates. Richard Nixon had once said, "A Vice President can't help you; [s]he can only hurt you."

In 1988 it was two-term Reagan Vice President George Herbert Walker Bush's ironic turn, and his dilemma came out of what had been his fortune when presidential nominee Reagan selected him for the second spot. Even though Reagan was elevated to the nomination by an ever-increasing conservative and Moral Majority wave, the presidential nominee wanted the safety valve of an ideologically balanced ticket. Despite some bitter moments during the primary season, G. H. W. Bush, clearly a moderate, became Reagan's choice. Bush spent eight years of loyalty to Reagan, denying he had ever criticized Reagan's ideas (the most classic of which was Bush having referred to Reagan's economic ideas as "voodoo economics). Reagan was pleased with Bush, but Republican conservatives were still dubious. So when it was "Bush's turn," he turned to Senator Dan Quayle of Indiana, whose conservative credentials were pristine. On the campaign trail, Quayle began to be an embarrassment to the party and the ticket. Realistically, Dan Quayle was and is a much more intelligent and capable individual than has been credited. But he suffered at the time and things became somewhat of a self-fulfilling prophecy.

It was Senator John McCain's turn in 2000. Perhaps it will never be entirely certain what the outcome of that campaign might have been but for McCain's selection of Alaska Governor Sarah Palin as his running mate. Many say that McCain deferred to his advisers in the selection process, banking on having a female on the ticket to take women's votes away from the presumed nominee Hillary Clinton (which turned out, ironically) to not be the case. But perhaps in no other campaign has the phrase "a heartbeat away from the Presidency" been used as frequently as it was with Sarah Palin in that crucial line of succession. Spiro Agnew had gaffes; Dan Quayle had moments of being ill-at-ease and giving way to slips of the tongue. But Sarah Palin's utter lack of knowledge astonished all within earshot.

CONCILIATION:
"CRACKS IN THE GLASS CEILING," AND UNUSUAL CIRCUMSTANCES, AND THE SELECTION OF JOE BIDEN

Securing an early "win" of the presidential nomination affords the nominee what is typically the "luxury" of doing extensive vetting of potential running mates. That luxury can have the added advantage of free media coverage of the presidential nominee and his/her judgment. Jimmy Carter enjoyed that luxury in 1976. On the other hand, it may "backfire" and back the presidential nominee into a corner – as it did for Walter Mondale in 1984. For Mondale, as the process lingered, he experienced increasing pressure from women's groups to select a female running mate.

For Joe Biden in 2020, the extended time was a plus. A serious vice presidential vetting process not only continued coverage of the upcoming presidential nomination itself, just a week before the Democratic National Convention; it demonstrated the seriousness with which the "older" candidate approached the selection of the person who would be a heartbeat away from the Presidency.

Since Biden had already announced during the last primary debate with rival Senator Bernie Sanders that if nominated he would place a woman on the ticket, media and public speculation could focus on a narrow, but select, range of individuals who might be designated for the second spot. And the continuing circumstances of the Black Lives Matter movement further narrowed the speculation to women of color.

The selection of California Senator Kamala Harris was a brilliant one – a woman of color from two different racial groups – Jamaican and Asian American; a woman with extensive legal experience that balances judicial justice with law and order, a woman with senatorial background in the intelligence community, a well-spoken, charismatic woman, a woman that the Trump team seems difficult to effectively attack. If there was any doubt in anyone's mind, Senator Harris' acceptance speech at the Democratic National Convention put those doubts to rest, as did her enthusiasm on the campaign trail.

U. S. politics can have many surprises. In earlier eras, the notion that not one, but two, "minorities" would be the final candidates for a presidential nomination would have been scoffed at. But the 2008 Democratic Party primaries marked a pivotal turning point in U. S. electoral politics.

Having secured the Democratic presidential nomination after a bitter rivalry with former First Lady Hillary Clinton, Illinois Senator Barack Obama was in a difficult position. Senator Clinton had been seen as the likely nominee and had garnered eighteen million votes -- the "eighteen million cracks in the glass ceiling," as she would often call it, and so she would have to be accommodated with a place in the administration.

Under other circumstances, the conventional wisdom would have been to anoint her as the vice presidential running mate -- thus acknowledging those eighteen million votes and the place of a woman in national politics as well as healing party wounds. But the circumstances of 2008 Democratic politics made this move untenable. A Clinton Vice Presidency would have been a very difficult one for all involved. Besides the fact that the Obama-Clinton primary battle had been such a contentious one, having Hillary Clinton as Vice President would likely be akin to Lyndon Johnson's incumbency in the second office, with one added factor: there would have been the issue of what to do with the Vice President's spouse, former President Bill Clinton.

Moreover and ironically, the very inclusiveness of the Democratic Party's end results presented an "elephant" in the room, and that elephant had to be considered. Could two minorities on the ticket -- the first African-American male and a woman -- fare well in the general election? Would voters accept an entirely "minority" ticket? By contrast, the more conventional selection of a white male who also had extensive senatorial and foreign policy experience might perform better in the general election.

As Senator Joe Biden's name surfaced during the running mate selection process, an embarrassing moment during a campaign interview given by the Senator's wife, Dr. Jill Biden, was revelatory. It was an off-the-cuff comment, but it said it all. Dr. Biden remarked that presidential nominee Obama had asked the Delaware Senator if he would rather be Vice President or Secretary of State in an Obama Administration, both of which, of course, would demand extensive foreign policy experience. Dr. Biden indicated that her husband was not interested in being Secretary of State, and he unequivocal preference for the spot a heartbeat from the Presidency made it clear that Senator Clinton would not be offered that choice. In many ways, her place was a default position. The added safety is the fact the Cabinet members (as do White House Staff), as the unelected, serve at the pleasure of the President. Not so the Vice President -- an elected office who comes to office with a constituency of his/her own and cannot be easily removed.

So the Biden vice presidential selection continued the trend of balancing professional background and especially experience. Obama had extensive experience in many of the domestic problems facing the nation, experience that stemmed from his work as a community organizer. But with little experience as a U. S. Senator under his belt, Barack Obama's stature and training in the foreign policy arena would undoubtedly be a handicap to him -- especially in a general election the Republican presidential nominee Senator John McCain, a Vietnam veteran and POW and a long-term member of the U. S. Senate. Obama needed to bring to the ticket the expertise someone of comparable foreign policy experience as McCain's. That someone was Joe Biden.

On the campaign trail, Biden was a feisty, loyal running mate, who nonetheless had to explain some of his earlier views. But in contrast to vice presidential nominee George Herbert Walter Bush's shifts in views following his selection by presidential candidate Ronald Reagan in 1980, Biden finessed more smoothly and candidly. Recall Bush's comment in his primary battle with Reagan when the future running mate referred to Reagan's economic plan as "voodoo economics." Bush later claimed he had never said such a thing. In Biden's case, as CNN reported on August 25, 2008, almost immediately following the Biden selection, the McCain camp ran an ad that featured Biden during the 2007 primary battle proclaiming that Obama was "not yet ready" to be President. In response, "the scrappy kid from Scranton," as Obama called Biden, simply responded, "I think I stand by that statement," and went on to vigorously campaign for the ticket. Reminiscent of the Bush turnabout on "voodoo economics," once selected as Obama's running mate Biden closed ranks with the presidential nominee on Iraq. Indeed, Biden took on the job that usually awaits a Vice President: that of administration spokesperson, as he was able to take aim at McCain.**100**

THE TRUMP CANDIDACY AND PERSONAL BALANCING: THE SELECTION OF MIKE PENCE

Campaign 2016 was perhaps the most chaotic and divisive of campaigns this nation has ever witnessed. Former First Lady and Secretary of State Hillary Clinton seemed the heir apparent on the Democratic side but found a challenger in the populist Vermont Senator Bernie Sanders. The Republican who seemed the least likely to emerge as the nominee, Donald Trump, seemed to sense the populist backlash and know how to tap into it. The media coverage and his keen understanding of the power of social media helped him to secure the nomination against established members of the GOP.

Controversy has surrounded Donald Trump for much of his adult life and his theatrical capturing of the presidential nomination accompanied by ongoing publicity revolving around his relationships with and attitudes towards women warranted a careful choice of a vice presidential running mate. Trump's selection involved several considerations.

Enter Indiana Governor Mike Pence.

The conservative establishment of the Republican Party needed to be satisfied that the policies in which they are invested would be met. Beyond this, Pence was still popular among his former colleagues on the Hill, with support coming from House Speaker Paul Ryan and many other conservative Republicans. Pence was just what Trump wanted and needed – an across-the-board social and economic conservative far surpassing any conservative position or statement made by the presidential nominee, whose positions on issues varied dramatically over the years. Beyond this, as has been suggested by observers, "Pence is the inside man of the conservative money machine. On Election Night, the dissonance between Trump's populist supporters and Pence's billionaire sponsors was quietly evident."**101**

The contrasts between Donald Trump and Mike Pence could not be any starker. While Trump seems unabashed about his reputation for womanizing and vulgarity, Pence's image is that of gentlemanliness and decorum. Indeed, Pence is proud of his policy to never dine alone with any woman other than his wife. When the Trump campaign trail seemed to suffer a major setback with a steamy revelation, Hillary Clinton's Presidency appeared even more assured. The emergence of an "Access Hollywood" tape of Trump bragging about aggressive behavior towards women, it was said that Mike Pence thought of removing himself from the ticket. Instead, according to a report by *The Atlantic,* he set himself on a different course.**102**

Ironically, by contrast to presidential nominee George W. Bush's selection of Dick Cheney that largely included Cheney's clear-cut position that he would not be interested in seeking the Presidency on his own, Donald Trump's selection of Governor Mike Pence of Indiana took an almost immediate turn in the opposite direction. Actually, it was a turn that should have been anticipated. Trump's performance on the campaign trail strongly suggested that, if elected, he would set a divisive tone to an administration, coupled with his selection of a seemingly mild-mannered running mate, should have hinted that there would be discord within the administration and the government as a whole. Satirists had a field day with this. SNL, for example, had actor Alec Baldwin as Trump proclaiming that he was the 45th President of the U. S. and that in two months Mike Pence would be #46. But the evangelical, well-liked and calm-speaking conservative, former talk show host was just what Trump needed in a running mate.

Moreover, not only is Pence a conservative, but one with a consistent history of Tea Party conservatism. The American Conservative Union (ACU) ranked Pence as "America's most conservative VP nominee in 50 years," while ranking Democratic Party presidential nominee Hillary Clinton's running mate, Senator Tim Kaine, as "the single most liberal vice-presidential running mate in our lifetime."**103** Pence was still popular among his former colleagues on the Hill, with support coming from Speaker Paul Ryan and many other conservative Republicans. Pence was just what Trump wanted -- an across-the board social and economic conservative far surpassing any conservative position or statement made by the presidential nominee, whose positions on issues varied dramatically over the years. Pence was ideal in all of aspects. The characteristics Trump sought for a Vice President foreshadowed the role Pence began to play immediately and consistently. As we know, loyalty is a consistent expectation of vice presidential behavior, and Pence, except for the period of the "Access Hollywood" controversy, had demonstrated over and over again that he is willing to subjugate his views to Trump's. His acceptance speech at the 2016 Republican National Convention echoed the Trump's consistent presentation of an America that needed to be renewed. And, of course, he clearly understood the needs of Trump's ego. For example, in speaking of his own selection by Trump, he massaged that ego by the exaltation of Trump's personality and the self-deprecation of his own. This statement was clearly an indication of the subservient, almost servile, role Pence would play vis a vis the President, noting, "He's a man known for a larger personality, a colorful style and lots of charisma. And so, I guess he was just looking for some balance on the ticket.104 What Pence didn't say was that another observer has since reported, and that is that Melania Trump played a role in the Pence selection. As author Kate Brower noted, "At the final decisive meeting it was Melania Trump, the aloof former model married to the outspoken and impulsive real estate tycoon, who drew the bottom line. Whoever is chosen must be 'clean,' she insisted, and "Melania's shrewd instincts proved correct; Mike Pence was by far the least controversial on Trump's list of vice presidential candidates."105 Pence's incumbency has had him serving as an apologist for Trump; as a spokesperson for righteousness; as a liaison to a major component of the Trump (and no doubt Pence's future) political basis, the religious right.

As Trump's administration became embroiled in more and more controversy, speculation mounted that an impeachment was not out of the question. Meanwhile, the Pence persona seemed to be in stark contrast to Trump's. But perhaps Pence is the proverbial "wolf in sheep's clothing," as suggested by his softly spoken but consistent support of Trump's policies and extreme rhetoric, topics to be discussed in subsequent chapters.

THE TWENTY-FIFTH AMENDMENT: THE CASE OF RESIGNATION

Momentous events beginning with the Kennedy assassination and the succession of Lyndon Johnson have pushed the Vice Presidency to prominence. Concern continued to focus on the office with the casual section of Senator Thomas Eagleton, with its subsequent embarrassment to the Democratic presidential candidate, his party, and followers. Not long thereafter, during his second term as Vice President, Spiro T. Agnew, confronted by criminal charges, was forced to resign. The denouement of the "Agnew Affair" was the elevation of Representative Gerald Ford of Michigan to the Vice Presidency - the first to be chosen to fill that office in accordance with the provisions of Article 25 of the Amendments to the Constitution. This first test of the new amendment, adopted in 1967, added an entirely new dimension to the vice presidential selection process.

The Twenty-Fifth Amendment had been inspired by a quite different set of considerations from those that necessitated its first application, namely, a vacancy in the Vice Presidency due to the resignation of the incumbent President. The initial impetus for the amendment had been over the possibility of presidential disability and the lack of constitutional clarity regarding vice presidential disability and the lack of constitutional clarity regarding vice presidential behavior during such a period. Senator Birch Bayh, author and Senate floor manager of the amendment, reflected on the problem of disability as he spoke before the Senate committee considering the nomination of Gerald Ford as Vice President. "The events of Dallas reminded us of [a] tragic possibility. Had the assassin failed in his primary purpose, the...national specter arose of a once energetic President left physically or mentally disabled and unable to perform the powers and duties of his office. We all recall a tragic period of our history when Woodrow Wilson, a once-vigorous leader, was stricken by a stroke and left unable to perform the powers of the Presidency for many months."[106]

The Kennedy assassination focused attention on the dual problem of presidential disability and a vacancy in the office of the Vice Presidency. Four years following the assassination, an amendment to deal with these problems finally became part of the Constitution. The vacancy created by the resignation of Spiro Agnew caused the Twenty-Fifth Amendment to be invoked and the machinery for its operation to be developed and set in motion. Because of what it says about the evolution of vice presidential selection, the Ford selection warrants some attention here.

More than ever before in the history of the office, attention centered on the Vice Presidency, and in particular on concrete issues regarding it. No previous vice presidential candidate had ever experienced the scrutiny Gerald Ford underwent by Congress. Moreover, the review of his credentials for the Vice Presidency took place within a far wider set of circumstances than the startling ones that led to the Agnew resignation. As the new amendment was being tested for the first time, there was omnipresent a sense that the need for testing it had hung over the nation for more than a year. The Watergate scandals could not be submerged; added disclosure of possible wrongdoings had made the possibility of a presidential impeachment or resignation a matter of time.

Senator Bayh spoke to this point as well: "Is this nominee qualified, not just to be the Vice President, but is he fully qualified to assume the most powerful job in the world-that of President of the United States?" Bayh further stressed recent events by adding: "Who could have imagined the possibility of Vice Presidential resignation as a result of criminal charges. Who could have imagined that at the same time the future of the President would be subject to serious question?"**107**

The singular, dramatic circumstances under which the Ford confirmation hearings were being conducted poignantly emphasized the place of the Vice President within the scheme of American government, as well as the need for a cautious selection. The awareness that Congressman Gerald Ford, if confirmed for the Vice Presidency, would very likely be President increased both the stature of the second office and the gravity of the investigation for filling it. Throughout the hearings, the underlying question that Ford the vice presidential nominee was being asked placed him in the hypothetical role of President. "If you were President, what would you do if-?" Question after question delved into Ford's concept of the Presidency. Ford was being considered on the very grounds that the Founding Fathers mistakenly had thought all the vice-presidential nominees would be considered, namely, their fitness to be President.

Nixon's selection of Ford, as dictated by past vice presidential selections, was conducted within a framework of acceptability conditioned by circumstance. The troubled times dictated that he take the utmost care in his selection. Mindful of his own predicament with the long shadows it cast, Nixon had to choose someone who would soothe a disgruntled Congress and an increasingly disgruntled and angry public.

The resignation of Vice President Agnew was a rare event. (John C. Calhoun was the only other Vice President to resign.) Had it occurred prior to 1967, the nation would not have had a vice presidential replacement. In deciding to nominate Congressman Ford as Agnew's replacement, President Nixon wisely carried off an exercise in practical politics. Contrary to speculation that he would try to push for confirmation of his very controversial Secretary of the Treasury, John Connally of Texas, he geared his choice to conciliation extending to the far reaches of a troubled and disillusioned nation.

The selection of Ford, a congressman of some two decades, a Minority Leader, and a popular man with both parties in the House and Senate, noted one confidential informant, "seemed to be inevitable," and there was a very real practicality to selecting a House leader since "the impeachment business would begin in the House." The selection of a popular member of the House might produce more sympathetic treatment of the President if he were to appear to answer charges. In the past the House has been relatively neglected as a source of candidates. The President's announcement of his selection of Ford was made before a joint meeting of the Congress and prompted a standing ovation. Even before Ford's name was announced, Nixon's description of his nominee could only fit the well-liked House Minority Leader.

The confirmation hearings that led to the approval of Nixon's choice tested the effectiveness of the Twenty Fifth Amendment. Because of the times in which they were conducted, they also focused dramatic attention on the office of the Vice Presidency and the selection of the new incumbent. As noted earlier, no previous vice presidential candidate had been subjected to so rigorous an examination as Ford had been; his financial status and personal life, as well as his political philosophy, were thoroughly examined. The Ford hearings underscored the need to question seriously the procedure of the national convention. For those who advocate a major overhaul of our entire selection process, perhaps the solution is found in the existing primary system. In many cases the primaries clearly select a presidential candidate long before the convention meets and so in a very natural way can afford greater leisure and greater care in the selection of a running mate.

Other forces have contributed to the new awareness of a more through scrutiny of the nominating process. Only a year and a half elapsed between the time Senator Thomas Eagleton left the McGovern ticket and Congress approved Gerald Ford's nomination. In addition, two of the past five Presidents had died in office, thrusting the powers and duties of the office on men who, although they rose to the occasion, had been selected rather haphazardly and usually within just a few hours following the presidential nomination. The 1980 nomination and election of Ronald Reagan, at the age of sixty-nine, further highlighted the importance of the vice presidential selection in three respects: Reagan's advanced age suggested the very real possibility that his Vice President might succeed to the first office; it was speculated that if Reagan survived his entire first term, it would be uncertain whether he would choose to run for a second term at the age of seventy-three, thus making his Vice President the heir apparent; and if Reagan in fact sought reelection and won, as turned out to be the case, again the possibility occurred that his Vice President might succeed to the Presidency or be the heir apparent for 1988.

TRENDS IN THE SELECTION PROCESS

The criteria for choosing presidential and vice presidential candidates are constantly changing. New factors are added while others are discarded, and once a criterion has been tested it becomes part and parcel of the myriad of factors to be considered in the selection process. For example, well into the twentieth century it was widely believed that only a native-born American of Protestant faith could be elected President or Vice President.

This belief might have been discarded in 1928, when Democratic Party nominated Governor Alfred E. Smith of New York, a Roman Catholic, as its presidential candidate, but the success of the Republican Party candidate, Herbert Clark Hoover, tended to cause the idea to persist for another generation.

Once a Catholic became President in 1960, however, Catholicism as an obstacle seemed to evaporate rapidly. Developments following the assassination of President Kennedy gave added legitimacy to the desirability of a "Catholic spot" on the national ticket and the need for due consideration in the selection process. This consideration weighed heavily on Lyndon Johnson as pressure developed for selecting the deceased President's brother, Attorney General Robert F. Kennedy, as Johnson's running mate in 1964. Although the President found a way out of his predicament by his shrewd announcement that no Cabinet member would be eligible for the vice-presidential nomination, Johnson felt obliged consider the selection of another Catholic, Senator Eugene McCarthy of Minnesota, even though he was subsequently rejected.

The notion that only a Protestant was an acceptable national candidate has been thoroughly overturned in recent history. President Johnson's opponent in 1964, Goldwater, chose a Catholic as his running mate. In 1968, Humphrey's choice, Muskie, likewise was a Catholic. At least one of the factors entering the aborted selection of Senator Thomas Eagleton of Missouri as McGovern's running mate in 1972 was his Catholicism, and this was also a factor when Mayor Kevin White of Boston was considered Eagleton's replacement and Sargent Shriver ultimately chosen; both White and Shriver are Catholic.

In the rapidly developing political scene in the United States, not only had Catholicism ceased to be the proverbial kiss of death for national candidates, but also the stage was set for inclusion of wider religious and ethnic representation. Senator McGovern extended the horizon further in 1972 when he sought to persuade Senator Abraham Ribicoff, a Jew, to accept the vice-presidential nomination. And ethnic diversity was reflected in Nixon's selection of a running mate: Agnew, the son of poor immigrants, was of Greek ancestry. In 1968, the vice presidential candidate, Muskie, was the son of a Polish immigrant, and he had demonstrated capacity to win in gubernatorial and senatorial elections in the traditionally Republican Maine. On more than one occasion the name Edward Brooke former Republican senator from Democratic Massachusetts and an African-American, had been mentioned as a vice presidential possibility. Prior to the 1984 vice presidential selection of New York Democratic Congresswoman Geraldine Ferraro as the first woman, who was also a Catholic and of Italian background on a national ticket, speculation had already begun to surround future vice-presidential candidacies of prominent Republican women, such as Kansas Senator Nancy Kassebaum, Transportation Secretary Elizabeth Dole, and Supreme Court Justice Sandra Day O'Connor. And the 1984 Democratic vice presidential selection itself had included consideration of other women, such as San Francisco Mayor Diane Feinstein and Kentucky Governor Martha Layne Collins. McCain's selection of Alaska Governor Sarah Palin in 2008, speaks to the need to more carefully select a running mate and to not just attempt to balance gender. As former Vice President approached the 2020 campaign, he forthrightly announced that he would seek a woman as his running mate, prompting his opponent in the primaries, Senator Bernie Sanders, echoed this.**108**

The 2020 vice presidential selection process is a classic example of the broader environment shaping the options for a presidential nominee. On the Republican side, there is the incumbent Trump-Pence Administration. On the Democratic side, after a long, arduous primary season in which there were so many contenders for the nomination it appeared that the party would approach the general election too divided to wage a meaningful campaign, former Vice President Joe Biden's candidacy went through a resurrection. Beyond this, his former rivals for the nomination rallied behind his candidacy in a united attempt to get Donald Trump out of the White House. And one thing Biden promised in his final primary debate was that if he gained the presidential nomination he would definitely select a female running mate.

The issues that a year prior seemed uppermost were upstaged by two critical unexpected events: the COVID 19 pandemic and the tragic death of yet one more unarmed black man at the hands of police officers. These two in combination carved out the "framework of acceptability" for Biden's vice presidential selection process.

While seemingly two different events there was an ironic linkage. The COVID 19 pandemic disproportionately hit the African American community, and it was readily apparent why: more health problems in that community; impoverished living standards; the ability to "social distance" the way many more affluent whites could; and countless other insidious conditions made it painfully evident to thinking individuals that despite all of the movements and legislation, the African American community was still suffering from inequality. Meanwhile, the Trump Administration's failure to take early action months prior when it was clear that there was indeed a pandemic and that the U. S. would soon suffer as much of the rest of the world was suffer became an even greater rallying cry to remove Trump from the White House.

In the midst of the pandemic, the heinous murder of George Floyd in Minneapolis, Minnesota over Memorial Day weekend – seen on a pristine videotaping of an eyewitness – went viral. As Mr. Floyd lay gasping for breath on the ground, a police officer persisted in pressing his knee on the Black man's neck, while three fellow officers watched. A nationwide – and worldwide – wave of protest ensued and the incumbent Trump-Pence Administration seemed unable to grasp the importance of what was happening. Indeed, Trump himself seemed to inflame the protests with his words and actions.

A new "framework of acceptability" for the 2020 vice presidential selection was thus set by these two events. It was a given that Biden would select a female running mate; but now came the calls for him to select a Black woman for the second spot on the ticket. Such a selection would signify the former Vice President's empathy for the needs and demands of the African American community. Moreover, as had been learned from past elections, if a candidate cannot get Black voters to turn out to vote and form for him/her victory at the polls was less likely. The Democrats lost control of the House of Representatives in 2010 because Black voters, who had turned out in 2008 to give Barack Obama a victory, did not turn out for the congressional elections in 2010. And if Black voter had turned out in key areas, candidate Hillary Clinton, who actually won the popular vote in 2016 but not the Electoral College vote, would have also beaten Trump in the Electoral College.

PROPOSALS FOR CHANGE IN THE SELECTION PROCESS

Numerous proposals, both in the literature and from individuals closely associated with the second office, have been made to change the vice presidential selection process. Many opinions have been offered, but there is no consensus as to what, if anything should be done. An overview of the proposals should give a clear indication of how far-reaching the thought has been on the subject. Although most are not particularly well thought out, it is worth to briefly see what has been proposed.

1. *Select a vice presidential candidate prior to the selection of the presidential candidate*109

    This suggestion ignores some basic facts about American presidential politics. Whatever significance a Vice President has depended entirely on the incumbent President. A Vice President chosen without, at the least, the approval of the presidential candidate might very well find himself/herself at odds with the President. While greater independence would have been gained within the confines of the nominating *process*, the functioning of the Vice Presidency would suffer.

Unless we are prepared to make substantial changes in what a Vice President is constitutionally and otherwise assigned to do, this proposal would increase the likelihood of a Vice President who would not be congenial with the President or with whom he could not work. Although theoretically this is possible even with the current nominating process, the likelihood of it would be greater with the prior selection of the Vice President. It might also create the possibility that a presidential candidate would be chosen to balance the vice presidential candidate.

2. *Have a separate election of the Vice President and President*

The worst outcome of this arrangement would be the election of two individuals of different political parties, which would be contrary to one of the underlying intentions of the Twelfth Amendment. Numerous additional problems would ensue.

First, the President would have a Vice President at his/her side that would owe him/her no allegiance whatever. While a Vice President should not be bound hand and foot to a President, the administration should speak with relative consistency. A separately elected Vice President raises the possibility of confusion and, quite likely, irreconcilable points of view, each directed to disparate constituencies. An additional problem would occur in the event the Vice President succeeded to the Presidency, as ensuing chapters will indicate. Succession by a Vice President of a different party would almost certainly produce dramatic policy and staff shifts.

3. *Require that the presidential and vice presidential candidates seek nomination as a team*110

This "package deal" suggestion has numerous drawbacks. For one thing, it ignores the complexities of presidential election politics. The vice presidential nomination, as has been said, is one of the presidential candidate's most significant resources for achieving party unity. A candidate needs the full duration of the primary battles to see the development of party and electoral lines; requiring the candidate to bind himself or herself to a running mate at the outset would be a disservice to party unification. Were the candidate to make a "mistake" in an early choice, the result might be a divided convention and an ideologically tense election campaign.

Another drawback to this package deal is the remote possibility of finding a top contender who would be willing to settle for the second spot at the outset of a preconvention battle. It is doubtful, for example, that a Lyndon Johnson, Hubert Humphrey, Walter Mondale, or George H. W. Bush would have been willing to do so, and thus individuals of high caliber would be lost to the Vice Presidency.

4. *Expand the pool of vice presidential potentials by agreeing to allow the Vice President to retain a previous office.*

The adoption of this suggestion would increase what has already been the trend during the past twenty years: that top-notch individuals would be willing to make themselves available for the office. Allowing a Vice President to continue, for example, as a senator or a governor, would attract individuals who might otherwise be reluctant to trade a substantially busier occupation for much of the frustrations of the Vice Presidency.

There are several objections to this proposal. First, it constitutes a breach of the constitutional doctrine of separation of powers. It might be countered that the constitutional position of the Vice President is already a breach of the doctrine, since it places a member of the executive within the Congress as presiding officer of the Senate. Not only is this *part* of the Constitution, but also assigns to the Vice President a relatively passive role, with a vote allowed in the rare instance of a tie. To allow a senator to serve in both the executive and legislative branches of the government would be to compromise the separation of powers doctrine. It would allow a legislator representing his or her state or district in the national legislature to have access on an active basis to the executive branch. In addition, it would give the Vice President two votes in the event of a tie, which is what the Founders wanted to avoid. Unless this suggestion were considered within the framework of an open review of the entire Constitution and many of the principles on which it is based, it would have no validity.

Second, a key goal of any changes in the selection process should be a Vice President capable of assuming the office of the Presidency if necessity demands it. Reducing the office's workload to enable its incumbent to fill some specific position would make that individual less familiar with the policies and procedures of the administration. If anything, the workload must be substantially increased in meaningful directions. That undoubtedly would increase the attractiveness of the position to qualified individuals.

Third, this suggestion misses the point that the proximity of the Vice President to the President as heir apparent and successor has already made the office attractive and appealing to individuals of national stature.

5. *Select the vice presidential candidate via an open contest within the convention*

Few presidential candidates, Adlai Stevenson in 1956 being the most recent, have chosen this existing option. To make an open contest mandatory raises many of the same problems as many other suggestions for change. While increasing internal party democracy, it enhances the possibility of a severely imbalanced ticket and a splintered party, thereby endangering the party's ultimate goal, election to office.

6. *Select the vice presidential candidate from among the top three contenders for the Presidency*

This suggestion raises the fewest obstacles or objections, the major one being that any of the individuals might be reluctant to settle for the Vice Presidency (although recent contenders have seemed quite pleased to do so). A second concern might be what this forced selection might mean for the party in the general election, especially if the candidates available who fit this criterion do not balance the needs of the party. A third possible problem would be, once again, the incompatibility of the two candidates. And let's keep in mind the near disastrous election of 1800, when Aaron Burr almost became President, but served as Vice President.

Once elected, the successful presidential candidate would submit the name of his vice-presidential choice for congressional approval. While this proposal would allow more careful inquiry into the qualifications of a vice-presidential candidate, it is one more unnecessary departure from the direct, democratic selection and election of candidates. Such a change would mean that the nation's voters would have no hand in the selection of the individual "a heartbeat away" from the Presidency.

7. *Have separate selections for both the presidential and vice-presidential candidates via a national primary*

This proposal has widespread appeal throughout the nation, for it promises a more direct and therefore democratic selection process. There are major flaws in it, however, including the possibility of poorly constructed tickets. While both the presidential candidate and the delegates in a national convention have the opportunity to weigh electoral realities, the random pairing of candidates via a national primary would do no such thing. Thus, neither coalition building within the party nor conciliation of the party's diverse interested would be very likely. In addition, a national primary system would increase the likelihood that only the better-known candidates would have a reasonable chance of winning, thus reducing the possibility of a gradual development of a candidacy, such as occurred in 1972 with the candidacy of George McGovern and in 1976 with that of Jimmy Carter. Beyond all these flaws, such a system would undoubtedly require a runoff primary, which would add to the burden of an already too costly electoral system.

8. *Allow the presidential candidate to select the vice presidential running mate within a designated time period after the convention has convened and have the candidate approved by the national committee.*111

Gerald Ford made this suggestion while he was Vice President. Ford proposed that the vice presidential nominee-designate be put through a screening process by the party's national committee similar to the one he experienced during his confirmation hearings by the Congress.

This suggestion has obvious merit, for it would allow a presidential candidate sufficient time in which to examine his or her options and would then permit a party organ to serve in an overview capacity, This was the process followed in the aftermath of the "Eagleton Affair" when, following Eagleton's resignation from the ticket, McGovern named a replacement, Sargent Shriver. Shriver's candidacy had to be approved by the Democratic National Committee, since the national convention was over. The major objection to regularizing this process is that it is one more step removed from the people.

9. *Abolish the office of the Vice Presidency*

The most radical suggestion relating to vice presidential selection is to abolish the office entirely. Following the Agnew resignation, several legislators and political scientists voiced this notion. Perhaps Arthur M. Schlesinger, Jr., gave this idea its widest airing. In the second edition of <u>The Imperial Presidency</u> (1974), he added material on the Vice Presidency with a concluding recommendation to abolish that office. Such suggestions overlook the reality that the Vice Presidency is the symbol of continuity of the executive branch. To claim that the Vice President does very little of significance is to misunderstand the evolution of the contemporary Vice Presidency. Any demarcated delineation of vice presidential functions misses the point that a Vice President's role emerges with the context of every administration.

While numerous suggestions have been made for revising the vice presidential nomination process short of abolishing the office, none of them is completely acceptable. No one has fully considered the nature of the Vice Presidency and the nomination process. The inherent dilemma is that, while the office is potentially very powerful, it is nevertheless the *second* office. If the paramount consideration is to select a candidate capable of serving as President, the dilemma lies in finding a person who would be willing to settle for the second office. Until the Presidency itself is out of reach, candidates of high caliber are not likely to want to volunteer to spend their days as faithful and loyal troopers.

In summary, then, the above proposals are attempts to solve a series of related problems:

1. The need for time to scrutinize a vice presidential candidate.

2. The need for compatibility between the President and Vice President.

3. The desire for conciliatory or balancing factors in a Vice President, which may not be recognized until the convention.

4. The need for party, and, ultimately, all voters' approval.

5. The time factors involved in the sequence of events.

Chapter 3

———∾∾———

THE VICE PRESIDENCY
AS A STEPPING STONE

The Vice President is in a sense a stand-in for the President. He is an alter ego or he is an echo, or he is nothing…It depends upon what the President wishes to give him in terms of responsibility and authority. Remember, this office is vested with all the responsibility in the world but no authority… You're not the President, and yet you're the Vice President - you may be President. **1**

THERE ARE TWO ways the Vice Presidency might be a stepping stone to the Presidency. The most obvious, of course, is in the event of the death, resignation, or impeachment of the President. Resignation has occurred only once in the history of the Presidency, with the resignation of President Richard M. Nixon in 1974 and the succession of Vice President Gerald R. Ford. Three Presidents have been impeached (Andrew Johnson, Bill Clinton, and Donald Trump) with Johnson and Clinton not having been convicted by the Senate and as of this writing the Trump impeachment about to go to the U. S. Senate, where

Republican Majority Leader Mitch McConnell steadfastly maintained that there will be no conviction, which was indeed the end result of the Senate trial in 2020.

The second way the office might be a stepping stone to the Presidency is if a Vice President rises to the presidential nomination following his/her experience in the second office, and Chapter 4 concentrates on that route. This chapter focuses on the office as a stepping stone as a result of the death and resignation a President.

The statistical yardstick confirms that a Vice President is indeed a "heartbeat away" from the Presidency: eight Vice Presidents have become President following the death of a President and one has succeeded following a President's resignation. Thus, the Vice President enjoys a one-in-five chance of entering the Presidency through the "backdoor," and at least in this regard the Vice-Presidency has become a stepping-stone to higher office. The death of a President is a traumatic event in the life of a nation. How the successor deals with this event is crucial to the continuity of and trust in the American Presidency. During the period of the modern Presidency and Vice-Presidency, the American people have learned that their chief Executive is indeed mortal. In the three instances of succession examined in this chapter-those of Harry S. Truman in 1945, Lyndon B. Johnson in 1963, and Gerald R. Ford in 1974 - a comparative approach will be taken in exploring both common and divergent themes and actions.

THE TRUMAN SUCCESSION TO THE PRESIDENCY: THE KING IS DEAD

On April 13, 1945, just three months following his inauguration as Vice President, Harry S. Truman, Franklin D. Roosevelt's third Vice President, was called on to provide national leadership. In the months preceding FDR's death, Truman had seen the rapidly increasing strain on the President and the deterioration that twelve years in office had wrought. In his memoirs, Truman explained his own reactions to what he knew was unquestionable a steep decline in the President's health, but recalled, "I did not allow myself to think about it after I became Vice President."2

The nation as a whole was not fully aware of Roosevelt's condition, nor did it prefer to think about it, and the press seemed mercifully kind and considerate in avoiding discussion of the subject. The effect was a prevailing Roosevelt mystique, which is perhaps best summarized by the statement made by one citizen, "I would vote for him even if I knew he was going to die tomorrow. I hope he will stay President as long as he lives."3

Polls conducted during the 1944 presidential campaign indicated relatively little concern over the question of Franklin Roosevelt's health4 as did the thrust of the Democratic party's major campaign theme- the inadvisability of abandoning Roosevelt's experience.5 Truman later recalled in his memoirs that his campaign travels during the summer and fall of 1944 made him fully aware of the people's reluctance to chance leaders during a war.6 And as Truman journeyed, he vociferously cautioned the people about the inherent dangers of expecting a new President to be able to learn his job in less than a year. Certainly, argued Truman, this danger was all the more pronounced when the country was at war, and only Roosevelt fully understood "the objectives and the inner thoughts of such divergent personalities as those dominant leaders who have guided the destinies of our courageous allies."7 Truman, it seemed, could see no further than being FDR's running mate, and yet as the nation's thirty-third President, Truman was faced with the task of finding the time to learn-and learn quickly- all that he had not been told or given the opportunity to learn during his brief incumbency in the Vice Presidency. The Roosevelt experience and expertise Truman had described while campaigning in 1944 A Roosevelt's running mate underscored a Presidency so personal, so individualistic, that the transfer of power was clearly jeopardized; the virtues of the Roosevelt Presidency contained the seeds of its own defects.

Many people shuddered at the thought of Harry Truman being

responsible for the future leadership of the country. No one else but FDR had been called "President" since 1932. The June 1945 *Current History* noted that Truman lacked "the magnetic personality of his predecessor." The May 19, 1945, edition of *The Nation* commented that the American public, in reaction to the death of Roosevelt and the subsequent Truman succession, "tended publicly to hope for the best and privately to fear the worst." *Time* magazine on April 23, 1945, reported that Truman's friends seemed to agree "that he would not be a great President," *Time* went on to say of Truman, "He is frank with himself as the ordinary, honest politician grown to stature through patience, hard work and luck. He believes in strict party responsibility, a politician's reward for work done, and complete loyalty to friends."[8] Students of American politics will not fail to notice the similarity of this gratuitous comment to what has been said about Truman's succession as a "backdoor" to the White House as akin to Gerald R. Ford's succession following the Nixon resignation, a subject to be discussed elsewhere in this work.

To many people FDR's third and last Vice President appeared to be nothing more than a compromise candidate, hardly worthy of succeeding to the Presidency merely because the people around FDR at the 1944 Democratic Convention wanted to avoid Henry Wallace as a running mate and needed a candidate amenable to labor. And now, this candidate himself was having difficulty adjusting to the notion of holding the first office in the land. As Harry Truman faced newsmen during the first hours of his Presidency, he said, "Boys if you ever pray, pray for me now…I've got the most terribly responsible job a man ever had." And when the newsmen wished him "Good luck, Mr. President," he responded, "I wish you didn't have to call me that."[9]

The prompt and orderly transition from one leader to another is one of the great achievements of the American political system. Under normal circumstances, the transfer is provided for by fixed terms of office and regularly scheduled elections. When the system is disrupted by uncertainties and sudden crises, the transfer of power has added significance. Political circumstances of the moment condition the steps that must be taken by a Vice President assuming the Presidency.

As Harry Truman succeeded to the office vacated by Roosevelt's death, a world war raged, albeit a war that had already insured victory over the Axis Powers in Europe and in which the tide in the Pacific was shifting rapidly in favor of the Allied Powers. Harry Truman described the environment in which his succession took place.

> The presidency of the United States in recent times, even in the prewar period, had become a highly complicated and exacting job. But to this already heavy burden the war had added new and crushing responsibilities. Not only did the President now have to function as Commander in Chief of the armed forces of the United States, but he also had to assume the major share of the leadership of a far-flung coalition of allied nations. As I took the oath of office I was conscious of how vast in scope the presidency had become.**10**

Any unscheduled succession to the presidency is a crisis; Truman's was a crisis in times of gravest crises. There is much American experience to demonstrate that a crisis government, particularly in wartime, is executive government, and FDR's Presidency had responded to crises characteristically. The majority of the American electorate had been willing to accept Roosevelt's forthright leadership. FDR's firmness in his policy convictions and capacity to lead and his support by his fellow Americans prompted his decision to fly in the face of custom and risk a third and then a fourth term. Roosevelt was always very much the Commander; no one around him had any doubt that he was completely in charge. For thirteen years, Roosevelt *was* the Presidency - and a crisis Presidency throughout. In responding to the exigencies of war, however, Roosevelt had dealt a serious blow to his successor.

Roosevelt's participation in Big Three conversations pertaining to the postwar world had been conducted in the same close-mouthed manner that had been the hallmark of his Presidency. He continued to drive himself, and he persisted in doing things single handedly, failing to share the leadership that would inevitably have to be passed on.

When Harry Truman took over the Presidency, he did not know what decisions Roosevelt, Churchill, and Stalin had reached. The first President in the Atomic Age had but three months' incumbency as a member of the fourth-term Roosevelt Administration before he had to take the reins of government. It is doubtful whether he would have been any better-prepared if he had served longer. FDR had never done very much for Vice Presidents. Indeed, the peculiarly uncertain position of the Vice President, partially in the executive branch, partially in the Senate, but enjoying authority in neither, has set the scene for all incumbents of the office, although the Truman experience itself focuses on the need to rectify the level of vice presidential preparation.

In the period beginning with the presidential campaign of 1944 and ending with his three months as Vice President, Truman had seen the President only eight times. On these occasions, little of substance had been transmitted to the future President. Although Truman was not without access to the President, being able to contact Roosevelt, for example, if absolutely necessary, during his secret briefings in the Map Room, Truman was not present for these briefings; he knew that Roosevelt preferred to go to the Map Room alone. The deterioration of the President's health and his fragile condition make it understandable that he doubtless felt more comfortable when he was by himself. These same circumstances in retrospect make it seem the more lamentable that the Vice President was to remain so ignorant of what was occurring in the prosecution of the war as well as in other public policies. Truman had to play "catch-up" on the piles of paper to which he had not been privy. He spent the early days and months of his Presidency conferring with the powerful that had surrounded Roosevelt, slowly piecing together a picture of the Roosevelt policies. Secretary of State Edward R. Stettinius, Jr., who briefed Truman on diplomatic matters and the upcoming United Nations Conference at San Francisco, presented one of the first pieces of business. Stettinius informed Truman of the daily briefing papers Roosevelt had had prepared, and Truman received reports from that point. These reports, recalled Truman, were "immensely helpful in filling gaps in my information. In fact, these were indispensable as aids in dealing with many issues, and from the first I studied them with the greatest care.11

Information vital to the conduct of the war revealed to Truman only after he became President. Under any circumstances this would now be astonishing. This was information to which he should have been granted access not only throughout his brief Vice Presidency but also from the moment he received the 1944 Democratic vice presidential nomination. The danger in neglecting the Vice Presidential and failing to share information was so obvious, and remedial measures were gravely needed.

The most astonishing piece of information transmitted to Truman was given to him following a special meeting of the Roosevelt Cabinet which Truman convened immediately after he took the oath of office as President. Following this meeting, Secretary of War Stimson lingered; he told the new President that a new explosive was in the works. Recalled Truman, "It was the first bit of information that had come to me about the atomic bomb, but he gave me no details."12 Not until the next day did Truman learn of the immensity of the new weapon. Only a handful of men had known about the project; the Vice President of the United States was clearly not one of those men. In fact, Truman, as chairman of the Senate Committee to Investigate the National Defense Program (more popularly known as the Truman Committee), had been asked by Stimson not to investigate plants in Tennessee and Washington since a very critical project was being undertaken. To this, Truman had agreed.13 Later, as President; Truman was the individual to render the final decision of where and when to use the atomic bomb that was the product of the secret project.

Truman's preparation for the Presidency was, in a word, deplorable. Although he had attended Cabinet and Big Four meetings (consisting of the Vice President, the Speaker of the House, the Majority Leader of the House, and the Majority Leader of the Senate), few of these meetings were held during his brief Vice Presidency.14 Besides, Roosevelt had been notorious for accomplishing little in larger meetings, which more closely resembled social gatherings than meetings to deal with substantive matters; the President had preferred dealing on a one-to-one basis, especially with Cabinet members.

While Truman's own background had fortunately provided him with some preparation, especially his tenure as chairman of the Truman Committee, he had little of the information he would need to win and conclude the war in an Atomic Age. In addition, he knew virtually nothing of what had happened at the Yalta Conference; nor did he have any information on FDR's personal agreements with Churchill and Stalin.15 Once again, despite the fact that crisis government demands central decision-making, secrecy, and continuity - a demand amply met by Roosevelt - the four-term President performed a disservice not simply to the man who was to take up the burdens of the Presidency but to the nation as a whole. In his memoirs, Truman very graciously sought to rationalize what Roosevelt had failed to do.

> No Vice President is ever properly prepared to take over the presidency because of the nature of our presidential, or executive, office. The President is the man who decides every major domestic policy, and he is the man who makes foreign policy and negotiates treaties. In doing these things it would be very difficult for him to take the second man in the government...completely into his confidence. The President, by necessity, builds his own staff, and the Vice President remains an outsider.

The Vice President, Truman continued, is a politician, and "the

President cannot afford to have his confidential matters discussed in Senate cloakrooms" where the Vice President has a presence.**16**

While this is true, it would appear far from ideal with respect to the stability of government. The situation suggests *a fortiori* that a remedy be found to shorten the distance between the offices of President and Vice President and to foster greater confidentiality between them. In the long run, it would seem far less detrimental to risk possibly information leaks from the Vice President than to have a repetition of the Truman transition. Moreover, the alleged notion that a Vice President, in mingling with senators as he or she presides over that body, may make slips or betray presidential or executive department confidences is a very lame excuse for not keeping him or her informed. The argument is further weakened because of the far greater opportunities for and likelihood of leaks from within the burgeoning White House staff, privy as it is to so much classified information. In this regard, Truman spoke of the constitutional inadequacies in the preparation of a Vice President.

> I was beginning to realize how little the Founding Fathers had been able to anticipate the preparations necessary for a man to become President so suddenly. . . . Under the present system a Vice President cannot equip himself to become President merely by virtue of being second in rank. Ideally, he should be equipped for the presidency at the time he is elected as Vice President. The voters, instead of considering a vice presidential candidate as a sort of appendage to the presidency, should select him as a spare Chief Executive. As such he should be kept fully informed of all the major business transacted by the President.**17**

Truman stated two basic principles of enduring validity: The Vice President must be presidential timber and be recognized as a likely substitute for the President; once s/he is elected as Vice President, unless s/

he is kept fully informer, whatever assets s/he brings with him will not suffice.

The history of presidential succession reveals that the passage of power is marked by uncertainties great and small. When the circumstances involved the death of a popular leader, the accession of the Vice President is accompanied by a public sense of inadequate substitution, the Truman experience. In due course, Harry Truman was able to rise above the handicaps of his elevation to the Presidency. His painful experience contributed markedly to the evolution of the Vice Presidency, which has witnessed the development of safeguards to ensure that Vice-Presidents need not rely so heavily on God and good fortune.

Truman was also hampered because he followed the charming and charismatic FDR, and comparisons could not help but be made. While FDR had been "aristocratic," Truman was considered "side street American stock." Whereas "Roosevelt talked and people listened, [people] talk and Mr. Truman listens."**18**

Truman realized the difficult task lying ahead of him but was persistent in being himself. A humble man thrust into the shoes of a man who even on leg braces loomed tall, Truman felt and often expressed his awe at his sudden inheritance.

While his total lack of preparation for the job weighed heavily on Harry Truman's mind as he assumed the office of the Presidency, he saw the necessities before him. He would have to retain and rely on many of the Roosevelt people in order to forge a sense of continuity across a grief-stricken, distraught nation; besides this, the information these men could provide was invaluable. For some of the Roosevelt staff, as would be true of a greater number of the Kennedy people during the Johnson succession eighteen years later, it was impossible to transfer or even attempt to transfer loyalties that had been bore years previously and nurtured through time. This is a critical problem that stems from the very nature of the Presidency. It is indeed a personal office, and any President succeeding to that office discovers how difficult a task awaits him in the delicate balance that must be struck between assuring stability and continuity by retaining the former President's staff to ease this process and putting together a working staff of his own.

On Truman's immediate agenda appeared the San Francisco Conference on Post-War Organization and the establishment of the United Nations, the surrender of Germany after years of bloody fighting, the Potsdam Conference, the birth of the Atomic Age, the surrender of Japan, and the restoration of a disheveled Europe. The short shrift he was obliged to give to domestic affairs plagued him.

Besides the necessity of keeping Roosevelt's staff on to assure the nation of continuity and stability, Truman needed the benefit of their information and experience to help see him through those first few overwhelming months during which he not only *served* as President but also *prepared* himself to serve as President. And so, to Samuel Rosenman, long-time counsel to Roosevelt and his personal representative in London, Truman turned for information regarding the late President's agreements on war criminals, about which Truman knew little.[19] He turned to Harry Hopkins, probably one of the most loyal of the Roosevelt aides, for insights into the working relationships among Roosevelt, Churchill, and Stalin.[20] Truman asked Hopkins to journey to Moscow, and he was an invaluable source of information and support to the new President. Truman recalled that as a "close [aide] to Roosevelt throughout his administration, [Hopkins] had performed many confidential tasks, and, as the President's personal representative, had carried out a number of secret missions."[21] Hopkins had been in a position occupied by few Vice-Presidents or vice-presidential candidates; he had information and insights from close contact and involvement with the President. That information and insight again proved beneficial once Truman succeeded to the Presidency.[22]

To James Byrnes, Roosevelt's former director of War Mobilization and the man who had desperately attempted to gain the 1944 vice-presidential nomination, Truman turned for a report on the events at Yalta, since Byrnes "had personally made shorthand notes of all the secret meetings he had attended."[23]

The late President's advisers served, on the one hand, as the strongest link in the chain of continuity. On the other hand, because of the personal loyalty that advisers feel to a President, they may also be the weakest links, for it becomes extremely difficult for these men and women to abruptly transfer personal loyalties. Harry Hopkins summed up the dilemma Truman was in. "Truman," he said, "has got to have his own people around him, not Roosevelt's. If we were around him, we'd always be looking at him and he'd know we were thinking, 'The *President* wouldn't do it that way."**24**

Hopkins expressed not only Truman's dilemma, but also the very nature of the Vice Presidency when its incumbent is summoned to the Presidency. While continuity and stability warrant the temporary retention of former presidential staff, that staff is a personal staff, and all new Presidents eventually and as expeditiously as possible develop one of their own. Fortunately, Harry Truman was able to strike a balance between these two disparate needs. Perhaps the most natural thing for him to have done would have been to have relied so heavily on FDR's aides' advice ass to become dependent, but Truman maintained his independence by managing to sift through the advice he received and reacting with his own judgment.**25** That another Vice President *cum* President might have acted otherwise underlines the dangers of the lack of preparation behind Truman's succession to the Presidency. Truman's understanding of the Presidency and Vice Presidency as well as of the demands of succession contributed to a successful transfer of power.

Beginning his Presidency during the turbulent war years and at the beginning of the Atomic Age and painfully aware that he was following a leader who had captured the hearts and minds of the American public and electorate for the past four presidential elections, Truman emphasized the importance not only of continuity but of openness as well. The Roosevelt Administration had not been a particularly open one, as Truman knew from first-hand experience, and the new President desperately felt the need to establish open relationships in order to assume full occupancy of his new office. Truman, who had spoken to members of the press with awe on the day after he assumed Roosevelt's place, pleased them at his first official press conference and again later on by the appointment of Charles G. Ross as his new press secretary. On May 17, 1945, Truman struck a theme that was to resound almost thirty years later in the words uttered by Gerald Ford upon his ascension to the Presidency. The Truman policy was open relations with both the press and the Congress.

All three Vice Presidents who succeeded to the Presidency during the time period under study behaved in similar fashion in relationship to their constitutionally coequal branch of government, the Congress. Certainly, the circumstances under which each succession took place - all three different - contributed significantly to the tone of press and public reaction to each.

A rush of emotionalism and sympathy, especially for Truman and Johnson, met these men, for the poignant circumstances of their successions to the presidency were quite different from those of Gerald Ford. All three new Presidents, in varying degree, nonetheless experienced the customary legislative honeymoon attaching to any new President. And Harry Truman struck the note of continuity necessary to the abrupt transition as he addressed a joint session of Congress shortly after assuming the Presidency.

Truman began his Presidency, as would Gerald Ford, by redefining the lines between the White House and the Congress. He asserted his desire for a co-operative relationship with the legislature and his intention to consult with Congress before reaching major decisions.26 This was in stark contrast to the Roosevelt days of personal government.

Truman was fully aware from the start that he would have to deal with international affairs unfamiliar to him; he would have a cooperative Congress. From the first day onward, he met informally with congressional leaders, allotting considerable time and attention to the legislature with which he would have to work. Truman's down-to-earth, common-man approach, his willingness to go to *them*, even for a casual chat, pleased the congressmen. He talked with employees, pageboys, anyone in sight. Everything Truman did during those early days was geared toward cementing a working relationship with the Congress.**27**

The need and desire for congressional cooperation was linked to the theme of continuity which Truman had enunciated in his first address to the congress as President. Reflecting on his preparation for the address, the new President admitted his realization that it was "imperative to let the nation know through Congress that I proposed to continue the policies of the late President. I felt that it was important, too, to ask for continues bipartisan support for the conduct of the war."**28** The speech was well received.

A problem faced by any Vice President called on to complete the term of his predecessor is the extent to which he is bound by the policies and programs of that predecessor. Truman appreciated this problem; he realized that both the nation and the world would be concerned about the directions, both domestic and foreign, which FDR's successor would take. For Truman, continuing Roosevelt's policies was not a problem, as he assured the nation and the world. He had always supported the late President's program and had easily run on the 1944 Democratic platform. In his reaffirmation of support for the United Nations, in his message to the Armed Forces, and his determination to gain support from congressional leaders, Truman built a structure of continuity.**29**

Truman followed the precedent established by his six predecessors who unexpectedly became President: dealing with problems according to the late President's designs, commitments, and policies while slowly moving to make the Presidency entirely his own. It is theoretically possible for an incumbent of the Vice Presidency who succeeds to the Presidency to abruptly alter policies and programs, as some of the Founding Fathers had feared. In practice, the policy of midterm Presidents has been to stress equilibrium and continuity. This is doubtless due to several factors: The Constitution seeks to ensure that there be no hiatus in the exercise of governmental power; the government and the nation are proud of American's history of orderly transition;

and vice-presidential candidates increasingly have been chosen who have been in basic agreement with the presidential candidate. Such factors, written and unwritten, make up the parameters within which a new leader may react in accordance with or diverge from the policies and programs of the leadership he has just replaced. Collectively, those parameters have developed in the direction of continuity. Thus, the American presidential type of government has evolved its own alternative to the solemn proclamation of continuity and longevity of its parent hereditary monarchy: "the King is dead; long live the King!"

The 1956 Committee for Economic Development (CED) study on "Presidential Succession and Inability" advised that "the Presidential successor should be basically sympathetic to the plans and aspirations of the incumbent President. Continuity and consistency require that he should not undertake abrupt shifts in governmental policy. To do so might disrupt public confidence in the aftermath of a succession crisis." Elsewhere, the CED report stated, "There must always be a full-time Vice President intimately associated with the president...In line with this view, there has been an increasing tendency for Presidents to use their Vice Presidents for a variety of important assignments."**30**

The next Vice President to succeed to the first office would come to that task ass the most thoroughly prepared Vice President to that date. But his succession would nonetheless have much in common with the 1945 Truman succession.

THE JOHNSON SUCCESSION:
ESTABLISHING THE RIGHT TO GOVERN

Lyndon Baines Johnson, following his sudden ascension to the Presidency in Dallas immediately following the tragedy of November 22, 1963, echoed the thoughts and deep emotion reminiscent of the Truman experience. Understandably, like Truman eighteen years earlier, he invoked the Deity to help sustain him.

"All that I have I would gladly give not to be standing before you here today,"31 Johnson said in an earnest voice in 1963. The emptiness of holding the highest office in the land had poignantly robbed both Truman and Johnson of the moment of glory that makes worthwhile all the hard years of work for presidential aspirants. Johnson, in marked contrast to Truman, however, became President as the best-prepared midterm Vice President in history. Despite this wide difference in the preparation of the two men, the Truman and Johnson successions have much in common. Although John Tyler's succession to the Presidency in 1841 established the undisputed precedent of succession to the office as well as to its duties in the fullest sense and no Vice President's right to do so has been questioned, the problems of transition remain.32

Regarding his own succession to the Presidency, Truman wrote, "It is astonishing how much was crowded into those first few days. I felt as if I had lived several lifetimes. Among the burdensome duties and responsibilities of a President, I soon experienced the constant pressure and necessity of making immediate decisions.33 Lyndon Johnson expressed this same sentiment as he stepped into the shoes of the assassinated John F. Kennedy. The new President reflected: "I feel like I've been here a year already."34

The history of the Vice Presidency reveals that all six Vice Presidents prior to Harry Truman who succeeded to the Presidency had "mediocre administrations."35 For Harry Truman, following the popular, overbearing FDR, the question had been whether he would follow in that "tradition" set by his predecessors. By all estimations, he had met the test; now it was Lyndon Johnson's turn.

Much as Truman had found himself with the seemingly insurmountable task of measuring up not only to the office but also to the *image* of the man who had been its previous incumbent, Johnson's problem was poignantly similar. The charismatic, attractive Kennedy in death became a larger-than-life myth. Johnson found himself haunted by that myth throughout his White House years. As with the Truman succession, Lyndon Johnson could lay claim to no national mandate. Vice Presidents are the also-rans, the product of a national convention and its presidential candidate. Such Presidents by succession must therefore face the major burden of gaining the authority of the Presidency in their own right.

The first days of the Johnson Presidency were filled with the confusion, the sense of urgency and crisis that had filled those days of the Truman succession eighteen years previously. Once again, the American governmental structure and political system were tested by the unscheduled passage of power and responsibility from one leader to another.

Unlike Truman, however, Johnson was prepared for the test; he always maintained that there was nothing more President Kennedy could have done to keep his Vice President better informed and thereby prepared. Moreover, the events in Dallas dictated the first and immediate acts of the new President. He had first to preside over the chaos; he had to be sworn in forthwith; he knew he had to act immediately in all respects as the Chief of State.

The jolt that had struck the nation would linger for months, probably years, to come, and Johnson knew it. Immediately following the Kennedy assassination, the conspiracy theories began to circulate; the doubts, fears, and anxieties of the shaken nation were suddenly thrust upon Lyndon Johnson's shoulders. He thought his first and most immediate task was to quell those fears and to reinstate a sense of trust and confidence in government; aware of a "need for a renewed sense of national unity," he set about "building a consensus."**36** Johnson knew, too, that these tasks must begin immediately, even before Kennedy's burial. And so mourning and meetings alternated.

Confronted by the nation's tears and sorrow, Johnson believed above all else that the prime need was for consensus. In emphasizing this from the start, Johnson struck a major theme that would prevail throughout his Presidency. He also emphasized continuity-continuity in thought, in substance, in purpose, in personnel. One of his first acts was to ask, and in some cases, to plead, for the Kennedy team to stay on, at least for a while. He did not need them to fill an information gap, as Harry Truman had needed the Roosevelt men, but to retain "the experience they had gained in nearly three years at the seat of power"**37** and to bridge the emotional gap from the Kennedy Administration under John F. Kennedy to the Kennedy Administration under Lyndon B. Johnson.

The personal nature of the American Presidency emerges strikingly when a Vice President succeeds to that high office. While the machinery of that institutionalized office continues to operate in the usual manner, the personal nature of the office echoes the abrupt passage from one leader to another. Indeed, immediately following the death of a President, even the late President's files are sealed and emptied; until recently, presidential papers have been personal, not state, property. In 1963, this process began within one short hour after the world learned of the Kennedy assassination.**38**

An inherent and critical aspect of the American Presidency as an institution is that the personnel who surround the President exercise power and are powerful only at the pleasure of one person - their President. No one elected these people; only the President can guarantee their length or type of service. Understandably, there is a jealousy between those who surround the President and those who sit in the shadows waiting to take over with a change of Presidents. Should change come by way of succession, animosity of the same sort prevails, although it is more difficult to perceive the full extent of it. Former Vice President Hubert Humphrey has provided some interesting and fresh material on this subject, derived from his experience in the Johnson Administration.

> If one became too popular or too effective, whoever the Vice President, the President says, "What's he up to?" Not so much the President-his staff. One of the things that happens to a President and a Vice President is that the presidential staff looks upon a Vice President as an extra wheel that ought not to be on the vehicle of government-it's a fifth wheel, so

to speak. And as far as that staff is concerned, it never needs a spare, you know. To them, a spare is extraneous; it's surplus baggage. And that staff will cut you out time after time- almost without malice. It's just sort of subconscious. They just say, "Well he isn't really needed." I remember Johnson, from time to time, exploding to his staff, saying, "Why didn't you have Hubert over here?" "Oh, I didn't know you wanted him, Mr. President." "Well, I want him around here," he'd say. And I used to wonder, is he doing that as an act or what? In fact, I found out that sometimes they'd just plain forget.**39**

As Vice President, Johnson, too, had experienced either neglect or malevolence at the hands of the Kennedy staff, and Gerald Ford, when serving as Vice President, admitted to this writer that staff can be a problem. He added that the staffs of a President and his Vice President seem to be more concerned with their respective bosses' prestige and power than are the officeholders themselves.**40**

While tension is common and pervades the staffs of both the President and Vice President, it reaches a fever pitch at the moment the Vice President assumes the Presidency. Staff tension was relatively nonexistent during the Truman succession since the Vice President had little staff. It was not until the second Nixon term as Vice President that the office of the Vice Presidency began to acquire any sizable staff of its own. As vice presidential assignments and activities increased, the Vice President's staff was increased accordingly, accompanied by growing animosities. By the time Lyndon Johnson succeeded to the Presidency, tensions between presidential and vice presidential staff members had reached an all-time high.

Lyndon Johnson had never enjoyed a congenial relationship with the Kennedy staff. As discussed earlier, much of this animosity was a holdover from the 1960 presidential nomination race; many Kennedy staffers had never forgiven Johnson for some negative remarks made by the Texas senator. But despite this deep-seated dislike, Johnson deemed the retention of the Kennedy staff necessary to promote a smoother transition and stability when confusion and mistrust in government were widespread. In addition to the peculiar circumstances of his succession, the new President had to contend with the general problems resulting from the doubt and suspicion surrounding the Kennedy assassination. Johnson described the special problems attending his succession. "In spite of more than three decades of public service, I knew I was an unknown quantity to many of my countrymen and to much of the world when I assumed office. I suffered another handicap, since I had come to the Presidency not through the collective will of the people but in the wake of tragedy. I had no mandate from the voters."**41**

Toward this end, the Kennedy staff played a critical part in achieving a sense of continuity, which President Johnson realized was so vital. While many of the Kennedy people stayed on, others could not. That very *personal* nature of staff, unlike the Cabinet, made the transfer of loyalties virtually impossible. President by accident, Johnson was as acutely aware of the Kennedy people's negative feelings toward him as he was of their intense loyalty to the deceased President. He knew, too, that he would have to earn their respect as well as that of the nation.

Johnson's first order of business was rapprochement with Congress, to which Johnson extended his efforts at consensus and continuity. As the former Majority Leader of the Senate, Johnson had been on intimate terms with most of the men who now sat before him as he delivered his first address as President to a joint session of Congress the day following John Kennedy's funeral. Millions, who in the preceding four days had watched on nationwide television a President and later his alleged assassin shot to death, and who had watched Lyndon Baines Johnson take the oath of office to become the nation's thirty-sixth President, now watched the new President address their elected representatives in the Congress. Johnson, his voice saddened but firm, began his determined course of action. He was aware of his legislative ability, as well as of the sentiment pervading the country. Thus, he set about establishing a national sense of legitimacy with the ringing statement, "Let us continue."

Johnson, as had Truman years before him, knew that he would enjoy a honeymoon period with the sympathetic Congress. But he knew, too, that that period would be brief; if he were to make the most of it, he would have to act quickly. Without hesitation, he made a major effort during those early days of transition, stressing the need for legislation in the critical area of civil rights-legislation, he added, which had been dear to the late President's heart and which would be a fitting tribute to the slain President. Seizing the opportunity of the moment, Johnson spelled out his request for legislation that he hoped would forge that sense of continuity and consensus that the nation, and he, so urgently needed. Not only did the stability of the system make consensus an imperative; Lyndon Johnson also needed to demonstrate an ability to achieve consensus to overcome his image as both a Southerner and an un-elected President.**42**

In his congressional address, Johnson called for quick legislative action on much of the Kennedy program: medical care for the elderly, youth employment, and education. He also stressed the administration's continued commitments to its allies abroad and to the maintenance of a strong-indeed, the strongest-defense system. As Johnson recalled, "The people were ready for action. And when I looked inside myself, I believed I could provide the disposition to lead."**43**

Thus, Lyndon Johnson linked himself to the Kennedy men, policies, and programs, meeting almost immediately after the assassination with the Kennedy Cabinet, civil rights groups, and other interest group leaders as well as congressional leaders, assuring the continuation of the Kennedy policy in both domestic and foreign affairs. With "Let us continue" as the keynote of his advent to the Presidency, Johnson was expressing a plea to allow him to begin.

Johnson had not only inherited Kennedy's policies; he gladly embraced them. As had Truman before him, as well as the six other Vice Presidents who had succeeded to the Presidency, Johnson wanted to avoid any abrupt change. "I never lost sight of the fact," reflected Johnson, "that I was the trustee and custodian of the Kennedy administration."44 He had spent three years in the shadow of the young man from Massachusetts whose death had given him the office he probably could never have obtained on his own. He was acutely aware of that as well as of the contrast that would frequently be made between himself and the deceased President. Throughout the course of his Vice Presidency, he had been the target of the Kennedy people's jokes and abuse; in his Presidency, he received more of the same from a wider source. As he sadly reflected in his memoirs, there were numerous "derisive articles about my style, my clothes, my manner, my accent, and my family... I received enough of that kind of treatment in my first months as President to last a lifetime."45

Much as Truman had, Johnson faced the seemingly insurmountable task of filling another man's shoes. Once again, a nation would make comparisons. Johnson, suggested Tom Wicker of the *New York Times*, was "something of a throwback to another time,"46 and the new President knew it. His task, in succeeding to the Presidency, was to create the "right to govern." In stressing consensus, Johnson had begun the arduous task of solidly building that legitimacy.

THE FORD SUCCESSION:
PRESIDENTIAL RESIGNATION

As had Truman and Johnson, Gerald Ford needed to assure the nation that the Presidency and government do indeed continue under stable conditions following the exit of a particular President. Unlike his predecessors, however, Ford had to strike resounding chords of change rather than promote continuity with the preceding administration, for it can be aptly said that Gerald Ford's succession to the Presidency began the day Richard Nixon nominated him for the Vice Presidency.

In early November 1973, as the Senate Rules Committee began to hold hearings on the confirmation of Congressman Ford of Michigan as the fortieth Vice President of the United States, a grave drama was unfolding within the other branch of the national legislature. This drama, which was to extend throughout months of agonizing investigation, opened when the House Judiciary Committee's meetings explored the possible impeachment of President Richard M. Nixon. Not for over 100 years had this question been addressed. Its movement to the fore coincided with the Ford confirmation hearings and set the stage for those momentous vice presidential hearings.

Two constitutional provisions were being tested simultaneously, one for the second time and the other for the first. Each was theoretically and constitutionally distinct from the other, but in this case, they were bound inextricably together, that is, the power of the Congress to impeach a President for misconduct in office and the exercise of the recently adopted Twenty-Fifth Amendment providing for the filling of a vacancy in the Vice Presidency. The seriousness of each underscored the urgency of the other. As the impeachment of Richard Nixon became an increasing possibility, it became all the more critical to have a ready standby in the Vice Presidency. A delay in the Ford confirmation might either hinder the willingness of impeachment forces to carry forth vigorously or would make likely the succession of House Speaker Carl Albert, a Democrat, thereby raising the possible outcry of political motivations behind the Nixon ouster.47 Many feared that impeachment under these circumstances would appear to have been forced by the Democrats in order to take the White House from the Republicans. It was considered likely, however, that the mild-mannered Speaker, with no presidential aspirations, would have resigned the office of the Presidency once Ford had been confirmed, handing the White House over to the newly selected Vice President.48 Clearly, the Ford hearings and confirmation needed to be conducted with all deliberate speed if presidential continuity and stability were to be maintained. Throughout the lengthy confirmation hearings, the inevitable linkup was made between the question of confirmation for the office of the Vice Presidency and succession to the office of the Presidency.

The Ford nomination, coming just two days after the first resignation of a Vice President, Spiro Agnew, for criminal charges, was accompanied by a promise from President Nixon that the nomination was "a new beginning for America."[49] Nixon undoubtedly hoped it might be a new beginning for him, as well. This promise held prophetic irony for the President: it was made on the very day the U.S. Court of Appeals for the District of Columbia upheld a lower court decision requiring Nixon to release taped Watergate conversations.[50]

The Agnew scandal and resignation were just two more element in the growing Watergate-related climate of lost confidence and questioned legitimacy in government. The resignation of the Vice President provided an unforeseen opportunity for the President to offer a conciliatory gesture to the Congress and nation. In considering a vice presidential replacement, Nixon toyed with controversial Republican figures such as John Connally, his former Treasury secretary; Governor Nelson Rockefeller; and Governor Ronald Reagan. All of these men, however, were regarded as potential presidential candidates for the 1976 election and would, therefore, evoke hostile reactions from both the Democratically controlled Congress and the Republican aspirants to the 1976 nomination. Among other candidates who seemed to be acceptable were several senators: Barry Goldwater of Arizona; Hugh Scott of Pennsylvania; and Robert Griffin of Michigan, as well as White House counselor Melvin Laird. The President finally settled on the House Minority Leader, Gerald Ford, who was not widely known nationally but was very well liked across the board in Congress. Moreover, House Speaker Carl Albert himself had recommended the Minority Leader.[51]

As the machinery for the Ford hearings moved into gear, it became more and more evident that the man under scrutiny could conceivably spend very little time in the Vice Presidency. Ford would not only be "one heartbeat away" from the Presidency, but also one impeachment away. The hearings produced some novel experiences in the history of American government and politics. For the first time, a President had been able to handpick his successor; for the first time, a Vice President, un-elected by the people, was instead confirmed by their elected representatives, filling an existing vacancy; and most importantly, for the first time a vice-presidential "candidate" received most careful and deliberated public scrutiny.

Gerald Ford by most accounts lacked charisma and was not particularly inspiring or qualified to be Vice President or, if fate so chose, President. Nonetheless, as the hearings demonstrated, he had no serious flaws in his political or personal background.

A steady questioning as to what Ford would be like as President, more so than all others throughout the Republic's history, marked the Ford Vice Presidency. The Vice President was therefore placed in an extremely difficult position and was forced to walk a political tightrope much of the time. He could not ignore the political environment in which he was moving as Vice President, but as Richard Nixon's choice he could not appear to be eager to grab power by engaging in public criticism of or commentary on the floundering Nixon Presidency. Thus, Gerald Ford seemed to be constantly hedging two positions: one critical of the anti-Nixon forces and the other semi critical of the course the Nixon people themselves were following. The Ford Vice Presidency fluctuated between assertions of loyalty to Nixon and innuendoes against the President.

Following his Atlantic City speech only a month after he stepped into the Vice Presidency, in which he criticized the partisan effort to hurt Nixon via "massive propaganda," Ford himself was accused of being nothing more than a White House puppet, another Spiro Agnew.52 In response to this criticism, Ford snapped back that he was running his own show. His actions, however, were far more indicative of his new position. As the President's future became more and more doubtful, Ford increasingly became the rallying point for an embarrassed and jeopardized party. As Ford jetted about the country campaigning for

Republican candidates in an effort to overcome the damage wrought by Watergate, his emphasis moved from a defense of Nixon to a salvaging of the Republican Party. Above all else, Gerry Ford had been a staunch party man; initially, that meant his solid support of the President. But ass conditions worsened, solid support of the President became antithetical to solid support of the party. Something had to give, even if within the confines of his delicate position as the likely beneficiary of a Nixon impeachment or resignation. Thus, in early March, it was Vice President Gerald Ford who was the first top official within the administration to state publicly that the secret report of the federal grand jury should and must be handed over to the House Judiciary Committee.[53] But still the Vice President felt obliged to hedge. During mid-March, Ford criticized the Judiciary Committee in its attempt to gain access to forty-two tapes, saying that the Committee had allowed its staff to "dictate proceedings," a charge that was then being made by the White House itself.[54]

As Ford's short term as Vice President progressed, he increasingly assumed party leadership, a position Nixon could not command. This made it imperative that Ford take a more independent and detached stand. While insisting that he fully expected to be Vice President for the duration of Nixon's full term.[55] Ford well understood that he might momentarily succeed to the Presidency. John Osborne, in a piece for the *New Republic* on April 13, 1974, indicated that Ford had actually gone as far as to speculate what his policies and personnel would be like as President-which members of the Nixon Cabinet and staff would remain. Osborne also indicated that Ford had expressed his impressions of the Richard Nixon then in office, especially in terms of Nixon's newly developed penchant for "small talk."

As he struggled to remain detached within his peculiarly sensitive position, Ford began to speak subtly against the Nixon Administration. For example, he admitted that he found portions of the edited White House transcripts "disappointing and disturbing."[56]

During the Ford vice presidential confirmation hearings, a House Democrat had been quoted as saying, "The Agnew thing has stirred up some feeling that we ought to get to the central question of Presidential succession. Gerry Ford won't have any trouble getting confirmed, but we're going to do it carefully. It's possible we could be picking a man who will be President nine months from now."57

This prediction proved to be very accurate, for nine months to the day that marked his assumption of the Vice Presidency, Gerald Rudolph Ford became the nation's thirty-eighth President. Thereafter it was revealed that a special Transition Committee had been operating on the Ford staff since April, in anticipation of a Nixon removal or resignation.

The Ford succession followed a week of political and personal turmoil for Richard Nixon during which a court ruling had forced his hand by ordering him to deliver a tape that indicated that he had, indeed, been lying about his part in Watergate. Following Nixon's public statement on the contents of the tapes, the President's support plummeted to an all-time low. Even his staunchest supporters on the House Judiciary Committee that was handling the impeachment hearings could no longer lend him support. Even more indicative of the approaching climax was his rapid loss of support in the Senate, which could anticipate the need to sit in judgment should the House vote for impeachment, which seemed likely. On August 8, 1974 Richard Nixon, after much deliberation and wavering, resigned. For the fifth time in this century and for the third time since World War II, an unscheduled transfer of power had taken place but under circumstances that were in sharp contrast to the two previous occasions. The Presidency on this occasion came to a man who had run for neither the Presidency nor the Vice Presidency.

Following his succession to the Presidency, Harry Truman repeatedly said he had achieved the Presidency by accident, that he had not sought the Presidency. In his initial speech to the nation as President, Gerald Ford repeated this theme, but for very different reasons. While Truman had not sought the office of the Presidency, he had run for and been *elected* to the office of the Vice Presidency. In contrast, Ford was elevated to the Vice Presidency by one man, the discredited President Nixon who was forced to resign. Before he could establish his "right to govern," Ford's initial task both as the first "appointed" Vice President to succeed to the Presidency was to legitimize his right to succession. He tackled the problem squarely as he spoke immediately following his talking of the oath of office as President. Ford stated, "I am acutely aware that you have not elected me as your President by your ballots. So I ask you to confirm me as your President with your prayers…I believe that truth is the glue that holds government together…That bond, though stained, is unbroken."**58**

Ford's actions during those first days of transition were framed, as had been those of Truman and Johnson, by time and circumstances. The nation, most observers agreed, was being slowly torn apart by political scandal; cynicism was rampant. As in all successions, the maintenance of stability was essential. Because of the unique events surrounding the Nixon resignation, however, the new Ford regime grasped the need for a sense of stability combined with restoration. "A national nightmare is over," Ford said in his first speech as President. His actions during those first days were calculated both to demonstrate the workability of the system in the transfer of power and to separate the Nixon Administration under Ford from the ills of the Nixon Administration under Nixon. The new President went on to say: "Our Constitution works; our great Republic is a Government of laws and not of men. Here the people rule." In short, the aim was to establish a new beginning for a tired nation, a new beginning that Richard Nixon had promised months before but had failed to deliver.

The Ford transition points to some interesting contrasts and parallels to the Truman and Johnson successions. Never before had a President resigned from office or been removed under the heavy weight of wrongdoing. Never had an un-elected Vice President assumed the Presidency. And both firsts had occurred simultaneously.

From the moment he uttered the words "So help me God," Ford had to represent the continuity implicit in the very existence of a Vice

Presidency. He also had to strike a critical chord of separateness, of in-dependence, from the bankrupt Nixon Administration**59** while avoid-ing any radical policy changes. Neither Truman nor Johnson had had to confront such problems.

One by one, in marked contrast to the paths followed by Truman and Johnson, most of the former President's men, tainted by Watergate, had to go. General Alexander Haig, Nixon's Chief of Staff, lingered awhile but was soon assigned abroad. Ford constructed a new admin-istration that was entirely his own; the tattered remains of the old had to be discarded.

Continuity in foreign affairs would be the keynote; Secretary of State Henry Kissinger would stay, as would much of the Nixon Cabinet. Ford himself admitted his rather paltry knowledge of foreign affairs. Like Truman in 1945, Ford would have to rely on the advice and expertise of others, and in this respect the presence of Secretary of State Henry Kissinger was critical. As one commentator noted, Ford " ha[d] a great advantage over Truman who had to scrounge around for some time be-fore he found the secretary of state he needed in George Marshall."**60** The Cabinet, unlike the Nixon staff, could remain for a while. Those of the Nixon Cabinet who had been sullied by Watergate had already exited. In his first full meeting with his inherited Cabinet, held on his first full day in office, Ford underscored the need for "continuity and stability," adding, however, that there would be a very different tone at the White House than that which had existed under Nixon.**61**

The Nixon staff was in a very different position, for it bore its own very negative identity. Unlike past successions, Ford could not ask the Nixon staff to stay on, even for a relatively short period of time as he planned a new beginning and a "clean" administration. Among the very first to go was one who had been very negatively associated with the Nixon debacle, Press Secretary Ronald Ziegler. A well-like Ford man, Jerry TerHorst, replaced him immediately.

Ford noted that his administration would be an open one: "In all my public and private acts as your President, I expect to follow my instincts of openness and candor." As he worked through those first difficult days, openness, candor, and honesty because the keynotes. For this task the Ford personality and background were well suited; he seemed to embody personally the wholesomeness and descent aspects of American society, which a disillusioned nation most needed.

The advent of President Ford ushered in a new open relationship with the public media for which the press had long thirsted. This in turn was productive of a new presidential image that the public as well as the media had long sought. As Truman had done, Ford promised a new, free flow of information with the press. Cabinet members were encouraged to be "affirmative in their press relations."[62] This was in sharp contrast to the Nixon Administration during which an Office of Communication had overseen all press releases.[63] Press conferences were to become more frequent and more candid, and the press was elated. The love affair with the press that followed had been absent from presidential politics since the early part of the Johnson Administration. Gerald Ford seemingly could do no wrong. His folksiness, his common-man demeanor, his down-to-earth approach-all became part of the material used by the press to reestablish the idealized image that has come to belong to the American Presidency. For an allegedly non-charismatic (some said quite colorless) individual, the press attempted to establish some distinct personality. What it developed was a glorification of the Ford "style"- everything from carrying his own briefcase to making his own breakfast. For a short period, at least, the benevolent leader, the father figure, had returned.

As with past successions, part of the sense of continuity and stability involved a "renewal" of relationships with the Congress, and here Ford again seemed to do no wrong. In the midst of his "inaugural" speech, he casually asked the congressional leaders to remain for a few minutes following the speech to confer with him. In a subsequent address to the Congress, Ford's demeanor was in sharp contrast to that of his predecessor. At every juncture, he seemed humble. For example, he referred to his "privilege of appearing before Congress."[64] Among his fellow Republicans, he was viewed as the possible savior of what had appeared to be an inevitable debacle; among the Democrats, he was viewed as the likable former House leader, even though his succession to the presidency had altered the prospects of a Democratic victory in 1976.

For a Congress that had spent the several years in confrontation with the Nixon presidency - the impoundment of funds, the secret bombings of Cambodia, the Watergate tapes, and ultimately the impeachment process were among the largest issues - the Ford Presidency appeared to mark a positive reconciliation between the two branches of government. Leaders on both sides of the fence applauded the new President, predicting a honeymoon period of two to three months and a Presidency far more willing to engage in consultation and cooperation with Congress than the preceding one had been. Within the framework of a renewed spirit of cooperation, Ford solicited suggestions from both parties regarding possible vice presidential nominees to fill the newly existing vacancy.**65** Ford, whose entire political life had been spent in the lower house of the legislature, "understands Congress in a way that Nixon didn't," noted Republican Senator Charles Percy of Illinois. "He knows the workings of the Congress, he'll work with the Congress, and more importantly he listens and will take political advice from the political sources he respects," echoed Massachusetts Republican Senator Edward Brooke in 1974. Gerald Ford had adroitly established his right to govern.

PROBLEMS OF THE HEIR APPARENT: DISABILITY, SUCCESSION, AND THE NEED FOR PREPARATION

The growth of the power, primacy, and prestige of the Presidency during the modern era has focused considerable attention on a two-sided coin: the questions of disability and succession. One result has been the swift enactment and ratification of the Twenty-Fifth Amendment, providing remedies for instances of presidential disability as well as for potential vacancies in the Vice Presidency. This section offers a critique of this amendment as well as a commentary on the preparation of the heir apparent.

The Twenty-Fifth Amendment was a response to a long-overdue gap in the Constitution. Unfortunately, in attempting to fill that gap, it also created a Pandora's box of additional gaps and dangers, only one of which came to fruition in the Ford-Rockefeller Administration commencing in 1974 - that of the first entirely unelected administration in the history of the Republic. Two hundred years of democracy culminated in moving that democracy one giant step backward-and away from the people. But this is only one of the problems.

The history of the amendment is a long one.**66** If the Constitution, as is evident from even the most cursory reading of it, is relatively mute on the parameters of the Presidency, it is a veritable deaf and dumb stone on the question of the ramifications of the dual problems of succession and disability.

The Founding Fathers, for all their foresight and wisdom, frequently omitted clarifications precisely because they could reach little agreement. The Presidency as a whole was one area of non-agreement, as is evidenced by the ambiguity of Article II.

The Twenty-Fifth Amendment's object of clarification (ironically, filling a vacancy in the Vice Presidency was only a secondary function of the amendment) was the role of the Vice President during presidential disability. The clause reading "In case of the Removal of the President from Office, or at his Death, Resignation, or Inability to discharge the Powers and Duties of the said Office, the same shall devolve on the Vice President..." is one of several muddled inclusions by the Framers. In this clause, they have managed to include a variety of states of being that are both temporary and permanent, and therefore had provided the basis for confusion.

Death, removal, and resignation are all one-time and permanent events, but not so disability. Yet the Constitution assigns the Vice President the task of discharging the powers and duties of the office under all of these conditions. From a reading of the records of the Constitutional Convention, it would seem that the Founding Fathers had *intended* the Vice President merely to *act* as President, but they did not clearly say so. Of even greater importance is the Tyler precedent that interpreted the role of the Vice President otherwise. (See Chapter 1 for a discussion of this precedent.)**67**

Because of the resulting uncertainty over whether a temporarily disabled President could return to office once recovered,**68** no Vice President seemed willing to test the question, and during periods of presidential disability the problem lingered. Vice President Thomas Marshall refused to pick up the constitutionally ambiguous gauntlet of the gap in the Presidency; as a result, the nation endured an absence of leadership while President Woodrow Wilson lay incapacitated.

President Eisenhower himself was well aware of the ambiguities of the Constitution regarding disability, but despite a brief flurry of attention to the question following his three disabilities, it was not until the shock of the Kennedy assassination that the dangers of constitutional ambiguities were again underscored.**69** While Kennedy and Johnson had entered into an informal agreement (as had Eisenhower and Nixon, and later Johnson and Speaker of the House John McCormack) providing that Johnson would *temporarily* assume the Presidency upon presidential disability, that agreement was not a legal or a constitutional document, carrying the legitimizing weight of neither.

Within four years following the Kennedy assassination, the Twenty-Fifth Amendment had been formulated and ratified, and the question hanging over the head of the executive branch had been answered. The Vice President, says the amendment, temporarily assumes the powers and duties of the office during periods of presidential disability. Furthermore, it provides a solution for those potential instances in which a President is unable to, or won't declare himself temporarily disabled, and here is another area in which the Pandora's box has been opened.

Wanting to keep the determination of presidential disability within the executive branch of government (to keep, for as long as possible, within the basic tenet of the system of separation of powers which guides the Constitution),**70** the authors of the amendment empowered the Vice President and a majority of the Cabinet to declare a President temporarily disabled, upon which declaration, of course, the Vice President acts as President, and herein lies the absurdity of this part of the amendment. Is it likely that the beneficiary of a presidential disability would be willing to put himself in the position of being criticized for acting out of self-interest? In addition, would the members of the Cabinet, whose very jobs are tied to the President, be likely to risk inquiring into the President's capability of running the Presidency? A President disabled by a gunshot wound and unable to speak is a clear-cut candidate for a determination of disability by the Vice President and the Cabinet; a President who is suspected of being insane presents an entirely more ambiguous and politically more cautious case. And there are numerous gray areas of disability. One might argue, for example, that Richard Nixon, in losing his "right to govern," as seemed to be indicated by the public opinion polls, was, in a very important way, disabled. Yet there was never any indication that Vice President Ford or any Nixon Cabinet member was moving to utilize the Twenty-Fifth Amendment. In short, under less than glaringly blatant circumstances of presidential (physical) disability, it is unlikely that this part of the amendment will be utilized. Could it not be argued that, in fact, having such a provision is far worse in that the very disuse of it seems to imply a stamp of approval on the state of physical and, more importantly (because less clear-cut), mental well-being of a President? This is a question that loomed large over the erratic Presidency of Donald J. Trump. Indeed, as the 45th President's behavior became more and more outrageous, with seemingly no intention on the part of Vice President Pence and a majority of the Cabinet to invoke the disability clause of the Twenty-Fifth Amendment, the value of this clause of the amendment became even more dubious.

And if a Vice President and the Cabinet should be willing to explore the question of presidential well-being, what of the potential disagreements a President may have with their findings? What recourse does a recovered President have if his examiners disagree that he is ready to assume his office? The Twenty-Fifth Amendment has an answer for this as well. It is at this point, says the amendment, that separation of powers takes a secondary role to a determination. The dispute is sent to Congress, which must decide, by a two-thirds vote, for or against the President and within a period of three weeks. Once again, the unknowns of the Pandora's box are set loose, particularly in the form of the overriding questions: What is the state of the nation during the controversy? What is the level of national confidence in a "recovered" President who has barely received his two-thirds vote in Congress? What is the level of national confidence in a Vice President acting as President because a President has failed by just one vote to be restored to office? Certainly, these are hypothetical situations, but recent American politics has taught us that the hypothetical does occasionally come to pass, and we should be ready for it.

The Ford-Rockefeller Administration was clearly an aberration that departed widely from a basic principle of American government, that is, that the President is elected by and represents all of the people. This is a deviation not to be repeated. If the Twenty-Fifth Amendment is to remain an operative part of the Constitution, it should be qualified by a further amendment that will provide for a special national election in the event an *unelected* Vice President succeeds to the Presidency for a remainder of the presidential term exceeding two years. This would help assure the stability of succession via the Vice Presidency and minimize the length of time a President by succession (who had not been elected to the Vice Presidency) would be apt to serve as the only national leader of the United States.

The Twenty-Fifth Amendment contains the vices of its virtues, and its flaws are obvious. On the one hand, there must be a mechanism to deal with disability, but the mechanism should be more clearly delineated. While it requires immediate reexamination, its defects should not work against the Vice Presidency.

Arthur Schlesinger, Jr., argued that the only function of the Vice Presidency is to provide its incumbents with a jumping ground to the Presidency, or at least presidential nominations. While this is obviously true, what Schlesinger perceives negatively may be viewed alternatively as a slowly evolving solution to the challenging problem of the position of the Vice Presidency: how to find individuals capable enough to be President who are willing to spend several years in the second office, virtually at the mercy of the President's whim. Precisely because the Vice Presidency provides a built-in advantage, the office has appealed to individuals of the stature of Hubert Humphrey, Nelson Rockefeller, Walter Mondale, and, George H.W. Bush, Dick Cheney, Joe Biden. What appears superficially to be a negative result, with gains from exposure accruing only to the incumbent, is, in reality, a positive gain from which the national community may benefit. Moreover, politicians who show interest in the Vice Presidency today are aware that the office has far more public interest and potential than it had a generation ago. Those who come to occupy the second highest office, even though they may never succeed to the Presidency, are much less likely to remain remote political figures than was often characteristic in the past.

Whatever formal changes may be made by constitutional amendment, statutory elaboration, or presidential order, the evolution of the Vice Presidency will be conditioned by the history of that office and by the actions of its past occupants as well as by the opportunities and challenges which the unfolding of future events will provide. It may be said that such developments as do occur in the foreseeable future will continue to depend in large measure on the person who occupies the Presidency and on what that President is willing to share with and assign to the Vice President.

THE GROOMING OF THE VICE-PRESIDENT

The dual question of presidential disability and succession implies an even deeper problem in the Vice Presidency: the events of the pas thirty years have emphasized that the Vice President must be fully prepared to assume the Presidency. The extent of such preparation is vital in considering presidential succession.71

The highly inadequate preparation of Vice President Harry S. Truman dramatized the need to ensure that no future Vice President would find himself so ill equipped to assume the highest office in the land. Truman as President was mindful of the important potentialities of being in line of succession and of the need to possess information relative to those potentialities. He and each of his successors have been aware of vice presidential needs, regardless of the varying roles assigned to them. While preparation in an informational sense is distinct from policymaking and administrative activity, each subsequent Vice President has been provided with considerable basic knowledge of affairs of state from the start.

Truman began this process of information sharing by having the Vice President listed as a statutory member of the National Security Council. He also invited his Vice President, Alben Barkley, to participate in Cabinet meetings.72 The next Vice President, Richard M. Nixon, in addition to serving on the National Security Council (NSC), had the opportunity to preside over its meetings during the Eisenhower illnesses.73 Nixon had been a very active Vice President, and his incumbency marked a significant turning point in the office. Benefiting from Eisenhower's staff system and his disdain for politics, Nixon soon developed a national and international forum. Nixon similarly was involved in NSC meetings and developed a keen training in foreign affairs, a training that would greatly enhance his political future.

Even in those instances in which the Vice President had no actual participation in decision-making, he was kept informed of proceedings and developments at home and abroad.74 Subsequently, Nixon would stress the wealth of information made available to him, along with his intense knowledge of issues and policies, as a précis for his own presidential campaign during which he emphasized that "experience counts."75

Eisenhower's illnesses gave Nixon the opportunity to assume greater executive duties. They pointed up the need for a Vice President who would be ready, if necessary, to take over in an emergency. They also drew attention to the continuing need to resolve the question of what action should be followed in the event of sudden and lingering presidential disability. (The last question was not dealt with until the Kennedy assassination revived it so dramatically.)

During the Constitutional Convention, John Dickinson, a delegate from Delaware, had asked the question, "What is the extent of the term 'disability' and who is to be the judge of it?"76 The question went unanswered for nearly two centuries. Eisenhower's three illnesses called attention more than ever to the confusing state of the term "disability" and the question of what was to be done in the face of it.

President Eisenhower's views on the office of the Presidency, as well as his application of these views to his own administration, provided the framework for special administration arrangements and applied during the three periods of disability that occurred while he was President. A hallmark of the Eisenhower Administration was its emphasis on staff organization, responsibility, and co-ordination. Eisenhower brought to the White House his years of experience in military life and the chain of command organization. In true military fashion, the White House Chief of Staff became the most important link in the communications chain of the administration, with the top man, the President, communicating all decisions and orders via his Chief of Staff. In this respect, even the nationally elected Vice President was subordinate to the Chief of Staff.

During the Eisenhower Administration, it became increasingly apparent that the President preferred to delegate authority to a select group of top assistants, in particular Sherman Adams, his Chief of

Staff, on the domestic side, and Secretary of State John Foster Dulles on the foreign. Adams and Dulles soon took the two critical centers of responsibility under the President. The "Eisenhower Team" was thus ready to keep the machinery of the Presidency running without its general, if the necessity arose.

When Eisenhower experienced his first heart attack on September 23, 1955, he was quite aware of the dangers inherent in the situation. The President, determined to avoid a repetition of the secrecy that surrounded Wilson's disability, ordered total honesty in reporting his condition.[77] In addition, upon Dulles' suggestion, he agreed to have Sherman Adams reside at Fitzsimmons General Hospital in Denver and directed him to serve as a conduit for critical matters[78] Again, to avoid a repetition of the confusion surrounding the Wilson disability, Eisenhower made it clear that he wanted the Vice President to chair all meetings of the NSC and the Cabinet and that all heads of departments be kept regularly and fully informed of world affairs.[79] Eisenhower's most important and frequent visitor, aside from family members, was Adams.[80] Adams, remembering those frequent meetings, said that the President "Had never given me directions for such an emergency, but then he had never given me many directions of any kind and we had gotten along all right. By that time, after working with Eisenhower for three years, I was able to rely upon a good deal more than instinct in deciding what he wanted done."[81]

Attorney General Herbert Brownell, after consultation with Eisenhower's doctors, had already ruled that the President's illness was not severe enough to warrant a constitutional claim of disability.[82] Moreover, the relative political calm of the moment did not seem to warrant such action.[83] This calm allowed a relatively trouble-free presidential disability. This additional reprieve, while fortunate in assuring the nation, was unfortunate in that it destroyed the momentum for seeking a satisfactory solution to the grave issue of presidential disability.[84] As Adams remarked, "It was only good fortune that carried the government without crisis through that last week of

September of 1955,"**85** and the Eisenhower team was well aware of this. Government by "committee" prevailed- a committee consisting of Vice President Nixon, Dulles, Brownell, George Humphrey, Jerry Persons, and Adams. As Adams himself has noted, however, this group was "well aware that a national or international emergency could have arisen during the President's illness to make this unofficial government by 'community of understanding' entirely inadequate."**86**

Without doubt, the Eisenhower team was in charge. During a period of presidential disability, as throughout his incumbency, the President's men are aware of their unique relationship to one man. Their power stems from his power, and it is highly unlikely that they would easily hand over the reins of government to another. As one observer remarked during the Eisenhower disability, "All of the men around Eisenhower did not wish to take any step that could result in giving Mr. Nixon greater authority or even in giving Mr. Nixon the impression that greater authority was soon to be his."**87**

Nixon's own reflections in his book *Six Crises* indicate his under-standing of the necessities of the moment. "My own position as Vice President," wrote Nixon, "called for maintaining a balance of the ut-most delicacy. . . . Any move on my part which could be interpreted, even incorrectly, as an attempt to usurp powers of the presidency would disrupt the Eisenhower team, cause dissension in the nation, and dis-turb the President and his family." Such a Vice President is caught in a dilemma, as Nixon indicated. "My problem was to provide leader-ship without appearing to lead."**88** Nixon also realized that his posi-tion was further affected by the timing of the Eisenhower illness. The Republican National Convention was almost a year away, and specula-tion already had it that the President would not be a candidate, leav-ing Nixon as the heir apparent. To be perceived as attempting to seize power during the Eisenhower disability would have cast Nixon in a particularly negative light.

The business of government went on relatively smoothly. Meanwhile, Adams, stationed by the President's side in the Denver hospital where he was recuperating from the attack, served as the "sole official channel of information between Eisenhower and the world outside of his hospital room."**89**

Eisenhower suffered two additional disabilities during his incumbency. However, neither his ileitis operation during June 1956 nor his cerebral occlusion of November 1957, which impaired his speech temporarily, was as severe as the 1955 heart attack.**90**

Following his initial heart attack, Eisenhower worked out an agreement with the Vice President whereby Nixon, if necessary, could assume the Presidency on a temporary basis until Eisenhower's disability was over. The second and third disabilities were not severe enough to warrant use of the agreement, and again Adams served as "captain of the team resum[ing] his 'caretaker' role" since Attorney General William Rogers had ruled out the necessity for Nixon's temporary succession to the Presidency, inasmuch as the President remained "capable of making emergency decisions."**91** It would seem that Sherman Adams was "the central figure in blocking the rise of Nixon to a position of greater power."**91**

Nixon's active Vice Presidency, coupled with the President's poor health, continued to emphasize the need to prepare the Vice President in order never to repeat the Truman experience. And apparently a lesson was learned, for both Lyndon Johnson and Gerald Ford were very well-informed Vice Presidents.

President Ronald Reagan's designation of Vice President Bush as the head of a special "crisis management" team- prophetically just prior to the assassination attempt on the President in 1981 - underscored the President's appreciation of the Vice President's position. Bush's comportment during the crisis -calm, assured, and part of the Reagan "team"- gained him the respect of the White House staff. Although the Twenty-Fifth Amendment was not invoked, underscoring the argument above regarding the amendment's flaws, and there was no official declaration of presidential inability, Bush's good working relationship with the President allowed him at least to unofficially assume the reins of government and to serve as the President's stand-in during the crisis. This instance further underlined the importance of the Vice Presidency, to which that administration, with the oldest elected President in history, had pointed from its outset. Perhaps it was because of President Reagan's age, ironically, that there was what many would consider to be an irresponsible failure to invoke the disability clause of the Twenty-Fifth Amendment during the period of time Reagan underwent surgery to remove a bullet perilously close (we later learned) to ending his life. His subsequent invocation of the clause under far less drastic circumstances should not distract us from an understanding of the serious disservice done to the nation during what could and should have been the testing of the disability clause in March of 1981. Since the Reagan Administration, Presidents have utilized the clause in the way it was intended. For example, the Bush Administration's matter of fact temporary transfer of power to Vice President Dick Cheney in July of 2007 when President Bush was under anesthesia for a routine colonoscopy should serve as a reminder to future Presidents that nothing should be taken for granted. The Bush-Cheney Administration properly used the Twenty-Fifth Amendment.

In conclusion, while the Twenty-Fifth Amendment evolved from a gnawing need to fill a gap in the Constitution and ensures that the United States has a Vice President ready to take up the presidential reins if the need arises, only the incumbent President can insure that the Vice President will be ready. While all Vice Presidents since Truman have been briefed and marked progress has taken place in this area, consideration should be given to the rather casual and flexible method for vice presidential preparation. A more formal standardization of the critical process of vice presidential grooming as the heir apparent would be desirable.

Chapter 4

—❧—

THE VICE PRESIDENT
AS HEIR APPARENT

Once there were two brothers. One ran away to sea,
the other became Vice President, and nothing was
heard of either of them again.

THE VICE PRESIDENCY has come a long way since Thomas Marshall, Woodrow Wilson's Vice President, told this story. A backwards glance over the period of the modern Vice Presidency is testimony to the new position of that office. Three Vice Presidents have succeeded to the Presidency: Harry Truman, Lyndon B. Johnson and Gerald R. Ford. Former Vice President Richard M. Nixon defeated another Vice President, Hubert H. Humphrey, for the Presidency. Spiro Agnew and subsequently Gerald Ford were seriously discussed from the outset of having taken office as Vice President as the potential nominee of the Republican Party in the next presidential election. The same held true for Vice President Dan Quayle as President George H. W. Bush's Vice President, even though the 1992 Bush-Quayle ticket lost. Al Gore,

President William Jefferson Clinton's Vice President, was an obvious heir apparent, despite opposition in the 2000 primaries, and there would have been far fewer Republicans interested in the 2008 primaries if Vice President Richard ("Dick") Cheney had decided to make himself available. And some Vice Presidents, thanks to name recognition and other factors, were able to seek the presidential nomination at a later date, such as Richard Nixon in 1968 (despite his defeat to John F. Kennedy in 1960), Walter Mondale in 1984 (after the 1980 re-election defeat of the Carter-Mondale Administration), and Vice President Joe Biden's aspirations to the 2020 presidential nomination.

Even before this, once it became abundantly clear that the aging Ronald Reagan would be the 1980 Republican presidential nominee, great attention was focused on his choice of a running mate, with former President Gerald R. Ford in unprecedented consideration for the second spot.

Indeed, the only incumbent Vice Presidents during the period of the modern Vice Presidency not to have been given considerable attention as a potential presidential candidate were Alben Barkley and Dick Cheney because of their advanced age, and Joe Biden in 2016, who did not make himself available because of the recent death of his son.

Clearly, the modern Vice Presidency has come to be the heir apparent and the party standard bearer, and constitutional change has contributed to this trend. The Twenty-Second Amendment, limiting presidential eligibility to two terms, guarantees speculation regarding who will take over, as soon as the previous presidential election vote is cast.

In addition, when the source of potential occupants of the Presidency has oscillated between from the governors' mansions and the U. S. Senate, the number of hopefuls has dramatically increased. The Senate as a stepping stone is a logical direction, since both Vice Presidents and U. S. Senators are better versed than incumbents of other offices in what has become the dominant issue since WW II, foreign affairs. And following the unprepared succession of Harry Truman, Vice Presidents are better informed and prepared to assume the Presidency as a result of the daily and extensive briefings they receive. Another force at work has been the expansion of the Presidency itself. As Presidents since Franklin D. Roosevelt has experienced increasingly complex problems both at home and abroad, there has been a greater need to delegate responsibilities. Certainly, the greatest manifestation of this change has been the expansion and institutionalization of the presidential staff. The Vice President, too, has been given additional and significant duties and assignments, notwithstanding the tendency of the President's burgeoning staff to overshadow the Vice President and shunt him/her aside from the political mainstream. The image of the Vice President, together with the political potential accruing to it, has also been enhanced.

Clearly, then, the Vice Presidency, despite the political pundits' jokes, has become a stepping stone (some have gone so far as to call it a "springboard")1 to the Presidency. But it can be a stumbling block as well. For while the incumbent Vice President has advantages over other aspiring presidential candidates, there are great handicaps as well. There may be up to eight years of an administration's record to defend, a record the Vice President may have had very little hand in shaping. If the administration has done well, the Vice President can, of course, ride on that record. Vice President George Herbert Walker Bush's success in the 1988 presidential campaign can certainly be credited to the public perception of both President Ronald Reagan and the accomplishments of his Presidency. Vice President Bush was the first Vice President since Martin Van Buren to be directly elected to the Presidency. Of course, the economics of the Reagan period "caught up" with his former Vice President in seeking reelection in 1992.

On the other hand, a Vice President may be saddled with the blunders and setbacks that may have occurred. The Vice President must simultaneously strike an independent note and not alienate the President under whom s/he has served. The President still wields power that can help or hurt the heir apparent, as Vice President Hubert H. Humphrey learned during the 1968 presidential campaign.

A large part of the incumbent's problems stems from the nominating process itself. Since the vice presidential candidates are selected with one end in mind – winning the White House – s/he must help unite an extremely heterogeneous party as well as round out the ticket's appeal to a very diversified and complex electorate. The presidential nominee will seek the person who manages to do both. Usually, even if the views of a vice presidential candidate are within range of those of the presidential candidate, their policy preferences will differ. President Ronald Reagan and Vice President George H. W. Bush were reflective of this, as were President Bill Clinton and Vice President Al Gore, especially on environmental issues, with this having a serious impact on Gore's presidential bid in 2000.

In many cases, the "second person" has been seen as a necessary evil, someone to be utilized for the election but later to be ignored or subjugated to the whim of the President and the presidential staff. With the Vice Presidency becoming more prominent and with individuals of greater renown occupying the office, many a Vice President will have been a competitor for the presidential nomination, as indeed was the case with the 1980 vice presidential nominee, George H. W. Bush, the 1992 vice presidential nominee, Al Gore, the 1992 vice presidential nominee and the 2004 Democratic vice presidential nominee, Senator John Edwards.

In accepting the vice presidential nomination, a candidate actually engages in a trade-off: a place in the national arena in exchange for little or no power within that arena. As the Vice Presidency has steadily become a source from which presidential candidates are nominate, the trade-off has become more appealing to individuals of prominence, and the office has increasingly been sought-after. For some, it involves a diminution of power and prestige, and for others it is a step upward. Lyndon B. Johnson's acceptance of the nomination was a demotion of sorts. On the other hand, for a relatively obscure governor like

Spiro Agnew it was quite the promotion. Other nominees probably fall somewhere in between these two extremes. To speak only of the winners of the vice presidential office, Truman's willingness to give up, even if reluctantly, his Senate seat, Alben Barkley's desire for the office at the expense of his position as Majority Leader, Humphrey's quest for it, and Nixon's rapid rise to it, all indicate the increasing desirability of the office.2 Others have sought the office and lost, such as James Byrnes, John F. Kennedy, Eugene McCarthy, Robert F. Kennedy, and Endicott Peabody. Even former President Gerald R. Ford entertained the idea of serving as presidential nominee Reagan's vice presidential running mate. As for the losing presidential vice presidential tickets, the name recognition achieved by the vice presidential nominee is certainly an advantage in approaching the next election season, such as with Senator John Edwards or Senator Joseph Lieberman.

Clearly, then, there has been a higher regard for the office since World War II, especially in its ability to place it incumbents within an arm's length of the presidential nomination.

Truman, having succeeded to the Presidency upon the death of FDR in 1945, received the presidential nomination of his party in 1948, despite his unpopularity. His Vice President, Alben Barkley although handicapped and "disqualified" by his age, was the subject of serious speculation for the 1952 presidential nomination once Truman had taken himself out of the running. Barkley had hardly received more than a lukewarm nod from the White House, but the speculation regarding his status as successor was present nonetheless.3 Since Barkley was not a presidential candidate, it is justifiable to limit this discussion of his short-lived attempt at nomination. Because the primary concern here is with the Vice President's liabilities and assets as party standard-bearer, the focus will be on Nixon's 1960, Humphrey's 1968, and Gore's 2000 presidential bids. Under discussion, too, will be Gerald R. Ford's and Spiro Agnew's early labeling as "heirs apparent."

RICHARD M. NIXON: PARTY STANDARD BEARER, 1960

As a result of the Twenty Second Amendment, Dwight D. Eisenhower was ineligible to service a third term, even if he wanted to. With a "lame duck" President in office, there was speculation regarding a successor through his entire second term, and Eisenhower's young, energetic, and politically minded Vice President was an obvious possibility.4

A President plays an important part in the incumbent Vice President's nomination quest. On the one hand, the President, whether s/he is ineligible to run or has taken himself/herself out of the running, is party leader; on the other hand, his/her Vice President is the party standard bearer. The President has all the resources of the office at his/her disposal; the Vice President has none. An incumbent President can be, and usually is, influential in the nomination and election of a successor.

Recent developments, however, have given the Vice President an edge toward the nomination, with or without the President's help. As early as March 1958, poll results indicated that Nixon was the Republicans' favored nominee for 1960,4 and soon he became the "obvious nominee."5 Thus, while Eisenhower did not overwhelmingly endorse Nixon for the 1960 presidential nomination, the Vice President, as a result of his performance in a party capacity, had built up a considerable cache of political IOUs. For example, as early as the New Year of 1950, Nelson Rockefeller had indicated his feeling that Nixon would undoubtedly be nominated as the 1960 Republican presidential candidate.6 And conservative Arizona Senator Barry Goldwater, in March and April 1959, had come out in support of Nixon as a "legitimate conservative," worthy of Southern support for the Presidency.7 Eisenhower, however, was not convinced that Nixon was presidential timber. He would have much preferred someone like Treasury Security Robert Anderson as his successor.8 The President circumvented the Nixon candidacy by stating at a press conference during the spring of

1960 that the selection of a successor was the business of the Republican Party and that he himself had "no responsibility for trying to groom [his] successor."9

Following Nixon's early January statement in which he threw his hat in the ring for the presidential nomination and indicated his intention of participating in all of the primaries, Eisenhower still said almost nothing. As a matter of fact, what he did say was more embarrassing to Nixon than if he had said nothing at all, especially when the President indicated, in a January 24 press conference, that there were "half a dozen, or ten, or maybe a dozen fine, virile men in the Republican Party that I would gladly support." It was not until March that Eisenhower gave Nixon a lukewarm endorsement.10

The more duties assigned to Nixon and the more public attention he received, the greater the enhancement of his claim to be heir to the throne, especially because of his extensive preparation in national affairs. To a large extent, it might be said that ultimately there was little else that Eisenhower could do. Ironically, it was the President himself who had done the most to bolster Nixon' position, which slowly but steadily gained in prestige.

Eisenhower's delegation of political chores11 held another irony – and this one with negative effects on Nixon's fate. Because Eisenhower was so apolitical, because he had so little interest in or real knowledge of politics, Nixon had been able to build an "empire" of sorts for himself. He had been able to go out and play party politics to its utmost. He was "the Republican Party's most energetic campaigner during the previous eight years," thereby slowly building his strength. The irony is that Eisenhower's apolitical nature also led him to give only minimal support to the Republican Party and thus to fail to transfer his own popularity to it.12 There has been considerable conjecture that Nixon might have won the 1960 presidential election had he had a strong party behind him.13

While Eisenhower did not particularly want Nixon for the 1960 nomination, he did not openly oppose him either. Nonetheless, the

President was troubled by the question of political succession in the Republican Party. He regretted his inability to convince Nixon to leave the Vice Presidency after his first term, and apparently he tried to deny the inevitability of Nixon's nomination as the party standard-bearer.[14] The President's early reluctance regarding a potential Nixon nomination became the Vice President's principal handicap, and it appears that Eisenhower eventually threw his support to Nixon only when no alternative emerged. Eisenhower took no particular role in the convention and was merely advised of the "master plan" which Nixon and his aides laid out for the campaign.[15]

If Nixon had a central approach in his attempt to capture the Presidency in 1960, it was his emphasis on experience.[16] He had enjoyed a rapid rise in his political life, with only four years of experience in the House of Representatives and two years in the Senate before achieving the Vice Presidency, a period shorter than his two-term tenure as Vice Presidency. Despite his relatively young age, he could present an image of experience and stress his superior knowledge over his opponent. John Kennedy had come to the national legislature in the very same year Nixon had, 1946; their length of governmental service was equivalent. But Nixon could and did boast of executive experience, which Kennedy could not.

Nixon had headed two intergovernmental bodies: the President's Committee on Government Contracts and the Cabinet Committee on Price Stability for Economic Growth. He stressed both appointments during the campaign to strengthen his position on the civil rights issue.[17] He had also built up an impressive record in foreign affairs: he was Eisenhower's good-will ambassador to some fifty-five companies, including South America in 1958, a trip that had brought him far-reaching publicity and sympathy, especially since his life had been endangered there.[18]

As one Eisenhower Administration official put it, as Vice President, Nixon was "mentally grooming himself for the Presidency."[19] His campaign against Kennedy highlighted an "Experience Counts" slogan, on the basis of his own record and that of his vice presidential running mate, Ambassador Henry Cabot Lodge.

Given Nixon's record, it would seem that a single event or unwanted remark would not likely damage his position. But in the strange game of presidential campaigning, such an event did occur. President Eisenhower, the man who had allowed Nixon to build his career, was the cause of it. A simple off-the-cuff remark by the President at a press conference on August 24, 1960, served challenger Kennedy well. In response to the request to "give us an example of a major idea of his (Nixon's) that you adopted . . . the President answered, "If you give me a week, I might think of one."[20]

The Nixon camp "damn near fainted, at the thought of such cavalier treatment."[21] Understandably, the opposition immediately seized on the comment. Most observers claim that the statement was not made with any malice on Eisenhower's part, but that it was his way of bringing the press conference to a close."[22] Eisenhower's comment was, one observer noted, "blown all out of proportion, and almost looked as though the President was demeaning any contribution Nixon had made in foreign policy."[23] Nonetheless, the idea that Eisenhower was striking at Nixon endured. Another interpretation suggests that the President was irked that Nixon was giving the impression that the President could not make decisions without his Vice President's assistance; the press conference statement was thus a way of striking back and humiliating Nixon.[24]

With or without the "give me a week" statement, Nixon was in a precarious position. On the one hand, he could point to his experience and knowledgeability, especially in foreign affairs. On the other, he had to prove he was not constantly in the shadow of the popular Eisenhower; that he had not been, and was not now, planning to ride on the President's lengthy coattails. He had to prove he was his own man.

While Nixon entered the presidential debates "because he was convinced he could win" and apparently never considered declining to participate, Kennedy managed to use the debates to counteract Nixon's major resource of experience.25 Perhaps Nixon's previous year's "success" in the "Kitchen Debate" with Premier Nikita Khrushchev had reinforced his belief that he could deal similarly with Kennedy. Eisenhower presidential adviser Emmet John Hughes has maintained that Nixon was undone primarily by his readiness to debate on television, for the debates erased the notion of the Vice President's superiority and maturity,26 a view held by many analysts. Before millions of television viewers, Kennedy was placed on an equal footing. Nixon himself admitted understanding that "the incumbent or whoever represents an incumbent Administration – will generally be at a disadvantage in debate because his opponent can attack while he must defend."27

Although the Vice President's position was not the volatile one that would plague Hubert Humphrey eight years later, he nonetheless had to deal with a number of events that reflected poorly on the Eisenhower Administration. The U-2 spying incident,28 the debacle of the Paris summit and Eisenhower's subsequent embarrassment at the hands of Nikita Khrushchev,29 the advent of a recession as the campaign approached,30 and an apparent missile gap in relation to the Russians31 – all had damaging effects on Nixon's campaign.

Nixon soon found himself in the unenviable defensive position.32 Saddled with the mistakes of the Eisenhower Administration as well as benefiting from its merits, he had to proceed cautiously, unable to assume the accusing stance of past campaigns. Kennedy could attach all he wanted and Nixon had to respond.33 The Democrats, aware of the unfavorable position Nixon was in, took every opportunity to refer pointedly to the mistakes not of the Eisenhower Administration but of the *Eisenhower-Nixon* Administration.34

While Kennedy could run on a "Let's get the country moving again" theme,35 Nixon had to protest that it *had* been moving under Eisenhower, whether or not he had entirely agreed with the President's policies. The Vice President attempted to defend the administration, in part, by transferring the blame to Congress. "Putting it bluntly," Nixon said, "there has been a political stalemate between the Administration and Congress over the past five years."**36** As one observer noted, "Kennedy was the challenger, the aggressor – everything to win and nothing to lose, really. Nixon had to fight a sort of *status quo* battle."**37** Nixon, as would Hubert Humphrey eight years later, struggled with the dilemma imposed by his split political identity; the quest for the Presidency requires the demonstration of a forceful single identity.

A more subtle complication for the incumbent Vice President seeking election to the Presidency is that he/she is usually privy to more information than his/her opponent. This distinction has been steadily fading, as more recent Presidents have provided comprehensive briefings for all serious contenders for the nomination and then for the two (or more, in some electoral campaigns) candidates themselves. But this was a very real problem for Nixon in 1960, especially in one area.

One of Kennedy's prime targets concerned the administration's policy towards Cuba. Kennedy, in taking the offensive, had begun with a general criticism of the Eisenhower-Nixon Administration for its seemingly lax stand on Castro. He ultimately became more specific and focused is criticism on the administration's lack of fortification for Cuban counterrevolutionaries.**38** What Kennedy did not know was that a covert operation was under way. Nixon, aware of what was taking place, could do nothing lest he endanger the administration's efforts.**39**

Nixon's attempt to maintain his positive identity with Eisenhower establishing his independence was complicated by the President himself,**40** who was very sensitive to criticism of his record.**41** Eisenhower expected, therefore, that the campaign would be run as a defense of that record. As early as March 1958, he had indicated he would refuse to support any candidates in 1960 "who failed to share his own views on the 'big issues.'"**42** As the presidential campaign got under way, the President's concern, as well as that of his staff, was to safeguard the Eisenhower record.**43**

Eisenhower did virtually nothing on Nixon's behalf throughout the major part of the campaign,**44** and when his help was requested, and came, during those last days of the campaign, it was too late.

With regard to Eisenhower's direct involvement, or lack of it, in the campaign, the picture is blurred. Only when the polls indicated that Nixon was losing did he turn to Eisenhower for help. He had probably not sought that help earlier because he felt it necessary to demonstrate an identity.**45** Nixon's purpose, noted Donald Paarlberg, a member of the Eisenhower Administration, was "to carry his own banner, to prove he could do it on his own."**46** Nixon wanted to make it on his own, with everyone else in supporting roles, noted another.**47** As Nixon aide Robert Finch observed, "I think it's fair to say that was quite a natural desire for Nixon to prove that he could do it on his own. He's been constantly subjected to the criticism that he had been sort of carried in by Eisenhower, in both the '52 and '56 elections.**48**

Nixon's solution to the dilemma – to establish his own identity – ultimately contributed to his defeat. He neglected the President as a potent political figure in his own right, and so the critical element in the development of the Nixon Vice Presidency, Eisenhower's apolitical nature, worked against Nixon in the 1960 campaign. For different reasons, Vice President Al Gore also made the fatal mistake of distancing him from President Bill Clinton during Gore's bid for the Presidency in 2000.

HUBERT H. HUMPHREY: PARTY STANDARD-BEARER, 1968

The incumbent Vice President not only cannot take the offensive, but is also handicapped by an inability to rally the resources available to an incumbent President seeking reelection – the powers and prestige of the Presidency itself. Such a person is in the same position s/he has often been in during his Vice Presidency: s/he continues to be subject to the President's whims.

Few Vice Presidents have been in as awkward a position as was Vice

President Hubert Humphrey during the campaign of 1968. On the face of things, it appeared that he had been involved in decision-making concerning the issue that was tearing the administration apart, the war in Southeast Asia, and had agreed with the administration. In reality, both his involvement and agreement had been limited. Although Humphrey had served as the administration's spokesperson, he had many moments of private disagreement.**49** In the mind of the electorate, these varying degrees of involvement and agreement blurred, and Humphrey seemed to be nothing more than a stand-in, a puppet, for the dominating figure of Lyndon Johnson. In this regard, Humphrey's personality played a critical role. He was, as former Secretary of State Dean Rusk once remarked, "a loyal fellow";**50** "an extremely loyal man," said former Johnson aide Walter Jenkins;**51** "loyal to a fault," observed former Kennedy aide Kenneth O'Donnell.**52**

Hubert Humphrey understood the uniqueness of the vice presidential office. He also understood what Lyndon Johnson wanted in a Vice President, and Johnson knew he could count on Humphrey to serve him loyally. In offering the nomination to Humphrey in 1964, the President had stressed the importance of loyalty, and Humphrey kept his promise. Despite some private disagreement, in public he was a solid Johnson man. Under normal circumstances, this association might have proven immeasurably beneficial; under the circumstances of 1968 America it was a disaster. One of Humphrey's major functions as Vice President, the defense and explanation of administration policy in Vietnam, contributed to his downfall in the 1968 presidential campaign.

Humphrey had bound up his fate with that of Lyndon Johnson; he was aware of the potential disaster of Vietnam, but he had had to make a choice. Johnson, he had decided, would make him or break him. Everything Humphrey had accomplished in his years of national service was somehow linked to Lyndon Johnson. "Humphrey is always aware of the political umbilical cord linking his fortunes with those of Lyndon Johnson," remarked one observer.**53** Humphrey himself noted his indebtedness to Lyndon Johnson. "I became Vice President because he made me Vice President. . . . I became Whip because he made me Whip. As a matter of fact, I've had a helping hand from Lyndon Johnson from the beginning. I remember him saying to me, 'Hubert, you should get better acquainted with more Senators,' and we'd have lunch with Walter George or Dick Russell or someone like that, in the private dining room."[54]

It was Senator Johnson who had placed Humphrey on the very important and prestigious Foreign Relations Committee, as well as on the Agriculture Committee,[55] two assignments Humphrey had coveted. When the possibility of the vice presidential nomination was presented to him, Humphrey yearned and vowed to serve Johnson loyally.[56] As he became increasingly involved in the Johnson Administration, Humphrey, formerly the darling of the liberal community, became identified as the one who had "sold out" all he believed in to become Johnson's "hatchet man."[57]

Humphrey, knowing that his greatest chance of being President rested in his relationship with LBJ, had compromised himself so that he could remain on Johnson's 1968 ticket. Ironically, when Johnson chose not to run in 1968, Humphrey's chance at the Presidency came even sooner than he had anticipated, but his past compromises, particularly his seeming support of Johnson on Vietnam, hurt his campaign.

In 1968, Humphrey had to defend an unpopular administration's record; he also suffered from an identity problem. His association and identification with Lyndon Johnson had become so fused that for all intents and purposes he *was* Lyndon Johnson.[58] His presidential campaign was a futile effort to sever that identification, to forge his own identity.

Humphrey himself, in a meeting with newsmen during the campaign, stated his basic problems: "My most serious dilemma, the thing that is at the core of our whole campaign is how on the one hand do you chart an independent course and yet at the same time not repudiate the course of which you've been part." And then he stated the essence of the vice presidential dilemma. "I don't think any Vice President is going to be able to fundamentally alter the policy of the country between now and January 20. Our advice and counsel may be sought, but *we are not in charge, any of us.* Comes January 20, high noon, 12:00 p.m. in the afternoon, then I will be in charge. And I will set the policy. And I will determine what we are going to do about our foreign relations and our national security, including Vietnam. And I have some rather strong ideas about it.**59** (italics added)

As Richard Scammon and Ben Wattenberg have pointed out, the "I'm displeased" feeling prevalent in 1968 American became an anti-Johnson and ultimately an anti-Humphrey feeling.**60** An "era of bad feeling" had set in, and Johnson and all those associated with him personified it.

Humphrey's problem was similar to Nixon's in 1960, but with a different twist. Whereas Nixon had to maintain his identification with the popular Eisenhower while showing that he was ready to win and take over the Presidency on his own, Humphrey had to avoid identification with Johnson.

During the campaign, Humphrey attempted to play down his association with the President. For example, he emphasized his independent choice of Maine's U. S. Senator Edmund Muskie as a running mate. In focusing attention as a contrast to Nixon's choice of Spiro Agnew, the strategy was to play up the Humphrey-Muskie team and to divert attention from the negatively perceived Johnson-Humphrey team. So, for example, Muskie was given wide coverage in a television program that associated him with famous Democrats, with Lyndon Johnson conspicuous by exclusion.**61** Indeed, it sometimes appeared that focusing attention away from the Johnson Administration and on Muskie was the only way out for Humphrey. This was a path followed by former Vice President Walter Mondale, who despite a four-year hiatus from the Carter-Mondale Administration was still associated with the dismal ending of that administration. For Mondale, the bold choice of the first woman as his vice presidential running mate was the Muskie equivalent.

Muskie, then, emerged as one of Humphrey's strongest assets. He handled himself well with demonstrators and hecklers; the press liked him; above all, Muskie had no opposition.**62** He was an even more potent asset because he represented a stark contrast to Nixon's running mate. Spiro Agnew rapidly emerged as a political incompetent during the campaign. Among some of his numerous faux pas of the campaign were his references to "Polacks," his calling one Japanese-American newsman a "fat Jap," and his claim that "if you've seen one slum you've seen them all."**63**

Humphrey was stifled in his endeavor to establish his own identity, limited by his own view of the Vice Presidency and its relationship to the Presidency, boxed in by his own determination to keep his word. The result was a sort of "hedginess" – a flirting with – an independent posture. Humphrey defended Lyndon Johnson's domestic policies but ignored Vietnam.**64** He announced Muskie as his running mate despite Johnson's preference for a candidate further to the right, such as Governor John Connally of Texas, and he made it clear that President Johnson was *"informed* of his choice of Muskie."**65**(italics added)

Humphrey's hedginess was characteristic of his remarks in the wake of the wreck of the Democratic National Convention in Chicago. "The policies of tomorrow need not be limited by the policies of yesterday."**66** said Humphrey. At the same time, he was obliged to support and run on the strong Vietnam plank adopted by the convention.**67** This was the only course possible for a man who had gone along with administration policy in that area and had to operate in the ominous shadow of Lyndon Johnson. Johnson was a master at cajoling, persuading, convincing, and intimidating. He had had years of practice at getting what he wanted. And in 1968, as he had during his entire incumbency, he wanted loyalty from Hubert Humphrey. Johnson seemed to be calling the shots; the nomination had been literally dangled before Humphrey, even though Johnson had seemingly kept his neutrality.**68** If Humphrey was to gain the nomination, it would be with Johnson's help, if not entirely Johnson's doing.**69**

Despite the fact that he was the front-runner for the nomination and the incumbent Vice President, Humphrey reportedly had little control over convention decisions. For example, although Humphrey wanted the convention held in Miami, Lyndon Johnson insisted on and got Chicago. When Humphrey asked Chicago Mayor Richard Daley for a special hall for demonstrators, it was to no avail; he did not even receive a reply. Reportedly, Humphrey even had difficulty getting tickets for the convention.70 Johnson might not have been running for the Presidency, but he certainly planned to control who would. In fact, he had insisted that the 1968 Democratic presidential nominee be, above all, someone who had followed and would continue to follow, the White House line on the sensitive issue of Vietnam.71

Incumbent Presidents have a vested interest in the continued support of their policies, and it is understandable that they will use the powers of their office to insure that end. Eisenhower had insisted on that in 1960; now it was Johnson's turn. But Johnson's position and his ability to command obedience were far different from what Eisenhower's had been. Both men had the perquisites of the office at their disposal; both had records about which they were sensitive. In sharp contrast, however, as President, Johnson had enjoyed both the heights and the depths of public opinion. A candidate running on a strong White House line in 1968 would not repudiate the Johnson Administration. Once Humphrey won the nomination, the Cabinet and White House staff began to join the campaign, further defending the Johnson record. Johnson was determined to control to the end.

Humphrey was in a peculiar position. He was the heir apparent to a President who could conceivably change his mind and seek reelection. Humphrey's only alternative, if he was to win the nomination, was to ride with Johnson, and it was the Johnson delegates who gave Humphrey the nomination.72

Having won the nomination, Humphrey began to engage in a battle that would bring many moments of doubt and hesitation. Johnson had helped him win the nomination, but would he lose the Presidency out of loyalty to Johnson? Was there any balance that could be struck that would establish Humphrey as an independent candidate and at the same time not alienate the man who was responsible for his being there and who still commanded vast political resources?

Some of Humphrey's advisers, fearing the disastrous effects of over identification with and defense of Lyndon Johnson, had recommended the most clear-cut method of severing ties: Humphrey would have to resign the Vice Presidency.73 Although he knew he had to extricate himself from the unpopular administration, resignation was not the answer for Humphrey; he had a contract with the American people, he told this author in a personal interview, and it would not do to break that contract.74 Besides, doing so might have cost him more in the long run.75 The President still wielded tremendous power.

And so he struggled through the campaign, attempting to concentrate on the administration's domestic achievements and to play down the debacle of Vietnam. His opponent was the benefactor of the dilemma. It has often been said that the Democratic Party's most effective unifying force was Richard Nixon. In 1968, the Democratic Party was Richard Nixon's strongest resource. Unlike his position in 1968, Nixon could retune to the campaign position with which he was most comfortable – the offensive – and Humphrey was the disadvantaged opponent.

Aware of the sentiment of disgust throughout the country and a general sense of dissatisfaction, Nixon employed his strategy. His strength, wrote Scammon and Wattenberg, was that "he was *not* Humphrey, and didn't have anything to do with anything that people were angry about."76

Nixon had little to say about Vietnam. Indeed, he had no need to say anything. The adoption of a strong Democratic Party plank (Hubert Humphrey would have preferred a more dovish one which would have enabled him to engage in a smoother break from Johnson) forced the Vice President into a position of defending the record. Moreover, Humphrey avoided bringing the issue into the campaign;

he knew it could only hurt him. Nixon was able to get a free ride on the most volatile issue of the year and perhaps the generation.

Nixon, with a united Republican Party behind him, attacked the Democratic record on all its vulnerable points. Vietnam, law and order, big spending, and the "security gap," an issue through which John Kennedy, at the turn of the decade, had put Nixon on the defensive.[77]

As the challenger, especially of an unpopular administration, Nixon had a flexibility Humphrey would have relished. As one Nixon aide put it, "Nixon was locked in in 1960. He was a member of Ike's team and Ike was a popular President, so he had to go along. Now he's freer."[78] Moreover, Nixon was the beneficiary of the "Social Issues" that pervaded the political environment, as Scammon and Wattenberg explained. "On the Social Issues that disturbed the nation – crime, race, student disorders, among others – the Republicans were perceived as somewhat "tougher" than the Democrats, somewhat more in tune with the attitudes of the electorate . . .. The feelings that Nixon capitalized upon were not part of a Southern strategy or a Border strategy – they were part of a national strategy that was attuned to a national malaise."[79]

Circumstances were working against Humphrey. Not only did he have to defend the record; he was also a Democrat at a time when Democrats were identified as being out of harmony with the issues outraging the electorate.

Humphrey's position, especially on law and order, had been worsened as a result of the assassinations of Martin Luther King, Jr. and the resulting riots, the assassination of Robert F. Kennedy and the turmoil at the Chicago Convention. The year 1968 was a violent year in American politics, and America was weary of violence – violence 6,000 miles away in Southeast Asia and violence around the corner. As Humphrey's position in the polls grew increasingly worse, it became obvious that he had to break or seem to break with Lyndon Johnson.[80]

Humphrey's September 30 speech in Salt Lake City represented the sharpest break from the Johnson Vietnam policy in the campaign and a marked deviation from his past policy of not disagreeing with the President in public.**81** It was an ambiguous speech at best, as had been all his attempts to establish an independent posture. Although Humphrey claims the speech "liberated him internally"**82** it failed to extricate him from his association with the administration's record or position on Vietnam.

Symbolically, Humphrey spoke from a lectern that bore no vice-presidential seal; he was not even introduced as the Vice President, and he began his speech by declaring, "Tonight I want to share with you my thoughts as a citizen and a candidate for President of the United States."**83** Throughout his speech, he remained not Hubert H. Humphrey, Vice President of the United States under Lyndon B. Johnson, but Hubert H. Humphrey, presidential candidate.

Humphrey's Salt Lake City speech is remarkable for its indication of the dilemma he was in. Although his advisers wanted him to openly declare his independence from the President, he realized he could not say anything that would jeopardize the President in the peace negotiations. He could, however, say what he would do as President. At the outset of the speech, he stated his pledge on the Vietnam War. There followed an assertion of his involvement in decision-making, but the indication was that Johnson, and not Humphrey, made the decisions. To avoid alienating Johnson, however, Humphrey added that "the choices have not been simple or easy." Then he reemphasized that Johnson's Vietnam policy to Johnson and that the "President . . . will continue – until January 20, 1969 – to make the decisions in Vietnam." The implication was that if Humphrey were President, things would be different; a Humphrey Administration would not be the Johnson Administration revisited. "The policies of tomorrow need not be limited by the policies of yesterday," voiced Humphrey. And then Humphrey returned to an appeasement of Johnson. "Neither vindication nor repudiation of our role in Vietnam will bring peace or be worthy of our country." Humphrey made another attempt to extricate the entire administration from bearing the full brunt of the war, and he cited the role played by the Eisenhower and Kennedy administrations in the development of the conflict. Having made clear, even if apologetically, that the policies of Johnson, Humphrey, Kennedy, and Eisenhower were *their* policies, Humphrey noted his opponent's link with past Vietnam decisions; he then set out to draw an identity of his own on Vietnam. This identity was designed to solicit from the hawks as well as the doves and all those falling somewhere in between.**84**

Johnson was livid.

Humphrey, who had consulted with the President on several occasions during the preparation of the speech, had "waited until the last minute, when the text of the speech was already in the hands of the reporters."**85** Johnson apparently had been reassured that there was nothing detrimental in the speech; nonetheless, the President reportedly warned his Vice-President: "Hubert, you give that speech and you'll be screwed."**86**

Humphrey, who had defended the Johnson policy almost to the death, had wavered. He had tried to hedge his bets, but he suffered the consequences of playing both ends against the middle; in the end, he satisfied neither.

Johnson's involvement in the campaign itself was rather mixed. On the one hand, he had considerable powers at his disposal. The entire thrust of the campaign could change in a moment depending on what Johnson decided to do, especially regarding the Vietnam bombing. For a "lame duck" President, he wielded tremendous potential authority. It was Johnson who had the power to halt the bombing of North Vietnam; it was he who had the power to enliven the Paris peace talks.**87** Humphrey's political fate was irrefutably linked to a man who was intransigent on Vietnam and who demanded loyalty. The combination was both compelling and frustrating.

Johnson was committed to do something about Vietnam and to vindicate himself. It is not possible to separate domestic from foreign politics, especially in an election year. What Hubert Humphrey was trying to achieve as a candidate in 1968 was not always compatible with what Lyndon Johnson was trying to achieve as President.**88**

Following Humphrey's Salt Lake City speech, Nixon, who had been quietly riding out the issue of Vietnam on the Vice President's difficult position, snapped into position. Nixon denounced Humphrey for "undercutting the United States position in Paris." Referring to the proposed bombing halt, Nixon hoped "Vice President Humphrey would clarify his position and not pull the rug out from under the negotiations and take away the trump car the negotiators have."**89**

Later in the campaign, when Nixon suspected that President Johnson might just pull a bombing halt out of his hat to aid Humphrey, he made a clever effort to head it off. Nixon offered his support to Johnson, should the President decide on a bombing halt to save American lives and bring peace. "The one man who makes the determination," said Nixon, "is the President of the United States. Let's let him make that determination, and if he makes it, we will support him because we want peace, and we do not want to play politics with peace."**90** Nixon killed two birds with one stone. He both anticipated Johnson's potential move, and he set up the conditions under which he would approve the bombing halt.

To further undercut the possibility of a bombing halt, Nixon rose to the President's defense in refutation of the rumor of a bombing halt, using it to his best advantage to stab at Humphrey as well.

> I am, told that this spurt of activity (meetings in the White House) is a cynical, last minute attempt by President Johnson to salvage the candidacy of Mr. Humphrey. This I do not believe . . .. At no time in the campaign have I found the President anything but impartial and candid in his dealings with the major Presidential contenders about Vietnam. I know this has not been easy for him. Beginning long before the Republican Convention in early August, influential elements within and outside his party have subjected him to

intense pressure to contrive what he has aptly described as a "fake peace." It is to his credit that he has withstood these pressures. . . .

In foreign affairs the President must be our nation's only spokesman. The Paris negotiations are critically important and exceedingly delicate. At such a time I believe every presidential candidate should mind his tongue to avoid weakening our diplomatic hand by irresponsible comments on the matters at issue. This has been my position throughout the campaign.**91**

Nixon both struck at Humphrey, whose reputation for not knowing when to keep silent was proverbial, and justified his own lack of a Vietnam position. Nixon used this same stance on CBS's *Face the Nation*: "I think we ought to be consistent on this and I think President Johnson has been consistent. I've been consistent. Mr. Humphrey ought to get in line, agree with his President for a change."**92**

Humphrey had been damned for agreeing, and now he was damned for disagreeing. It seemed impossible for him to win. He was locked in by even more confining circumstances than Nixon had been in 1960. The year 1968 was an unparalleled year in American politics, and Humphrey was its prime victim. Vietnam, ghetto riots, assassinations, all created a tense atmosphere fraught with impending eruption; all this was well before Humphrey went to Mayor Daley's Chicago, the city Johnson had thought would be safe for the Democratic Convention.

Vice President Humphrey, heir to the presidential throne following Robert Kennedy's death and the short-lived Jesse Unruh-Richard Daley movement to draft Senator Edward M. Kennedy,**93** came out of the Chicago Convention at about the same level at which he went in, which is a calamitous situation for any presidential candidate. Kennedy's death, while it virtually assured Humphrey the nomination, implicitly held other consequences for the Vice President. The assassination of the second Kennedy brother, just sixty days after that of civil rights leader Martin Luther King, Jr., was in large measure "a mental breakdown for the American political community."[94] A nation stunned by the events of a year only half over wondered what would come next. Humphrey's problem was to make certain that the nomination he got by default was worth having.

The traumatic events of the Chicago Convention further diminished Humphrey's possibilities of winning the election. Millions of Americans watched on nationwide television as police, national guardsmen, and demonstrators clashed on the Chicago streets, while divided Democrats clashed on the convention floor. As a candidate associated with an administration immutably tied to the violence of Vietnam, Humphrey's nomination was a hollow victory. While "law and order" was emerging as the principal issue of the campaign and the third-party candidacy of Alabama Governor George Wallace served to alter the strategy and position of both major party candidates,[95] law and order broke down for the Democratic party on the streets of Chicago.

The war and the bitter dissent and violence hurt Humphrey in a double way. Because of the turmoil during and following the Chicago Convention, the Democratic Party, which had been identified as soft on the social issues, was further identified as contributing to the crisis ravaging America. This did irreparable damage to the Humphrey candidacy.[96] Not only was Humphrey's liberalism compromised by his identification with President Johnson and his administration; the law and order issues also made him fearful of being branded a racist. Of all the candidates in 1968, Nixon appeared to be the most closely identified with the center in his enormous appeal to "Middle America."[97] Forced to take a stand but wanting to avoid the racist overtones associated with "law and order," the Democratic party chose to use the phrase "justice and law" in its plank, which declared, "In fighting crime we must not foster injustice. Lawlessness cannot be ended by curtailing the hard-won liberties of all Americans."[98]

Humphrey was plagued by dissension within his party. The

President's withdrawal from the race was symptomatic of the deep division within the party. Although Johnson claimed to have made his decision a year before, it is most likely that the challenge by Eugene McCarthy contributed in no small measure to the President's announcement on March 31 that he would not run for reelection.**99**

On March 12, the man who had not been taken very seriously almost won the New Hampshire primary, jeopardizing the President's re-nomination. Eugene McCarthy's strong showing prompted a heretofore reluctant and cautious Robert Kennedy throw his hat into the presidential ring as well,**100** and the stage was set for a confrontation among the challengers. In a wider sense, the confrontation was between the Old Politics (represented by the administration and Hubert Humphrey) and the New Politics (represented by McCarthy and Kennedy).**101** Humphrey, as Johnson's political heir, had the unpleasant and disadvantageous task of defending an unpopular administration in not just one forum, but two – one within his own party and one with the "out party." If Lyndon Johnson's nomination had been in doubt, this feeling was transferred to his Vice President. If Johnson was, as one observer referred to him, the "Anti-Christ of the New Politics,"**102** Humphrey's problem was that he was guilty by association. It is small wonder that Humphrey did not believe he could win the election.

Following his victory in the nomination battle, Humphrey was left with the tattered remains of a party. Only four years earlier, following the debacle of the Goldwater defeat at the hands of the Johnson-Humphrey ticket, it was wondered whether the Republican Party could ever pull itself together again. Now, the Republican Party was united behind its candidate, Richard Milhous Nixon, who was eager to enter combat with the shreds of its opposition. Robert Kennedy was dead; Eugene McCarthy was embittered; Hubert Humphrey was the nominee. In a society with little in the way of ideological politics, 1968 was the year of the flood. The additional burden placed on Humphrey as he waged an uphill battle against the opposition was to woo and win the disillusioned and disdainful Kennedy and McCarthy supporters.**103**

While many of the Kennedy people eventually fell into line behind the Vice President, McCarthy and many of his ardent supporters sulked and thereby widely advertised the dissension within the party. McCarthy was a tough man. If Humphrey was to win back the dissidents, something dramatic had to be done on the question of the Vietnam bombing.

The resulting Salt Lake City speech, however, had done little to change McCarthy's position; McCarthy felt the speech was too much the product of semantics and too little of substance.**104** McCarthy's support, coming only at the very end of October, on October 29, was too weak and, above all, too late. McCarthy merely said that Humphrey, even if unsatisfactory, was better than Nixon. The "establishment" had miscalculated, or possibly had not taken the time to calculate, the temper of the country,**105** and Humphrey suffered as a result. As one Johnson Administration official said, "Maybe Hubert Humphrey's situation is simply impossible. Maybe his dilemma on the war is just insoluble. Maybe he is bound to be nominated, but he can't be elected."**106**

In order to fully understand what happened to Hubert Humphrey in 1968, it is necessary to recall the traumatic mood of 1968 America. The war, the violence, the bitterness, the changed engulfed those who were seemingly responsible for it, and Hubert Humphrey was no exception. The year was a year of losses: Lyndon Johnson "lost" the right to seek reelection; Robert Kennedy and Martin Luther King, Jr. lost their lives; the Democratic Convention lost control; youth lost its faith in system; the system lost faith in itself. It is no wonder that in the midst of such events Hubert Humphrey lost what he had been striving for all his political life, the Presidency of the United States.**107**

THE HEIRS APPARENT:
AGNEW, FORD, BUSH, AND PENCE

Spiro Agnew's Vice Presidency was a very mixed one. On the one hand, he enjoyed national exposure, which few Vice Presidents have experienced; on the other, the controversial nature of that exposure made him the subject of severe criticism as well as adulation. Agnew became progressively a master at rhetoric and used it effectively. His promise, made at the Republican National Convention, to become a household word was overwhelmingly fulfilled. He had gone from a seemingly clumsy, inept campaigner to an adroit vocalizer of much of the nation's grievances. Agnew had almost single-handedly taken on the networks, radicals, liberals, Democrats, opponents to the war – whatever "enemy" plagued the administration. While alienating many segments within the electorate, he skillfully realigned others. At the same time that it was "political suicide to tackle the networks,"**108** for example, Agnew's attack on the media forged a critical link in his appeal to the more conservative element in America. Since Agnew was simultaneously a most idolized and most despised political figure, any attempt to reach for the Presidency in 1976 would meet mixed reactions.

During his Vice Presidency, Agnew utilized every opportunity to obtain nationwide exposure. He had successfully transformed himself into a star, however controversial. As he began to look to the next presidential election, other considerations confronted him. As one confidential source explained, "What the White House wanted and what Spiro Agnew wanted were the same thing, but for two different purposes. Agnew wanted to be in a good position for the '76 election. He wanted to be low keyed and to be a party person and the White House wanted someone to speak for the party, which is exactly what Agnew wanted." **(See Appendices A and B for Agnew's attack speeches)**

Following the 1972 election, with Richard Nixon as the incumbent ineligible for reelection and unable to remove his running mate, Agnew's attentions began to move in new directions. He began a more purposeful courtship of the party professionals and the press.**109** At the same time, however, the President was grooming his own successor, namely, John Connally, and began to reduce Agnew's staff, ominous signs that were not too propitious for his presidential ambitions.**110**

At this juncture, Agnew found himself the benefactor of events. The Watergate scandals, while tarnishing most of the administration, including the President himself, not only left Agnew unscathed but also made him appear more favorable. Agnew was emerging as the "Mr. Clean" of the administration, one who had had nothing to do with Watergate at any stage.**111** In addition, John Connally left the White House.

Agnew's position was singular. He had managed to achieve national prominence and to be the object of serious speculation for the 1976 Republican presidential nomination. Meanwhile, he avoided any commitment regarding his plans or goals for 1976 by maintaining that "Vice Presidents aren't automatically accepted as the logical successors of Presidents."**112**

In order to emphasize that he was presidential timber, Agnew had to show that he had an active role in the administration. But Watergate forced him to strike a peculiar sort of balance: he had to stay "above the Watergate battle"**113** while at the same time making the most of his experience in office. In this instance, *not* having participated in decision-making was decidedly more beneficial to Agnew's political fate. Regarding Agnew's role, Senator Barry Goldwater sarcastically remarked, "If there is one thing the Vice President can back up it's that he doesn't know what the hell is going on at the White House."**114** Agnew also had to keep the immaculate image bestowed on him by Watergate without displaying disloyalty to the President. The results were a very cautious posture. For example, while he expressed approval of Nixon's foreign policy, he said he would approach domestic problems differently.**115** In assuming this ambivalent stance, Agnew sought to avoid alienating the President by adding, "That doesn't mean my ideas are superior to those of the President."**116**

When questioned specifically about Watergate, Agnew, in a *Time* magazine interview of July 1973, strove to find a path that would do him the least damage, from whatever side. While asserting his confidence in the President, he cautiously based this sentiment on faith rather than fact.**117** Agnew was equally cautious in his statements concerning the President himself.

> I would assume that if he's human and fallible like the rest of us, he's made mistakes. But I think they have been very minimal. . . .

> Watergate does show one thing. In a job as big as the Presidency, you can't watch everything. You're at the mercy of the people carrying out your instructions. I don't think there's any foolproof way in which a person who heads a large enterprise can protect himself against people who work for him. You want people with initiative. You don't want people who check with you before doing anything, because that's of no value to you. There isn't any other way. We're all locked into the people we work for.

In laying out a suggested course of action for the President to follow, Agnew maintained that "it is important to get the President before the people. I think a freewheeling press conference would be a mistake. I don't think the President can be put in a position where there's an inquisition with people screaming and yelling the way they've been known to. Out of that volatile atmosphere comes an impression that's highly misleading sometimes."

But Agnew was cautious enough to add, "If you get some of the giants of your profession, you could figure out a proper kind of interview. You could screen out the matters that are highly improper . . . and concentrate strictly on information concerning the President's position." And with respect to the specific issue of "bugging," Agnew said, "The entire idea of bugging I find personally repulsive. . . . I would never sanction listening in on somebody else's personal conversations."

Moving away from specific Watergate issues, Agnew built on his immaculate image by striking a sanctimonious note on campaign spending. "No matter how good your reforms are and how ideal the method of financing campaigns, there will always be those who break the law. . . . [E]very serious candidate [should have] enough money to run a decent, respectable campaign without raising funds through private funds."**118** This response was in sharp contrast to President Nixon's policy in vetoing related legislation.

In short, by avoiding over identification with the administration, Agnew was attempting to spare himself the fate of past Vice Presidents who had become the innocent victims of presidential problems. The head of steam Agnew's political future gained throughout his incumbency and especially during the Watergate scandal was suddenly and completely and completely exhausted in 1973 by his *nolo contendere* plea in a criminal charge and his prompt resignation,

Following his appointment as Agnew's vice presidential successor, Gerald R. Ford was confronted by a similar mixed blessing. Thrown into the position of being one heartbeat, one resignation, or one impeachment away from the Presidency in the midst of the most devastating political scandal since Teapot Dome, Ford reacted similarly to past Vice Presidents: he was obliged to hedge his position. There was one important difference, however: Ford was confirmed after congressional hearings that pointedly and in advance sought out his credential to be President. Unlike Spiro Agnew who had *emerged* as the "Mr. Clean" of the administration, Ford assumed his duties with a clean slate. Thus, Ford began his Vice Presidency amid speculation of a Ford presidential bid in 1976, if not a succession before that.

As President Nixon's problems grew more complex, Ford's position became more uncomfortable and frequently more flexible. In the awkward position being the beneficiary of President Nixon's spiraling problems, Ford probably had little choice but to maintain a low-keyed, balanced line of support and defense of the President, with an occasional criticism of the Watergate state of affairs. He was at once linked to the President but free of him.

While he still relied on the President for his duties, Ford was also able to sound an independent chord. More importantly, he was expected to. However often his disavowed any interest in achieving the highest office in the land, he was in line for the Presidency, if not as a replacement for a denounced Richard Nixon, then on his own in 1976.[119]

With the events of the week of August 5, 1974, especially Nixon's announcement that he had lied to the American public and had halted the Watergate investigation, his impeachment or resignation grew more inevitable. As the President's remaining strength in Congress evaporated rapidly, the succession of the much-respected Ford became all the more imminent.[120]

Finally, on August 8, following several days of conferences with his staff and legal advisers, Richard Nixon, perhaps the most "imperial" President in American history, made his decision to resign from the Presidency. Gerald Ford thus became the first person not elected to office to serve as President.[121]

As Ford's short tenure in the Vice Presidency had made him the likely 1976 Republican presidential nominee, now his succession to the Presidency seemed to virtually assure him of that nomination. Having gotten the nomination, however, President Gerald Ford lost his bid for the Presidency in 1976, in no small part due to the pardon he gave to Richard Nixon.

In 1988, Vice President George Herbert Walker Bush was the first Vice President since 1836 to be elected directly from the Vice Presidency to the Presidency. That this occurred underscores the point that a Vice President is subject to the legacy of the President with whom s/he served. Ronald Reagan was a consistently popular President, and would likely have won a third term were it not for the Twenty-Second Amendment and its two-term limit on the presidency. Bush was able to ride the Reagan coattails and what seemed to be an era of peace and prosperity. Bush's defeat for reelection, however, further underscores the impact of a President upon a Vice President's future, with the seeming prosperity of the Reagan legacy catching up on Reagan's successor. Bush's opponent, Bill Clinton, was able to use a simple line leading to his victory. "It's the economy, stupid" was very effective.

In 2000, Vice President Al Gore was in a similar position as Bush had been. Following a charismatic, popular President, Gore rode the presidential coattails. Perhaps one mistake Gore made was in not recognizing just how long those coattails were. Unlike Bush in 1988, Gore believed he had one albatross hanging over his neck from the Clinton Presidency – the Monica Lewinsky affair. Gore's defeat in the electoral vote, despite his majority in the popular vote, might not have occurred had Gore more fully utilized President Clinton during the course of the campaign. This is reminiscent of Nixon's failure to more fully utilize President Eisenhower in 1960. Another interesting and poignant parallel between the 1960 and 2000 presidential elections featuring incumbent Vice Presidents is that both Nixon and Gore gave their opponent an extraordinary opportunity. Even though each was the frontrunner, Nixon and Gore failed to realize that the series of live debates to which they agreed harmed – perhaps doomed – their success in the general election.

Enter the Presidency post-2016 for another formerly unanticipated set of circumstances that seemed possible of propelling a Vice President to the forefront.

While the Vice Presidency has always had at least a subconsciousness of being a heartbeat away from the Presidency, perhaps it can be said that for the Trump-Pence Administration this aura began on the day the ticket rode to victory. With all of Trump's peccadilloes, many observers had the sense that for whatever reason, Trump would serve a shortened term. Perhaps this is what Vice President-elect Pence and the Koch brothers were thinking as they reportedly slipped champagne in their hotel room while the President-elect delivered his victory speech.122

This sense increased as Donald Trump's behavior in the highest office of the land became increasingly erratic and controversial. Day to day policy shifts and confusion, unusually frequent staff and Cabinet departures, increasing vitriolic tweeting against an array of assume enemies -- "crooked Hillary" as a continuation of Trump's 2016 campaign rhetoric; rants about "fake news" by many media sources; complaints about uncooperative Democrats in the Congress; a strange friendship with foes of the U.S. while distancing himself from the nation's allies; assaults on the judiciary and intelligence communities; attacks on special Counsel Robert Mueller; flagrant misunderstanding or misinterpretations of the U.S. Constitution; comments suggesting the President is above the law, and so many more) -- increasingly shed light on the prospects of impeachment and a resulting Pence Presidency.

Many commentaries on Mike Pence have suggested the Vice President has a belief that God has a plan for him and that the Vice Presidency is the route to that plan. There is a two-edged sword to his belief in this divine plan. On the one hand, to reach his goal he had to assume immediate and consistent support of and subservience to Donald Trump the candidate and the President. On the other hand, this very behavior might very well be Pence's downfall. From the outset, Pence was seen as "powerful" not because of assigned powers and duties. This assignation came in light of the perilous road Trump continued to travel both during the campaign and into his Presidency. Moreover, Pence's potential succession to the Presidency seemed more imminent than is typically the case. He was also in a position to attempt to influence and perhaps soften Trump's statements and behavior.**123**

The great irony for Trump is that Pence's very appeal to many Republicans -- both inside the Congress and within the general public -- has perhaps led Republicans to bide their time as Trump continues to be his own worst enemy. After all, a "true" conservative is next in line.

There is irony, too, in that Trump needs Pence to assuage the religious right, who many very well see Trump as a "necessary evil" towards the goal of achieving a Pence Presidency. He also needs Pence as a conduit to Republicans in Congress. With the Republican Party not only at odds with the Democrats in Congress but increasingly suffering an internal disaffection, from the outset Pence was perceived as a temporary salve.**124** Moreover, Pence enjoys "not having enemies in the White House" and a "steadfast" appearance.**125**

Meanwhile, Trump has had his own suspicions about a "Deep State" -- not entirely unjustified -- in which his Vice President was making all the "right" moves to step in.**126** Indeed, Pence had made himself available to do so in October of 2016 when the scandalous "Access Hollywood" tape became public and it appeared that would be presidential candidate Trump's downfall. In his fawning moments, Vice President Pence has compared Trump to Ronald Reagan,**127** hardly a compliment to ardent Reagan supporters. But there is certainly one way in which the comparison is apt. Reagan was often referred to as "the Teflon President," to whom nothing stuck. Is the 45th President also Teflon?

The Trump-Pence relationship is the polar opposite of the Obama-Biden relationship -- one that has been termed a "bromance,"**128** where the two had a true affection and a mutual respect for each other. Trump's utilitarian use -- and reportedly sometimes abuse and mockery of his Vice President -- and Pence's steadfast support for and feeding of the Trump ego is at the expense of his own integrity. Meanwhile, tales abound that the President consistently humiliates his Vice President, who has abandoned his most fervent beliefs to stay in that President's good graces. This relationship could not remotely approach the "bromance" between Obama and Biden, nor should it be expected to. While the office has grown its essential nature remains: the necessity of being loyal to a fault, of being viable by being invisible except when called upon, by attempting to build a record of service and experience by virtue of being strapped to all of the successes and failures of an administration.

VICE PRESIDENTIAL SELECTION EMBARRASSMENTS

Unfortunately for some presidential nominees, the choice for the second spot may turn out to be an embarrassment. This was what Nixon in 1968, McGovern in 1972; George Herbert Walker Bush in 1980, and John McCain in 2000 experienced. So much for a "learning curve."

In 1968, Richard Nixon thought he had found the perfect running mate in Maryland Governor Spiro T. Agnew. This was also a classic moment when the overall political environment dramatically affected the Agnew selection. Once third party candidate, former Governor George C. Wallace, an ardent segregationist, introduced what became the theme of the 1968 presidential campaign. Ironically, the Vietnam War took a back stage position to the Wallace theme of "law and order." The Wallace theme was clearly racist, and reflect a great deal of the resentment in many parts of the U. S. Humphrey's own strong background on civil rights put him under far less pressure than what Nixon felt. Nixon sought a running who was both strong on "law and order" AND civil rights, a very odd and difficult background to have earned. So Agnew it was. But no sooner had the general election campaign begun than Agnew's frequent gaffes served to embarrass the Republican ticket, as noted earlier in this work.

1972 proved to be a very good year for the would-be Democratic presidential candidate Senator George McGovern, whose direction of the post-1968 Democratic Party delegate reforms certainly helped him gain the presidential nomination. But what was to follow dramatically harmed his general election chances of success.

Several factors seemed to be at work as McGovern selected Missouri Senator Thomas Eagleton. McGovern seemed certain that Massachusetts Senator Edward M. Kennedy would accept the second spot. But Kennedy declined. Reports are that McGovern actually telephoned Kennedy several times throughout the night. By morning, it became quite clear that Kennedy's answer was still "no." McGovern turned to Eagleton.

When McGovern spoke with Eagleton, he asked the Missouri

Senator if there was anything in Eagleton's background that might embarrass or be harmful to the ticket. Eagleton said "no," and McGovern presented Eagleton's name to the convention delegates. But after the convention recessed, it became abundantly clear that McGovern had not done an adequate vetting process. The story broke; not only had Eagleton undergone psychiatric treatment – taboo in that era – but had also undergone electric shock therapy. Both disclosures were overwhelming for that period of time. McGovern made matters worse with his initial statement that he was behind Eagleton "1,000%" – only to drop him from the ticket days later.

So it was back to the drawing board for the Democratic presidential nominee. Recognizing the value of having a Catholic on the ticket, McGovern compiled a list of Kennedy alternatives (all of whom were of Catholic faith but one – Connecticut Senator Abraham Ribicoff, of Jewish faith). All declined. Finally, Kennedy in-law Sargent Shriver, former Peace Corps Director, agreed to be on the McGovern ticket. By this time, however, an already popular incumbent President Nixon (for whom "Watergate" had barely surfaced) was travelling a safe road to re-election.

Neither party seems immune from potential embarrassment, and in 1988 and again in 2008, it was the Republicans who suffered from the selection of running mates. Richard Nixon had once said, "A Vice President can't help you; [s]he can only hurt you."

In 1988 it was two-term Reagan Vice President George Herbert Walker Bush's ironic turn, and his dilemma came out of what had been his fortune when presidential nominee Reagan selected him for the second spot. Even though Reagan was elevated to the nomination by an ever-increasing conservative and Moral Majority wave, the presidential nominee wanted the safety valve of an ideologically balanced ticket. Despite some bitter moments during the primary season, G. H. W. Bush, clearly a moderate, became Reagan's choice. Bush spent eight years of loyalty to Reagan, denying he had ever criticized Reagan's ideas (the most classic of which was Bush having referred to Reagan's economic ideas as "voodoo economics). Reagan was pleased with Bush, but Republican conservatives were still dubious. So when it was "Bush's turn," he turned to Senator Dan Quayle of Indiana, whose conservative credentials were pristine. On the campaign trail, Quayle began to be an embarrassment to the party and the ticket. Realistically, Dan Quayle was and is a much more intelligent and capable individual than has been credited. But he suffered at the time and things became somewhat of a self-fulfilling prophecy.

Chapter 5

—∾—

THE ROLE OF THE
MODERN VICE PRESIDENCY:
GROWTH OF THE ALTER EGO

It's like being naked in the middle of a blizzard,
with no one to even offer you a match to help you
keep warm—that's the Vice Presidency. You are
trapped, vulnerable and alone and it does not
*matter who happens to be President.*1

ALTHOUGH THE MODERN Vice Presidency has developed significant roles
and duties, it is nonetheless subject to the frustrations that Hubert
Humphrey so aptly described. A Vice President soon learns what s/he
has to do to become a viable part of the administration. Thus, an in-
troductory comment on incumbents' perspectives provides an invaluable backdrop against which to view the development of the office.

Harry S Truman (Truman had no actual middle name, thus the
absence of a period after the initial "S"!) once called the Vice President

a cow's fifth teat,"2 and his own Vice President, Alben Barkley recognized that the second office could be used to get rid of competitors. Barkley, however, seemed to adapt well to the uncertainties of the office and was considerably more optimistic that the office was much more than the "fifth wheel on the machinery of government" that John Adams had proclaimed it to be.3 Adams had also referred to the office as "Your Superfluous Excellency."4

John Nance Garner, who had served as Vice President under FDR for two terms and had been ignored, advised Lyndon Johnson to decline the offer to be John Kennedy's running mate; the office, Garner said, "isn't worth a pitcher of warm spit."5 Johnson himself, as senator and Majority Leader, commenting on Vice President Nixon, said he does nothing in the legislature, and he (Johnson) was not about to trade a vote for a gavel.6 But Johnson did accept it, and once he did he was more frustrated by the office than he had ever imagined possible.7 Johnson had nonetheless astutely grasped the nature of the office: to be entirely at the disposal of the President.8

A Vice President, he would later emphasize, must above all be loyal.9 As he reflected in his memoirs, he had been the kind of Vice President he would want – loyal and self-effacing.10 Johnson clearly transmitted his expectations to his own Vice President, and just several days prior to be selected as Johnson's running mate, Hubert Humphrey indicated how well he understood the necessities of the office: "he must have a quality of fidelity, a willingness literally to give himself, to be what the President wants him to be, a loyal, faithful friend and servant."11 This understanding of the office was echoed in Spiro Agnew's statement, "Whatever the President wants is what I want. . . . I envisage this as the principal role of the Vice Presidency – to implement the policies of the Chief Executive."12

President Dwight Eisenhower was undoubtedly responsible for the turning point in the Vice Presidency. "I personally believe," he said "the Vice President of the United States should never be a nonentity. I believe he should be used. I believe he should have a very useful job."13

Eisenhower met with Nixon prior to the 1952 campaign to discuss what was promised to be a more active role for the Vice President.

Nixon seemed to fluctuate in his view of the office. "A hollow shell," Nixon had once said of the second office, 14 although he reportedly preferred the Vice Presidency to the legislature.15. As Vice President, Nixon felt the second office must be "given vast responsibility."16 As President, he stated, "Because of the burden of the Presidency, particularly with foreign policy problems becoming more acute than they had been previously . . . the Vice President can and should be used more than he has been in either the Kennedy or the Eisenhower administration."17

Emphasizing the need for and anticipation that future Presidents would make greater use of their Vice Presidents, Nixon noted the most critical duties of the office, "First, his participation in the deliberations of the National Security Council, his participation in the deliberation of the Cabinet; and then the increasingly greater use of the Vice President as a trouble-shooter and as a representative of the President in the field of foreign policy."18

While Nixon's view did not fully coincide with the assignments he gave to his own Vice Presidents, other expressions of his views emphasized the trouble-shooter function. "The Vice President," he said, "should sustain Presidential policy";19 he should clearly represent views of the President and be [someone] the President could trust to carry out very important assignments."20 As President, Nixon said of the Vice President, "He is dealing with expressing established policy to opinion leaders throughout the country."21

Vice President George Bush's two most recent predecessors, Nelson Rockefeller and Walter Mondale, both succinctly grasped the essence of the office. Despite the peculiar circumstances under which he had come to the Vice Presidency, despite his own notoriety which went far beyond that of the President [Ford] who had appointed him, Nelson Rockefeller knew what his future as Vice President would be. Commenting that he had known every Vice President since Henry

AMERICAN PRINCE(SS), AMERICAN PAUPER

Wallace, Rockefeller noted that "they were all frustrated, everyone one of them."[22] At another point, he said, ""I don't expect anything. This, I think, is my greatest strength."[23]

Walter Mondale, who had prepared himself for the office by talking with Rockefeller and Humphrey, immediately saw his job as that of the President's "advisor on crucial, broad issues affecting government; to be the bearer of bad news. . . . My future in public life really depends upon the success of the Carter Presidency,"[24] Just one month prior to this statement, the new inaugurated Vice President Mondale symbolically underscored another key understanding of his relationship to the President, and he talked about this in a February television interview. "When he walked in that parade . . . I told the President, 'I don't want to upstage you, I think I'll ride – I wouldn't want to take this away from you."[25] Mondale astutely knew that a low profile was crucial to the second office.

Vice President George Bush rather quickly and adeptly discerned this principle and behaved accordingly. He consistently defended the President and has spoken forcefully in support of administration policies. Candidly referring to his role, Bush stated, "I have a very low profile. Because I think that the way you become an effective vice president-have something substantive to do-is to have the confidence of the President. And if you are always out there in the newspapers or in some news conference and talking about your close relationship with the President-well, it just won't work." Early on, Bush anticipated having the same potential room for activity as had Mondale, 'if I don't blow it. Because the President is giving me every opportunity."[26]

THE GROWTH OF THE VICE PRESIDENCY: AN OVERVIEW

The understanding expressed by Mondale that a Vice President's success is inextricably linked to the President and his administration is at the heart of the office's growth. The growth of the Presidency itself has undoubtedly contributed to the role of the Vice President. A succession of events has likewise continued to call attention to the likelihood that a Vice President may be called on to lead the nation. Franklin Roosevelt's death left his new Vice President with the seemingly inhuman task of filling the shoes of a President who had been larger than life, who had single-handedly guided the United States through twelve incredible years of the Depression and war, and who had done little to prepare his Vice Presidents for the possibility of taking over. The Truman succession marked the beginning of a new Vice Presidency; henceforth, all Vice Presidents would be conscious of their responsibility to prepare for the smooth transfer of power and leadership should the need arise. Other events would continue to promote an increased awareness of the office.

The very active Nixon Vice Presidency of the 1950s coincided with the three Eisenhower disabilities, and the new image of the Vice Presidency was well on its way. Increasingly, individuals of stature would be attracted to it as candidates.

The hours of anxiety following the assassination Of President John F. Kennedy in Dallas on November 22, 1963 underscore the reassurance of having a Vice President available and ready to assume the reins of government. The Kennedy assassination definitively established the importance of the office; the death of the youngest elected President in the history of the Republic loudly proclaimed the mortality of all humankind. Lyndon Johnson, the man nobody has chosen for the Presidency, masterfully assumed the stewardship of the   country he inherited. The Kennedy assassination also created renewed interest in providing a mechanism for filing vacancies in the Vice Presidency, and thus three relative swift drafting and ratification of the Twenty-fifth Amendment. Never again would the country be long without a crowned prince, as it had been for practically the duration of the first Truman Administration following FDR's death in office.

The events of the 1970s – first the hasty selection of Senator Thomas Eagleton in 1972 as presidential candidate George McGovern's running mate and then the resignation of Vice-President Spiro Agnew in 1973 following charges of misconduct during his tenure as Baltimore County executive several years earlier, followed by the floodgates of Watergate and, finally, the protracted congressional hearings over Gerald Ford's nominee for the Vice-President, Nelson Rockefeller – would create unprecedented interest in the Vice Presidency. Politicians and average citizens alike would be hard-pressed to forget that one in five Presidents have come to that office via the Vice Presidency.

The development of the Vice President's role as administration spokesman, first during Humphrey's incumbency and alter during Spiro Agnew's tenure, established a new unofficial assignment that would have profound political reverberations. Serving as administration spokesman would have mixed blessings, as this work will explore.

That Vice Presidents often find themselves "naked in the middle of a blizzard" despite their own expertise and constituencies was especially true of the Rockefeller Vice Presidency. The office had come a long way, attracting the likes of Lyndon Johnson, Hubert Humphrey, and Nelson Rockefeller. The peculiar circumstances of the Rockefeller Vice President might have suggested that he would have had a freer hand in carving out a role for himself under the Ford Presidency. One of the most prestigious and influential men to serve in the second office, Rockefeller had an extensive interest and background in foreign affairs. He found himself serving under a President who admitted he had little expertise in that area. The figure of Secretary of State Henry Kissinger was dominant in foreign affairs, and personal relations between Kissinger and Rockefeller were friendly and harmonious. At the outset of his incumbency, Rockefeller did not seem apt to supper he same fate of many of his predecessors, who spent a good deal of time making good-will tours and raising funds for the party. In his initial functioning as Vice President, Rockefeller maintained a low profile, seeming deferring to the higher office of the Presidency. This is essentially the position any Vice President who hopes to survive must maintain, as Mondale noted.

Unlike many of his predecessors, too, Rockefeller, a major political figure for years, did not need to waste time attracting public notice, nor did he need to convince the President of his abilities or usefulness. Indeed, the President himself seemed awed by the Rockefeller power and talent. In short, the Rockefeller Vice Presidency was in many ways unique. Ultimately, however, Rockefeller's promise never fully materialized. Essentially, he was the victim of political considerations for the 1976 campaign. The conservative wing of the Republican Party took exception to Rockefeller and the Reagan challenge to the incumbent President Ford forced the President to award the running mate spot to a candidate acceptable to the right, Robert Dole. Rockefeller, too, was expendable, underscoring the nature of the Vice President, no matter whom its occupant. In the end, the interests of the President always prevail. Ironically, a Rockefeller presence on the ticket might very well have helped President Ford hold onto the office. Dole's "hatchet man like" performance during the vice presidential debate with Walter Mondale undoubtedly had a negative effect in the very close race. As for the inherent nature of the Vice-President, Hubert Humphrey's insights on the presidential-vice presidential relationship were well stated.

> In most instances you will find a President never remembered when he called on a Vice President. There is a love-hate relationship. There is a faith and doubt relationship. A comradeship and an adversary – if not an adversary, at least a competitor. It's just in the nature of it. It's a marriage, as Lyndon Johnson pointed out to me, but it's one in which both the husband and wife are constantly looking at each other, and saying, "What's he up he/she up to?" And in this sense, male chauvinism is supreme.27

Walter Mondale, Humphrey's protégé of many years, understood this relationship very well. He enjoyed the more active role Jimmy Carter had promised from the outset, but this increased role also reflected the basic fact of the Vice Presidency; the Vice President is entirely subject to the wishes of the President. Mondale was viable because he was not visible.

George H. W. Bush also discovered that this is what the Vice Presidency is all about. During his early incumbency at least the symbolic change brought by the Carter-Mondale White House continued. The Vice President's office remained in the White House, exactly where Mondale's was, and where it remains today.

Vice President George Bush's early assignments were to head a task force to investigate governmental regulations and later to deal with the growing tragedy of the serial murders of black children in Atlanta. President Reagan thus continued the historical precedent that Presidents initially promise an active role for their Vice President and fulfill this promise by assignments early on in the life of the administration. What follows, of course, is subject to all of the traditional variables. One of Vice President Bush's assignments – as head of the administration's "crisis management team" -- might have been made to undercut what had been the growing power of then Secretary of State Alexander M. Haig, Jr. Nonetheless, Bush's roles were the product of what the President of the United States wanted them to be. And this is what the future holds for all Vice Presidents.

THE IMPACT OF THE PRESIDENCY
ON THE SECOND OFFICE

By the time Harry Truman became Vice President, the office had experienced an enduring history of "Throttlebottomism."**28** As Vice President under Franklin D. Roosevelt, who had never treated Vice Presidents very well, Truman could expect little in the way of assignments. He realized that the office, especially under FDR, consisted of little more than ceremonial and social activities. His short tenure in office was not particularly busy, although there was the usual initial presidential promise of increased involvement.**29**

The lack of prestige and importance attached to the Vice Presidency during the FDR years is demonstrated by the public's lack of concern for a vacancy in the office of almost four years during Truman's first term. On a number of occasions in the past, the office had been left vacant and caused little worry.

During Truman's second term, his Vice President, Alben Barkley, was a congenial, very popular former legislator with a penchant for storytelling. Although he sought little power from the second office, he was not idle during his four years, and his devotion and wisdom, together with the public respect he commanded, served President Truman's needs very well. In addition to relieving the President of some of his social commitments and foreign travel,**30** Barkley participated in decision-making, notably in the President's decision to dismiss General Douglas MacArthur.**31** Through Truman's efforts, Barkley was better briefed than previous constitutional heirs to the Presidency. An astute and experience legislator who for years had served as Senate Majority Leader, Barkley was able to assist the President's legislative program.**32** Truman's laudable intentions and efforts to elevate the Vice Presidency did not produce spectacular results. Barkley's congeniality and light-heartedness during the 1948 presidential campaign and the Truman Presidency projected "Dear Alben" as primarily an attractive public relations man. His elevation to the second office was a tribute to an elder statesman who had served long and faithfully in the legislature and deserved the prestige of high executive office.**33**

Vice President Barkley's failure to take greater advantage of the statutory changes that were intended to widen the Vice Presidency is only partly to blame for the lack of spectacular developments. The main reason lies in the vast growth of presidential responsibilities, power, and influence, which has necessitated the astonishing expansion of the White House staff. As a result, the Presidency has become "dispersed," with a hidden arm of presidential aides and advisers responsible to no one but the President and extremely difficult, if not impossible, for him to assess or control.**34**

The second highest office has likewise expanded, with added office and staff facilities. This change signals added prestige for the Vice Presidency and is another indication of growth, diffusion, and increasing applicability of "Parkinson's Law" within the executive branch.

While the presidential staff has grown larger in both numbers and responsibilities and authority, the Presidency has become increasingly a singular job with increased constitutional obligations, powers, and responsibilities that cannot be shared. Because the President cannot delegate his office, he remains accountable for his staff. In *The President's Men*, Patrick Anderson discusses the problem of presidential staffing and the seeming paradox of vast increases in the number of presidential advisers in recent years paired with greater presidential duties. He states: "It is of the nature of Presidents to use many men, to need a few, and to love almost none."**35** The presidential aides perform the thankless thanks of the Presidency: "Credit flows upward and blame downward. . . . The President's good works are carved in marble; his aides' are writ on water."**36**

As noted earlier, Hubert Humphrey pointed out that a Vice President suffers a similar treatment. "In most instances you will find a President seldom ever remembered when he called on a Vice President as a spokesman." The Vice President can be a spokesman," Humphrey continued, because the "President can always disavow you . . . if you get too far out."**37** Presidents, then, use the people around them, be they aides or Vice Presidents.

In referring to President Roosevelt as an example, Anderson believes that "it is over simple to say that Roosevelt 'used' his advisers as shields of criticism – the system used them whether or not the President liked it. But it is true that he rarely spoke out publicly in their defense; he is expected to fight their own battles, or to suffer in silence if that suited his interested."**38**

FDR was not unique in this behavior, for there have been recent applications of the "silent treatment." There were notable similarities between Eisenhower's handling of Nixon's slush fund problems during the campaign of 1952 and Nixon's handling of Agnew's scandal in 1973. In the first case, Eisenhower was a presidential candidate, while in the second Nixon was an incumbent President with the Watergate atmosphere pervading. Nevertheless, both presidential candidate Eisenhower and President Nixon behaved similarly with regard to their second man. Neither said anything, preferring to leave their heirs apparent on their own. Thus, both Eisenhower and Nixon maximized their options.

In sharp contrast with Democratic presidential candidate George McGovern's initial and premature statement of "1,000 support" for vie-presidential running mate Senator Thomas Eagleton in the 1972 campaign when Eagleton's psychiatric record, previous unrevealed, became a public controversy. Despite his initial support, McGovern eventually came to a position similar to that taken by Eisenhower and Nixon. He began to be less committal in his support for Eagleton, until Eagleton found other alternative but to remove himself from the Democratic ticket. In 1952, Eisenhower had played a waiting game, watching public reaction to Nixon's problems and his television address to the nation, before any decision was made regarding Nixon's place on the ticket.

A President may, of course, eliminate those staff members who become a hindrance to him. In a very important sense, this is his ultimate check on them. Anderson notes that "one of Roosevelt's political ploys was to whisk controversial aides out of view at election. . . . Roosevelt's aides had to learn to accept such indignities; if they couldn't, their days were numbered."**39** The Vice President, however, is not so easily disposed of; bearing malfeasance, resignation, impeachment, or death, the Vice President is there to stay.

The Vice President, as an elected rather than an appointed official, brings greater status to the tasks a President may assign to her/him; similarly, s/he can more legitimately serve as a substitute for the President. For example, Kennedy dispatched Vice President Johnson to Berlin in 1961 in order to dramatize U. S. interest and concern in the political situation there, while at the same time not involving the full force of the presidential office. Similarly, Vice President Nixon was President Eisenhower's representative in the settlement or the steel strike of 1959.**40**

A President, it has been said, makes no new friends; s/he cannot afford to. The extent to which any President emphasizes loyalty depends on his own personality, yet he cannot function effectively in the absence of the crucial commodity, as President Jimmy Carter soon learned in his Presidency. Harry Truman's astute observation of the potential sharing of confidences between a President and the Vice President sheds additional light on just how much loyalty a President might be able to demand. Noted Truman,

> The President is the man who decides every major domestic policy, and he is the man who makes foreign policy and negotiates treaties. In doing these things it would be very difficult for him to take the second man in the government – the Vice President – completely into his confidence. The Presidency, by necessity, builds his [sic] own staff, and the Vice President remains an outsider, no matter how friendly the two may be. There are many reasons for this, but an important one is the fact that both the President and the Vice President are, or should be, astute politicians, and neither can take the other completely into his confidence.**41**

Because the Vice President, like the President, is a political being, a pragmatic President knows full well that even the best-intentioned Vice President might sometime be tempted to put his/her own interests above the President's.

Roosevelt had a "need for followers whose devotion was total," but he was not unusual in this respect. While it was Roosevelt who "stated the evolution of the White House staff toward the large and powerful extra-constitutional institution that now exists,"**42** that evolution was inevitable, and with it the evolution toward an increasing emphasis on personal loyalty to the President. Presidents Johnson and Nixon placed demands of loyalty on their staffs, which may have been due in part to their individual makeup; but they could do so with greater ease as a result of the evolutionary trends in the institution of the Presidency.[43] Two case studies, focusing on the Johnson-Humphrey relationship, illustrate this point well.

THE IMPACT OF PERSONALITY:
THE JOHNSON-HUMPHREY RELATIONSHIP

Lyndon Johnson described his relationship with John Kennedy by noting that "I serve him loyally, as I would have wanted my Vice President to serve me. We did not always see things in the same light. I did not always agree with everything that happened in his administration. But when I did disagree with the President, I did so in private, and man to man."[44]

Having experienced the frustration inherent in his vice presidential office, Johnson was, at least initially, determined to avoid having Humphrey suffer the same fate.[45] Whatever Johnson's intentions, however, a combination of forces worked to make Humphrey the frequently battered victim of the office.

In his psychological study of American Presidents, The Presidential Character, James David Barber has said of Lyndon Johnson, "The virtues were questioning loyalty, absolute servitude; Johnson was not given to praising his men for independence of mind." From the outset, Johnson has made clear to Humphrey that a precondition for his vice presidential nomination in 1964 was the promise of loyalty. Public disagreements were taboo. Barber notes that "from recruitment to subordination was a regular transition for Johnson," and "Humphrey was no exception to the process," for "the crux of Johnson's interpersonal style was the habit of turning occasions for mutuality into occasions for domination."[46]

As Johnson threw himself into his Presidency with a vigor he had not exercised since he had left the legislature for the relative impotence of the Vice Presidency, the true Johnson began to reassert himself. One observer noted that Johnson was "oversize."47 Johnson's aid, Walter Jenkins, said, "He drove his staff, but he drove himself; he drove everyone around him,"48 and former Secretary of State Dean Rusk pointed out "one forgave him for that because he was hardest on himself."49 Said one confidential source, "People worked under LBJ in fear." Frequently unable to delegate responsibility – not unlike his father figure in the Presidency, Franklin Roosevelt – Johnson engulfed the Presidency, living and breathing it inhumanly long hours of every day.

In describing the Vice President's role, Humphrey said,

[T]he office is dictated pretty much by the fellow who occupies it, by the nature of the man who is Vice President -- what he's like intellectually, mentally, genetically, his glandular makeup, and his background and experience. Number two, the Constitution and the public law that relates to the office. Number three, the relations – what the man himself wants to make of the office. The man himself. And number four, what the President permits -- responsibilities he gives.50

President Johnson was willing to give as long as Humphrey obeyed the ground rules, especially the one about loyalty. Continued Humphrey,

Now, my man, my President, the man that I worked for, Lyndon Johnson, gave me a very active [role] . . . . I think he knew me well. . . . He knew that I would be restless if I did not have duties. He knew that I had people that I could work with, that I had a constituency. I didn't come to the Vice Presidency as just a parochial figure. I had actually a national constituency – the labor movement, the civil rights movement, [and] and the education people that I had worked with. These were people that knew me, so he put me to work with these people, and I became sort of the eyes and ears of the President in many areas – without authority, without any great power, but reportorial. I reported; I coordinated; I was the President's spokesman to these groups.**51**

While Humphrey did indeed have an active Vice Presidency, he endured many periods of uncertainty, resulting from what Albert Eisele, Humphrey's biographer, has called the "hot-and-cold Johnson treatment," during which Johnson would praise Humphrey one day and damn him the next."**52** Johnson's unpredictability seemed to dominate the relationship; he was the President, and could afford to be unpredictable. The Vice President was just that, nothing more, and certainly not an Assistant President.

Humphrey's flexibility fit in well with Johnson's unpredictability. And so Humphrey would be "chewed out" for getting too much publicity, or when in an ebullient moment, which was so inherently part of the Humphrey character and personality, for accidentally leaking information Johnson had preferred to remain confidential a while longer. As examples, Humphrey leaked information regarding minimum wage increases when talking with labor leaders; in July 1965 at the Governors' Conference, he pleaded for their backing in the decision to expand this nation's combat role in Vietnam (a decision Johnson had not yet made public);**53** and he made his exuberant call, also in 1965, for a "Marshall Plan" for the troubled cities.**54** This was the Humphrey who frequently got carried away in doing his job and who suffered the consequences.**55**

Johnson, not about to share the limelight and "out to use whatever technique would confirm his own power,"**56** was frequently enraged by some of Humphrey's slips and did not fail to tell him so. The result was a self-imposed restraint by Humphrey, during which time the

Vice-President declined interviews and said little. The contrast was sufficiently apparent once to produce the remark that one could see the President more easily than his Vice President.**57** Humphrey's friends perceived Johnson as "the great emasculator," but the Vice President continued his unswerving loyalty.**58** From the time he assumed the Vice Presidency, Humphrey was sure he would be able to survive the demands and frustrations of the Vice Presidency and the particular problems of working under Lyndon Johnson.

Humphrey, however, diverged very early on from Johnson on one grave and controversial point. At the February 10, 1965 meeting of the National Security Council, Humphrey, departing from his promise to avoid any public disagreement with the President, questioned the intelligence of bombing North Vietnam.**59** He followed this public expression of disagreement by a memorandum to Johnson. The President was furious. According to Eisele, "His secretive nature and absolute insistence on avoiding any public display bordered on an obsession, and he upbraided Humphrey for committing his thoughts to paper."**60** The break marked for Humphrey "a critical turning point in his vice presidency," and he was now excluded from the "Tuesday luncheons," meetings of Johnson's closest advisers who participated in making decisions on the war.**61** Humphrey was lucky enough to have been left, at that point, with domestic chores. But Eisele astutely points out that "Humphrey's exclusion from Vietnam strategy sessions did not extend to matters relating to the impact of the war on the domestic front."**62** This fact represents one area in which the Vice Presidency has come to be used a great deal, particularly since the first Eisenhower Administration. Humphrey described the role he was expected to play.

A Vice President can [serve as] . . . a political spokesman for the Administration. President Johnson did not always want to get involved in all the campaigns and politics, so I was a political spokesman. I went to the party conventions. Obviously, he went to some – the biggest ones, but I was sent out to many of the state meetings, and I had to take on defending the Administration at the college campus level. The college campuses were [in turmoil] my Vice Presidency – and went through a terrific upheaval, unbelievable, but I was able never once ever driven from a platform. Most of the time despite all the heckling and all that it came off with a good reception.

Humphrey also mentioned the dilemma that this role posed.

The Vice President *can* be a spokesman – because the President can always disavow you, you see, if you get too far out. He can always say, "Well, that's the Vice President speaking. He wasn't speaking for me." If he [the Vice President] speaks well, and gets by, he was speaking for him, so it's really a no-win job. It's really being willing to do the Lord's work, you know? Whoever you are, I think that's the case.**63**

Humphrey defended policies he had no part in forging. He did so even after his relationship with Johnson had suffered a severe setback and the President, on many occasions embarrassingly pulled the rug out from under him. Humphrey, for example, did not participate in the development of, nor was he given an advance copy of, Johnson's 1967 State of the Union message. And Johnson's abolition of the civil rights coordinating council, which in effect eliminated one of the Vice President's jobs, came about in an abrupt, humiliating fashion.**64** As a result, Humphrey suffered a long-lasting setback with irremediable overtones, and perhaps "the full potential of Humphrey's vice presidency was never realized."**65**

Humphrey knew that his own personality and background and that of all Vice Presidents, helped shape his incumbency, both positively and negatively. The former Minnesota senior Senator was well aware that he brought with him how own constituency and the expertise of many years of governmental service. He knew a great deal about world affairs, and he had served as a United Nations delegate to the World Health Organization and UNESCO. He had attended the Geneva disarmament talks. He had met with Premier Nikita Khrushchev in 1958, during which time he had talked at length with the Soviet leader. Humphrey had served as chairman of the Senate disarmament sub-committee which performed preparatory work leading to the nuclear test ban treaty in 1963.**66** His expertise on civil rights and poverty issues, combined with his astute knowledge of the legislative process and close personal relationships with legislators, all served to condition his role as Vice President. Moreover, he was highly knowledgeable regarding urban affairs, which became a principal concern of the Johnson Administration. As the former Secretary of Housing and Urban Development, Robert C. Wood, pointed out, "There was nothing like the focus of attention to urban affairs in the Kennedy time as was characterized in the Johnson era."**67** Humphrey had a very long arm extended into the liberal camp – an arm Johnson would borrow to help him defend the administration's position on Vietnam and try to salve the alienated liberals.

The Vice President's personality itself was a critical ingredient in his survival. Eager and grateful to be nominated for the office, and genuinely appreciative to Johnson was assistance in developing his political career as a legislator, Humphrey was eager to please. His gravest misfortune was that he was ultimately swallowed up by a war that the administration he served had inherited and enlarged. Because of his identification with Lyndon Johnson, Humphrey's abilities and potential were never fully realized or utilized by the American people.

As his Vice Presidency progressed, Humphrey, fulfilling his pledge of loyalty, took on a hectic schedule of public appearances, speeches, political rallies, and legislative conferences. Throughout his Vice Presidency, Humphrey was keenly aware that Johnson would make or break him politically. Humphrey knew that the President was his "constituency of one."**68** The Vice President was stultified because he was at the time "almost totally dependent upon Johnson for his political future."**69** Yet, being subordinate to Johnson was not an unnatural role for him, for it was simply a continuation of their Senate relationship. Furthermore, his personality was far more flexible than Johnson's, and unlike Johnson, who rankled at his position under President Kennedy, total subordination to the President was not distasteful to Humphrey.

Johnson's domination of Humphrey gave rise to countless jokes in Washington. Allan Ryskind tells one story that circulated during the Johnson Presidency: "LBJ and Humphrey were attending a swank dinner affair when the President suddenly whispered into Humphrey's ear, 'Hubert, did I hear you belch?' To which Humphrey responded, 'No, Mr. President, was I supposed to?'"**70** And there was a great deal of truth behind these apocryphal tales. When Johnson criticized Humphrey for seeking publicity, Humphrey maintained a low profile; when Johnson criticized Humphrey for having a press secretary, Humphrey promptly fired him.**71** Throughout his Vice Presidency, Humphrey followed Johnson's cue, snapping smartly into line when called to order, and strove to maintain a low profile. Humphrey's subordination contributed to his loss of identity and doubtless contributed to his defeat in the 1968 presidential race, when he was perceived as being nothing more than a puppet under, and stand-in for, Lyndon Johnson.

THE IMPACT OF PERSONALITY:
THE EISENHOWER-NIXON RELATIONSHIP

In character and personality, Dwight D. Eisenhower represented the other end of the spectrum from Johnson. In stark contrast to Johnson, he not only was disinterested in politics, but also seemed to disdain politics and politicians. Among the few politicians in the Eisenhower entourage, the young Nixon rose rapidly as the politician par excellence.**72** Eisenhower was content to let Nixon take care of party politics, and the Vice President made the most of the opportunity. Commentators have said of Eisenhower that party politics "was not congenial to him. There was a feeling of disorientation."73 Despite the fact that the President never forgave or full trusted Nixon after the "Checkers" debacle, Eisenhower pushed off political chores on Nixon.74 It was advantageous to Nixon that Eisenhower never came to enjoy or appreciate the value of politics. Eisenhower went "all the way through feeling rather sorry for himself for having to deal with politicians; he felt demeaned by them."75

The Nixon Vice Presidency was strongly conditioned by Eisenhower's reliance on the staff system, which he had employed for so many years in the military. The dominant force of this staff system was the President's Chief of Staff, Sherman Adams, to whom the *London Economist* referred as "the most publicized hidden hand in Washington."76 The Chief of Staff received briefings and decided what matters should be brought to the President's attention. He also made specific assignments to specific people, and unlike other admin-istrations such as those of FDR, Johnson, and Nixon, Adams made assignments with very little overlap. These assignments helped isolate the President from members of his staff. Despite the limitations that had on the development of the vice presidential office, Nixon sur-vived and in many areas he even thrived, serving as a spokesman for the administration in foreign affairs, party affairs, and as chairman of the Committee on Government Contracts (the predecessor of the President's Committee on Equal Employment Opportunity). With the election of the popular Eisenhower, possibilities for Republican gains were ripe; the President, however, seemed unwilling to reap the harvest. Eisenhower's sweeping victory had carried his party with him. For the first time in years, the Republicans held control of both houses of Congress. New York's Republican Senator Jacobs Javits recalled that at first there existed a very "reverential" sentiment toward the President and the hope that he would actively work for the party "to make it a living force in our country" and "to give it a greater status as the alter-native in the two-party system."77 The party was soon disappointed. Former New York Republican Senator Kenneth Keating believed that

Eisenhower "could have built the Republican Party to a position where it would have been hard to get them out. If he had taken that attitude, I'm sure Dick Nixon would have been elected when he ran, because it was so close; any such little thing would have tipped the scales."[78]

Eisenhower, however, refused to work toward transferring his personal following into a party following.[79] As noted earlier, the task of being the party man fell to Nixon, who took on assignment after assignment. Nixon built an impressive reputation and acquired a long list of political obligations upon which he would later collect.[80] In addition to his party role, Nixon himself estimated that he spent more than 90 percent of his time on executive duties[81] – at National Security Council meetings, Cabinet meetings, as chairman of the Cabinet Committee on Price Stability, and as chairman of the Committee on Government Contracts.[82]

It was, nonetheless, in the field of party politics that Nixon was most outstanding. "Nixon was always a very strong party man," said Republican Leverett Saltonstall. Saltonstall added that Nixon "also tried to help where he could, without getting in conflict with the President, on all patronage and things of that kind. Now for eight years I sat beside him at these morning weekly conferences. . . . Nixon didn't speak very much at those meetings, but when he did speak, it was generally to express a political point of view on the feelings in the country in a certain section, as he got it, and as Nixon always does, he spoke very well."[83]

And he got things done. Nixon was aware of his position as Vice President, and he was careful not to go too far. He ultimately maintained the President's policy, and "in his first two years in office Nixon imposed a limited oath of silence on himself."[84] Some observers feel that his maintenance of the Eisenhower policy caused a "conservative affection-disaffection syndrome" within the Republican party.[85] Others have credited Nixon for being above all else astutely political. As "a very effective member of the President's team . . . he was very careful not to try to assume any of the prerogatives of the Presidency in carrying out functional responsibilities. . . . He didn't try . . . to go around the President, or to build himself to the exclusion of somebody else."**86** Nixon knew he could not, as some of his advisers had suggested, "stand up to Ike"**87** and strike out on his own. His staunch party convictions and political wisdom prevented such action.

When Eisenhower became President, the crusading senator from Wisconsin, Joseph McCarthy, was riding high in his attempt to purge the country of the "Red Menace." Little escaped his scrutiny. McCarthy's activities undoubtedly contributed to the selection of Richard Nixon as the 1952 Republican vice presidential candidate. A nationally known figure as a result of his long fight against the Communists within the United States, Nixon became the administration's spokesman on communism. While Nixon took no public posture on McCarthy, as Vice President, he served as a buffer between McCarthy and the administration."**88** In 1954, Nixon reluctantly responded to the President's order that he reply to Adlai Stevenson's attack on the Eisenhower-McCarthy division within the Republican party.**89**

Seeking to maintain his ambivalent ideological position in the party and to avoid alienating its right wing, Nixon responded to his problem by utilizing a speech form familiar to him since his run for his first political office, the innuendo. The Nixon formula was patterned as follows: "Men who in the past have done effected work exposing communism in this country have, by reckless talk and questionable methods, made themselves the issue, rather than the cause they believe in so deeply." This led up to his subtle attack on Stevenson whom Nixon did not name to avoid unnecessarily alienating the left.

> When they have done this . . . they have not only diverted the attention from the dangers of communism, but they have allowed those whose primary objective is to defeat the Eisenhower Administration to divert attention from its great program to these individuals who have followed these methods.**90**

It was a brilliant speech, jabbing at McCarthy and Stevenson simultaneously. It touched on what needed to be covered without blatantly alienating, although it did little to quiet McCarthy.**91** In terms of its importance for the Vice Presidency, Nixon's speech was symptomatic of a role that developed during the modern Vice Presidency, that of administration spokesperson.

Nixon could do little more about McCarthy without making himself appear hypocritical. His record and his claim to fame as an avowed foe of domestic communism set the stage for his reactions to McCarthy. For as long as possible, Nixon tried to remain on firm ground, balancing one move against another, playing to McCarthy and striving to keep the President from moving into a position apt to cause a party split.**92** Nixon's leitmotif seemed to be the unity of the Republican Party, above and beyond all else, for as long as possible. Throughout this battle, Nixon played both sides against the middle. As administration spokesperson, he served as a defender and buffer as he would be obliged to do throughout his incumbency as Vice President. Meanwhile, he continued to play the role of the party man.**93** "His effectiveness," noted one observer, "placed him in the line of fire," as it had in his successful 1953 confrontation with labor at the AFL Convention, a confrontation thrust upon him by the President.**94** Eisenhower even assigned Nixon and the Republican National Committee the task of dealing with Sherman Adams after the scandal involving gifts Adams received as Chief of Staff erupted; Adams eventually resigned. And, although Nixon ultimately worked toward the Senate's censure of McCarthy, Nixon's public reaction to the censure demonstrated "little policy and no principle . . . but there were displayed infinite adaptability and caution." He avoided any mention of what the censure meant to Eisenhower and the administration.**95**

Beginning in 1957, Nixon began to tone down his "hatchet man" role by utilizing a more subdued and moderate approach to political affairs. He doubtless was looking toward the next presidential election; the similarities in Nixon's behavior as a second-term Vice President and Spiro Agnew's in 1973 are striking.

Other developments helped make the Nixon Vice Presidency an active one. Hubert Humphrey noted that Nixon was "propelled into responsibilities that were unusual for a Vice President."96 Eisenhower's willingness, and sometimes preference, to have Nixon do the politicking for the party, his willingness to send Nixon on important diplomatic missions abroad, and especially his three illnesses gave Nixon immense exposure and prestige.97 As acting chairman of the National Security Council and the Cabinet during Ike's illnesses, Nixon successfully focused attention on his role as Vice President.

As Nixon's second term progressed, it seemed increasingly obvious that he would become the Republican presidential candidate in 1960. His Vice Presidency set precedents for future occupants of that office. Although he was defeated in 1960, his titular leadership of the party continued,98 and future Vice Presidents would build on the precedents he had set, especially as administration spokesman and in foreign affairs.

ADMINISTRATION SPOKESMAN:
THE JOHNSON INCUMBENCY AND A HIATUS

Nixon was well suited to the times of his Vice Presidency. His willingness to take to the road and mount the podium, to sing the administration's praises and chastise its enemies, carved out a place for him in American politics virtually unknown to his vice presidential predecessors.

In contrast, Vice President Lyndon Johnson's personality was not compatible to with the function of administration spokesman. Moreover, his position within the Kennedy Administration was far different from that of his predecessor, and he was neither called on nor inclined to fulfill his role as blatantly as Nixon. Some occasions did arise, however, notably within the delicate of civil rights. Viewed initially with suspicion and sometimes outright hostility by liberals, Johnson was able to get involved in some areas that few others in the Kennedy Administration could approach. Through the civil rights arena, Johnson greatly enhanced his image as an effective administration spokesman.

Johnson's work as chairman of the President's Committee on Equal Employment Opportunity (PCOEEO) helped him rebuild his image. While it seems quite obvious, as Tom Wicker pointed out, that "Johnson had no political choice whatever but to commit himself to the civil rights bill Kennedy sent to Congress,"**99** the Vice President had certain unique assets which rendered his support meaningful. He knew and understood the people whose minds had to be changed, especially within the legislature. As an astute politician, he knew that coercion was far less effective than persuasion. He also knew when and how to be forceful. Reflecting on the work of the PCOEEO in 1972, Johnson told Walter Cronkite,

> We used all the power and all the authority we had. I don't think we made a choice between what's hard-nosed and soft-nosed. I think we did everything that we had the implements to do. We created an awareness among the people in government that the minorities weren't getting a fair shake in employment in the government. We created an awareness in the employer groups in the country and the labor groups in the country that we had to move much farther in giving equal employment to all of our citizens. And we used every power that we had and some we didn't have. I don't think we had any compromise on it. We couldn't just go and wrestle with the fellow and say you've got to do this, or we'll do something to you. We tried to lead them with persuasion because that's all the power we had.**100**

The Vice President, Kennedy's elder in both years and government experience, was kept occupied by Kennedy, who was aware of Johnson's sensitivities. Kennedy well appreciated the need to insure "the care and feeding of Lyndon Johnson."**101** Arthur Schlesinger, Jr. recalled that during the Kennedy Administration "the problem remained of finding things for the Vice President to do."**102**

In addition to attending the seldom-held Cabinet and National Security Council meetings, Johnson chaired numerous committees, including the PCOEEO and the Space Council. Kennedy used him extensively in the area of foreign travel, journeying not only to Europe but to Southeast Asia and the Middle East as well, visiting thirty-three countries.**103** The exposure which those foreign assignments gave him, coupled with his work in the civil rights field, provided valuable experience and filled many gaps in his background.**104** The experience he gained in his thirty-four months as Vice President made him the best prepared man in the nation's history to that point in time to assume the burdens of the Presidency upon Kennedy's assassination. His vice-presidential incumbency continued the developmental trend in the Vice Presidency begun under Nixon.

Former Johnson Press Secretary George Christian noted that the comedown from the dominating position of Majority Leader to the "political limbo of being second man to John F. Kennedy for three years" was not an easy transition.**105** Despite Kennedy's sincere efforts to keep Johnson both active and informed, the Vice President's negative relationship with the Kennedy staff and especially with the second most important individual in the administration, the President's brother, Attorney General Robert Kennedy, set the tone of frustration for his Vice-Presidency.**106** The relationship between Johnson and Robert Kennedy was at best one of tolerance. Robert Kennedy was more than staff, more than aide, more than Cabinet member as Attorney General. He was above all the President's alter ego. His personal antagonism toward Johnson did not help Johnson's relations with the Kennedy staff. "Colonel Cornpone," as Johnson was derisively labeled by some members of the Kennedy staff,**107** did not fit the Kennedy image and "baiting the Vice President became the favorite indoor sport" of many Kennedy aides, as one high Johnson administration official confidentially recalled.

The emphasis of Kennedy's "New Frontier" was on youthful energy in the executive branch, and as the esprit de corps among the Kennedyites became almost visionary, the Vice-President, who had campaigned hard (and many felt unfairly) against Kennedy, was viewed as a throwback to another generation.[108] Johnson's aide, Walter Jenkins, described the difference succinctly: "Johnson was from Austin, not from Boston."[109]

Although harmony was lacking, Johnson requested and received a major role in the space program, an areas in which he had worked hard in the Senate.[110] This assignment pleased Johnson, and his association with the space program demonstrated President Kennedy's firm commitment to the program.[111] Future Presidents would also stress a particular issue or program by assigning the Vice President to it. Richard Nixon, for example, assigned Vice President Gerald Ford to the Committee on Privacy, and President Ford assigned Vice President Nelson Rockefeller to the committee to investigate the Central Intelligence Agency and to reorganize the Domestic Council. Similarly, President Reagan underscored the importance of de-regulation by assigning Vice President Bush to the area. Bush's Vice President, Dan Quayle, spearheaded the administration's conservative stance on family values.

Johnson deferred to the President and his men, avoided public disagreements, kept his opposition to administration policies private, and interjected his opinion "very quietly, unobtrusively."[112] Nonetheless, Johnson suffered the inevitable fate of Vice Presidents vis-à-vis presidential staff, which in his case was particularly negative. Former Kennedy press secretary (who also served Johnson for several months following the Kennedy assassination) describes Johnson's relations with the Kennedy staff as "distant and cool."[113] He was seldom asked to serve as administration spokesman as were his successors in the Vice Presidency.

THE VICE PRESIDENT AS ADMINISTRATION
SPOKESMAN: THE RISE OF SPIRO AGNEW

Perhaps the most striking utilization of the Vice President as administration spokesperson occurred during the Nixon Administration. Referred to frequently as "Nixon's Nixon," Agnew managed to draw audiences politicians only dream about, accumulating ardent fans and equally ardent enemies wherever he went and on whatever issues he pursued. Unlike his fictional predecessor "Throttlebottom," few could be unaware of, or neutral toward Spiro ("Ted") Agnew. The relatively obscure former governor of Maryland indeed fulfilled his 1968 campaign promise of becoming a household word. In a role comparable to that performed by Nixon during the 1954 congressional campaigns, Agnew took on the "unsavory politician assignments" which the President shunned.114

Judging from his seemingly inept performance in the 1968 presidential campaign, Agnew seemed to be the last person one would expect to launch a frontal attack on behalf of the Nixon Administration. His tasteless ethnic references to "Fat Japs"115 and the like had made him the butt of campaign ridicule, with the Democrats taking full political ad advantage of Agnew's gaffes.

For a while following the inauguration, the Vice President was kept under wraps. Thereafter he began to speak out as no Vice President had before. Agnew's early May 1969 address before the Young President's Organization in Honolulu foreshadowed the themes that would develop in the ensuing months. Agnew criticized the "continual carnival on the streets of . . . [the] cities and the campuses of the nation" that was taking place at the hands of "young adults hell-bent on 'non-negotiable' destruction," while college administrators stood by "confused and capitulating" and "sophisticated faculties" were "distraught and divided over issues as basic as the criminality of breaking and entering, theft, vandalism, assault and battery." Agnew had begun to take on the campus protest of the Vietnam War; subsequent speeches would build on these early remarks, and a theme which he ad woven into this speech would gradually come to be the focus of the administration's attention: the "vast faceless majority of the American public in quiet fury over the situation." Agnew continued with an analysis of the "anatomy of violence" that had begun to pervade this nation, beginning with the civil disobedience of the civil rights movement, and cited as "prophetic" Supreme Court Justice Hugo Black's 1966 statement, "Once you give a nervous, hostile and ill-informed people a theoretical justification for using violence . . . it's like a tiny hole in the dike . . . and violence becomes a normal, acceptable solution for a problem."

The Vice President then, in the same speech, turned to a theme to which he would return repeatedly in the months ahead: permissiveness. This society, had been entirely too tolerant: tolerant of "the new politics which campus radicals have pushed to the furthest extreme"; tolerant of "group[s] assert[ing] rights without commensurate responsibilities." Agnew was clearly echoing themes he had proclaimed as Maryland's governor. As Vice President, however, he expanded this theme to appeal to the "majority . . . bewildered by present irrational protest."**116** The temper of the times caused Agnew's statements to strike a responsive chord among a vast segment of America frightened by the growth of crime and rioting in cities and disturbances on college campuses. In response to these fears, "law and order" had been the major issue of the 1968 presidential campaign. In this first speech as a spokesman for the Nixon Administration, Agnew attempted to find a resolution to the problem of "law and order." Responsibility, he asserted, fell to nongovernmental institutions to do their jobs better; the administrators and faculties who 'capitulate before "storm-trooper tactics" were creating the very environment of permissiveness that led to riots and disorders.**117**

The battleground had been determined. The permissiveness of the liberals, the permissiveness of the college environment, and the permissive of the new politics would be the enemies. But before Agnew completed his speech, another enemy was identified, and the

Vice President charged that "the Fourth Estate, which would rise in righteous fury against any demagogue attacking freedom of the press, has been far more gentle with demagogues in the established order."118 In a commencement address the next month, Agnew included florid statements in an otherwise moderate speech. To the graduates he said, "A society which comes to fear its children is effete. A sniveling, hand wringing power structure deserves the violent rebellion in encourages. If my generation doesn't stop cringing, yours will inherit a lawless society where emotion and muscle displace reason."119

These initial speeches in May and June of 1969, after a long silence, portended the active role the new Vice President was to play as administration spokesman. Opening his Ohio State University with a quotation from Cicero, "Young men hear an old man who whom old men harkened when he was young," Agnew advised the assembly in Columbus that his purpose was "not to castigate youth nor discuss why the generations differ . . . [but] to point out the case for American democracy."120

In July 1969, an event occurred which was to have a profound effect and recurring repercussions for American politics. The last of the Kennedy brothers, Edward M. ("Ted"), viewed as the inevitable Democratic challenger in the 1972 presidential campaign, suffered a grave setback. His involvement in the tragic death on Chappaquiddick Bridge, Martha's Vineyard, of a former campaign worker for Robert Kennedy eliminated him as a presidential hopeful for the Democrats. The controversy surrounding the actual events and motives involved in the fatal accident still lingers, as does the controversy regarding the impact the event had on the Nixon Administration, particularly Agnew's role in the administration.

Agnew assumed a more vigorous and petulant role in the months following Chappaquiddick, which some have interpreted as a windfall of relief from political pressures for the White House. With Kennedy no longer a presidential threat, the path was cleared for a stronger attack on the liberal segments of America to whom Kennedy most likely would have appealed. Some observers maintain that Agnew's new role was merely coincidental to the Chappaquiddick incident. This view is reinforced by the themes of Agnew's speeches made prior to Senator Kennedy's misfortune. Nonetheless, the Agnew crusade did not suffer as a result. As the Vice President's crusade expanded, greater efforts were concentrated on the circumstances that had produced the vote for third party candidate George C. Wallace, which had been so threatening in the 1968 campaign.

In response to the widely organized Vietnam Moratorium Day demonstrations on October 19, 1969, President Nixon declared that such manifestations would in no way influence his policies. This infuriated large segments of the press, to which Agnew responded four days later in a speech in New Orleans. "The young," said the Vice President, "overwhelm themselves with drugs and artificial stimulants. . . . Life is visceral rather than intellectual, and the most visceral practitioners of life are those who characterize themselves as intellectuals." Slowly, over the course of several speeches, Agnew polarized the "majority," the masses, from those who disagreed with administration policy, "an effete corps of impudent snobs who characterize themselves as intellectuals."

Agnew was careful to note that not all the young wee maliciously motivated; rather, they were "well-motivated young people, conditioned since childhood to respond to great emotional appeals, [who] saw fit to demonstrate for peace." They were misled, however, by the Moratorium leaders, claimed Agnew, "the hardcore dissidents and the professional anarchists within the so-called 'peace movement.'"121

Agnew then turned to the situation in Vietnam by first reviewing the progress that had taken place since Nixon took office, and then he resumed his attack on the enemy. "There's a constructive program [in Vietnam]. What do the marches in the Moratorium offer in place of that? Nothing . . . except an emotional bath for the people of the United States. And then Agnew logically concluded that those who "prefer to side with an enemy aggressor rather than stand by this free nation" were less that patriotic.**122**

The "effete corps of impudent snobs" phrase established the kind of rhetoric that would typify the developing Agnew crusade. Criticism of the speech began to reverberate, and to many the comparative silence of the White House**123** signified at least tacit approval of Agnew's colorful new role. With Teddy Kennedy out of the 1972 presidential picture, Agnew zeroed in on the many who now most threatened Nixon's reelection.

In the 1968 presidential campaign, Alabama Governor George Wallace's candidacy had greatly influenced the strategies of the two major party candidates, particularly in their decision to speak to the "law and order" issue that obsessed the country. As the presidential campaign continued, Wallace's potential strength became so formidable that some began to doubt whether either of the two major party candidates would receive the required majority of the Electoral College votes.**124** Wallace's strength with the electorate and the likelihood that Edward Kennedy would be the Democratic candidate in the next election forced the Nixon Administration to look forward prematurely to 1972. To some extent, perhaps "political schizophrenia" best characterized the reaction of the Nixon team, as they contemplated how to kill both the Wallace and Kennedy threats, one on the right and one on the left. After Chappaquiddick, however, factors bearing on the 1972 campaign were more limited, and only George Wallace remained a problem. Thus, the administration's strategy could be aligned with the Agnew crusade.**125** Several days following his grandiloquent New Orleans incursion, Agnew spoke in similar fashion in Jackson, Mississippi, saying "This Administration will never appeal to a racist philosophy. . . . However, a free government cannot impose rules of social acceptance upon its citizens. . . . The point is this – in a man's private life he has the right to make his own friends." The Vice President continued with a disavowal of "the Southern Strategy" – that is, the administration playing to Southern issues in hopes of forging a new alignment. Despite this avowal, Agnew proclaimed that "for too long the South has been the punching bag for those who characterize themselves as liberal intellectuals. Actually, they are consistently demonstrating the antithesis of intelligence."

The Jackson speech is an example of Agnew's masterful rhetoric. Disclaiming any racist policy on the part of the administration, Agnew championed the right of the individual to remain unshackled by "rules of social acceptance." Calling for an ideological "alignment—an exhortation to which he would give greater emphasis in his October 30 speech in Harrisburg, Pennsylvania – Agnew emphasized the need for a "positive polarization" from leftist adversaries. In subsequent speeches, Agnew continued his denial of an administration "Southern Strategy," but lashed out against the "Northeastern liberal community." The "liberal intellectuals with their admirers in Congress," said Agnew, are also the "arrogant ones" who "are bringing this nation to the most important decision it will ever have to make."

Agnew's cleverness with words enabled him to draw the battle lines against those who were "asking us to repudiate principles that have made this country great." The liberals who protested the war, he maintained, were "more comfortable with radicals." Stringing together words such as "the liberals," "Congress," "war protesters," the "New Left," the "Democratic party," and "the media" had the effect of labeling them individually and collectively as "the enemy" of the country.126

Agnew shortly became of the most sought-after speakers in the country. Whenever he spoke, the pubic awaited his vituperative rhetoric, which he was certain to deliver.

The "majority" of Americans of whom Agnew had spoken in his Jackson speech and whom Richard Nixon had mentioned in his acceptance speech at the 1968 Republic National Convention gradually made up the audience to whom Agnew's remarks and appeals were addressed. In his October 30 Harrisburg speech, Agnew defended his New Orleans speech and repeated his call for a polarization of political views, because "it is time for the preponderant majority, the responsible citizens of this country, to assert their rights. It is time to stop dignifying the actions of arrogant, reckless, inexperienced elements within our society."

The audience, Agnew assumed, was a "preponderant majority" comprised of "the responsible citizens." The enemies, on the other hand, were the arrogant, reckless, inexperienced," who engaged in tantrums that were destroying American society.

Taking advantage of the widespread fear of crime and violence in American society, Agnew labeled the activity of these "elements" as "unbridled protest," and suggested that our democracy was withering at its hands. The Vietnam protect, which had had its most recent expression in the Moratorium a few days earlier, he suggested, was a deception of the well intentioned by "political hustlers," an "evil cloaked in emotional disguises." In demanding the exposure of these "elements," Agnew yet again called for the polarization of the American people and utilized a "we/they" or "them/us" pattern of words in his speech: "*They* would have *us* believe that *they* alone know what is good for America; *they* would have *us* believe that *their* reflexive action is superior to *our* reflective action; that *their* revealed righteousness is more effective than *our* reason and experience."**127** [italics added]

Agnew continued to polarize as he appealed to blue collar workers, saying of the critical "unpatriotic": "Most of them disdain to mingle with the masses who work for a living." "They mock the common man's pride in his work, his family and his country." Agnew further invoked the "masses" and the "common man" to form a "positive polarization" to obliterate those "avowed anarchists and communists who detest everything about this country and want to destroy it."**128**

In what came to be known as "The Media Speech," delivered on December 13 in Des Moines, the Vice President unleashed an unprecedented torrent of criticism against the "Fourth Estate," a long-time Nixon "enemy." In December of 1968, shortly after Nixon won the presidential election, an ironic account entitled "Will the Press Be Out to Get Nixon?" appeared.**129** On the contrary, as it turned out, Nixon's Vice President was out to get the press. In response to the networks' negative reaction to the President's November 3 Vietnam speech in which Nixon had pleaded for the support of the "silent majority," Agnew asked Americans, "Are we demanding enough of our television news presentations. . . . Are the men of this medium demanding enough of themselves?"

The President's address, claimed Agnew, had its "words and thoughts characterized through the prejudice of hostile critics before they [could] even be digested." Referring to a "gaggle of commentators," Agnew attacked the media for being able to "elevate men from local obscurity to national prominence within a week." Pointing to the hidden persuasive power of the nation's commentators, the Vice President noted, "A raised eyebrow, an inflection pf a voice. A caustic remark dropped in the middle of a broadcast can raise doubts in a million minds about the veracity of a public official or the wisdom of a governmental policy." Not only do the media distort, claimed Agnew. Living and working in "the geographical and intellectual confines of Washington, D. C., or New York City . . . they . . . bask in their own provincialism, their own parochialism."**130**

The reaction, at least on the part of the media, was an uproar. Nonetheless, the Vice President got considerable support. The "silent majority" had been aroused. Responding to the charge that he was nothing more than Nixon's mouthpiece, Agnew again invoked the silent majority theme: "I spoke out . . . because, like the silent majority, I had had enough. . . . It was not that I suddenly launched a spiritual crusade nor that I was handed the White House standard, but that I was speaking my thoughts and . . . those thoughts abraded some revered dogmas of the Fourth Estate."**131** Thus, the "Fourth Estate" was the silent majority's enemy as well.

Whether or not the administration commanded Agnew to be its spokesman remains unclear. It is clear, however, that the White House did little to silence him. Perhaps Agnew did embark on his program of oratory on his own. It is possible that those elements in American society which Agnew chose to take on as enemies happened by chance to correspond to the age-old Nixon enemies and to issues then besetting the administration. It is also possible that what Humphrey had to say about the relationship between a President and a Vice President – "The President can always disavow you . . . if you get too far out"**132** – was on Nixon's mind as his Vice President administered whiplashes on his behalf. It seems obvious that Nixon did not believe that Agnew had gotten "too far out," for the President did not disavow Agnew. Moreover, Agnew's role in the subsequent 1970 congressional campaign was at the explicit instruction of the White House.**133**

Agnew played a critical role as administration spokesman during the off-year campaigns, a role Nixon had played for Eisenhower. In undertaking that role, Agnew apparently took a cue from Nixon's commentary on the April 8, 1970, Senate defeat of his nomination of G. Harrold Carswell for a Supreme Court seat. Irate over the Senate's rejection of Carswell, which followed closely on the heels of the Senate's rejection of another Nixon Court nominee, Clement Haynsworth, Nixon told reporters, "I have recently concluded – with the Senate presently constituted – I cannot successfully nominate [individuals] from the South." Haysnworth and Carswell," claimed the President, "have been falsely charged with being racist."**134** Agnew had a similar point tucked away in his Jackson, Mississippi speech. The subsequent congressional campaign gave him the opportunity to assume the personification of a purifier. The President had expressed his belief that Congress, especially the Senate, would be cleansed ideologically. The White House seemed pervaded by the sense that ideology was more important than party.

A great deal of literature has been written depicting the rise of a new Republic Party majority during the Nixon Presidency. Two tracts of the times are Kevin Phillips' The Emerging Republican Majority and Richard Scammon and Ben Wattenberg's The Real Majority.

According to the prophetic Phillips analysis, a new majority coalition of voters "centered in the South, the West, and in the Middle American urban-suburban districts would emerge in the 1970s.**135** This was the "silent majority" that claimed the close attention of both Nixon and Agnew despite denials from the White House of such a preoccupation. Moreover, this presumed new majority dictated the Republican campaign strategy for the 1970 elections and became the evolving theme of the Nixon Administration and the Agnew crusades.

Scammon and Wattenberg 's insightful study pointed out that the typical voter was not among any of the categories to which Democrats had appealed since FDR. In describing the so-called social issues, those writers identified the typical voter as being generally "unyoung," "unblack," "unpoor," and one who felt very strongly about what was perceived as the upheaval of all that had been good and clean in America. This group of voters felt very strongly about law and order, violence on college campuses, what was viewed as America's new permissiveness, and the cost of social welfare programs. All these subjects had been touched on in Agnew's speeches, and the analysis of the "typical voter" provided an ideological framework for his political thrusts.

Committed to an ideological rather a party majority, Agnew's congressional campaign crusades began. No one from either party was immune; the liberals had to be purged, especially those in the Senate. American politics had seen little of this type of vigilante political since Roosevelt's failed attempt in 1938 to purge the Democratic Party. Few Presidents would be willing to undertake such a politically hazardous task. Richard Nixon found it unnecessary to do so until the very last weeks of the campaign, for his Vice President was doing it for him. Agnew not only attacked but also suffered attacks. He campaigned vigorously for months, lashing out at critics within his own party as well as within the Democratic Party. Striving for ideological purity, he stressed the necessity of polarization. One of his typical attacks backfired. Governor Nelson Rockefeller of New York had appointed Charles Goodell to complete the term of the late Senator Robert F.

Kennedy. The liberals attacked Rockefeller for the Goodell appointment because they regarded Goodell as a conservative. He turned out to be less conservative that had been expected, however, and the Nixon Administration soon came to regard him as a liberal threat.

In keeping with the White House technique in the 1970 campaign, Agnew was instructed to embark on a program that would make it clear to the voters of New York State that the conservative candidate, James Buckley, was far more appealing to the administration than Goodell. Apparently, the President told Agnew to attack Goodell at an opportune moment. Agnew was not slow in labeling Goodell a "radical liberal," a term that had emerged from and became part of the Vice President rhetoric.**136** Furthermore, he could not bring himself to support the senator from New York because Goodell posed a threat to Nixon's foreign policy and to the welfare of the nation as a whole. While Agnew did not come out openly in support of Buckley, he enhanced the conservative candidate's position as he continued his verbal attacks on Goodell.**137** In his most outlandish attack, he called Goodell "the Christine Jorgensen of the Republican Party."**138** Jorgensen, formerly a male, had recently undergone one of the first sex change operations ever performed.

The administration chalked up Goodell's defeat as a victory of sorts but its immediate and longer rave consequences for Agnew were ominous. The Vice President's willingness to engage in the purse had alienated an important segment of his own party.

Agnew's Vice Presidency was first and foremost a public one. There was a duality to his conduct of the office. As one observer pointed out, "When all his bureaucratic achievements are totaled, it is painfully obvious that he has not a great deal to show for his efforts – little, that is, beyond the public side of his Vice Presidency."**139** As Vice President, Agnew was so public that by 1972 he had developed a large independent following, for "Agnewism," which embodied so many of the grave social issues troubling America, had had a notable impact. (See Appendix A and Appendix B for the Vice President's full statements)

Agnew's place on the 1972 ticket seemed scarcely open to question, notwithstanding the widespread notion that President Nixon preferred the former Texas Democrat turned Republican, Governor John Connelly as Agnew's successor.**140**

By the time the Nixon-Agnew Administration had entered its second term, speculation concerning Agnew's future as a presidential candidate in 1976 had grown. However, with the Vice President's independent power base increased, Nixon chose to use him in the campaign less frequently.**141** Here again, Agnew seemed to suffer the fate of many of his predecessors in the office, subject to the whims of the President. Understandably, the Vice President became less abrasive than during his first term in order to broaden his acceptability over the next several years. For a time, Agnew found himself in a peculiarly advantageous position. As the President's Watergate-related problems increasingly engulfed the administration, Agnew, virtually alone, emerged unscathed. This image, coupled with his past reputation as a supporter of what was portrayed as right and good for America, would be of immeasurable help, it seemed, to an aspiring presidential candidate. Nor did his position seem to suffer when the White House cut his duties and staff. While the White House announced that new duties and responsibilities would replace them, little of anything new emerged. Rather than being a handicap to Agnew, in this one instance the Vice President's traditional lack of closeness with the President and his staff paid off. Agnew could point out convincingly that he had had precious little contact with the Watergate-implicated Bob Haldeman and John Erlichman.**142**

As a presidential hopeful looking to the 1976 national election, Agnew's task was twofold: to make the most of the experience and exposure gained from his role in the administration and to remain above the Watergate fray. Without the Watergate scandal, Agnew's position would have been little different from other incumbent Vice Presidents who has aspired to the Presidency while at the same time being obliged to remain loyal to the President and his policies. One can only speculate what Agnew's political future might have been if no one had searched out his record in Maryland government service, with "kickbacks" going back to his days as Baltimore County executive. His resignation, preceded by and admission to charges of guilt and his resort to plea bargaining to avoid further legal prosecution, abruptly ended a public career that might otherwise have led to the presidential nomination in 1976 and possibly the Presidency.**143**

Thus, the most "public" Vice President to that date in time made his exit from the second highest office in the land. Time and future circumstances will determine whether Spiro Agnew enhanced that office by adding to its dimensions or whether he will be remembered merely as the thirty-ninth Vice-President of the United States, who resigned his office in ignominy.

PLENIPOTENTIARY -- THE VICE PRESIDENT AND FOREIGN AFFAIRS: THE INFLUENCE OF THE "MODERN" PRESIDENCY

As noted earlier, the Vice Presidency is far more active than ever before. But, still, the Vice President's agenda continues to depend on the inclinations and needs of the President who, under the American constitutional system, alone must bear the responsibilities of "the supreme executive magistrate." As the Presidency has come to be dominated by foreign affairs, so too expansion into this arena has helped to develop the role of the Vice President.

Presidents have been willing to share certain functions with their constitutional heirs apparent, especially ceremonial duties and foreign travel.**144** Travel assignments and official representations abroad have often been regarded as mere exercises to preoccupy the prestigious and energetic individuals who have served as Vice President, but not all their travels have been busy work. On the contrary, they relieve the President of excessive travel and at the same time enable the President to meet the demands of protocol by sending a Constitutional counterpart. A notable example, discussed previously, was Vice President

Johnson's Berlin trip in 1961, where he stood in for President Kennedy. Johnson's presence underscored the administration's concern without arousing the attention implicit in a personal presidential visit.[145]

Richard Nixon's travels were of immeasurable help to the Eisenhower Administration. They also focused national attention on the Vice-President himself, especially Nixon's South American trip when rocks and an angry crowd assailed him and his wife and his 1958 trip to Moscow where he engaged in a well-publicized confrontation with Premier Nikita Khrushchev in the famous "Kitchen Debates."[146] Nixon's keen mind and his ability to withstand an exhausting schedule, as well as Eisenhower's own distaste for travel and representative functions, made Nixon's own role all the more vital. Nixon soon became known as, to that date, the most traveled Vice President, journeying to the Soviet Union, Latin America, Africa, and Asia. One newsman said that Nixon "became a very good traveling ambassador. I followed him through Africa, and I think he did a good job in many respects."[147] In his 1953 trip to the Far East, "an assignment that changed the while pattern of his life,"[148] the constitutionally elected Vice President could speak and act with presidential authority and prestige. Parmet has pointed out that "Ike's purpose . . . was to dramatize that American foreign policy was aimed at putting Asia on a par with Europe,"[149] and Nixon's visit was intended to emphasize that point. Nixon buried himself in preparatory material familiarizing himself with as many aspects as he could of the countries he would visit.[150] The trip was an overwhelming success. Nixon was the focus of attention, especially in his willingness, possibly even eagerness, to meet the common people in the huge crowds that greeted him. The reception upon his return home equaled the one he had received en route. A former Eisenhower associate said that in Nixon's report to the Cabinet the Vice President had given a "very impressive performance."[151]

Nixon's observations and suggestions were transformed into administration policies,[152] and "the occasion was a landmark in Nixon's career. From that moment on he became a respected participant in the

Administraiton."153 As he approached the 1960 presidential nomination and election, Nixon could point to his proven activity and expertise in the field of foreign affairs. This background was crucial to his campaign strategy.154

By contrast, Nixon's own Vice Presidents, first Spiro Agnew and then Gerald R. Ford, enjoyed few foreign assignments. Unlike Eisenhower, Nixon relished the Presidency's dominance in foreign affairs. He had chosen Agnew as his running mate in part to provide the domestic balance he thought necessary to a President who would concentrate on foreign matters; indeed, Agnew's few trips abroad were largely "cosmetic."155

When Gerald Ford was appointed Vice President, Nixon was even less willing to share his foreign affairs activities. Watergate upon him, Nixon sought to engulf himself more than ever in foreign relations since travel abroad could still bring him the cheering, excited, approving crowds at a time when he had little applause at home. In addition, Ford's background could not compete with Nixon's; Nixon, after all, had had the tutelage of Secretary of State John Foster Dulles.156 Had Ford continued in the Vice Presidency he would probably have been given few foreign affairs assignments in view of the dominant position of not only the President but also Secretary of State Henry Kissinger.

As discussed earlier, Vice President Lyndon Johnson traveled extensively for Kennedy; some of his trips were more successful than others.157 He journeyed to the Far East, to Southeast Asia, to Europe,158 and to India, carefully reporting his findings and recommendations to the President, but he never evoked as much interest and fanfare as Nixon. This was not for lack of preparation, for the State Department briefed him thoroughly for these journeys and he was determined not to go on protocol visits, but rather to discuss matters of substance.159 Perhaps the principal reason was "the excitement of the handsome era of Kennedy the King."160

President Kennedy, as would be true of President Nixon, became increasingly involved and fared far better in foreign relations than in domestic affairs. By sharp contrast, Johnson was much more adroit in domestic than in foreign affairs, and this remained true after he became President. It is understandable that Vice President Johnson regarded foreign trips as "one great escape."**161**

As Johnson's Vice President, Hubert Humphrey was given a role in foreign affairs that was linked to one of his most important domestic roles, that of administration spokesman, especially on Vietnam. In 1965, he made his first trip as Vice President to Southeast Asia, with Johnson watching closely, **162** but the real turning point in Humphrey's foreign affairs role came with his assignment to the funeral of India's Prime Minister Shastri and his second trip to Asia. These trips came in the wake of his outspokenness in the National Security Council criticizing the administration's Vietnam policies. Humphrey desperately needs to get back in Johnson's good graces, and these trips provided the opportunity. Humphrey's biographer Albert Eisele (who later served as Vice President Walter Mondale's press secretary), points out that those trips "established his credentials in Johnson's eyes as an able roving ambassador who could hold his own in the high-stakes game of international diplomacy." Moreover, as an administration spokesman, Humphrey could "effectively present Johnson's Vietnam policies to America's allies and to critics at home."**163** Humphrey readily accepted both tasks. The Vice President had learned an important lesson of the office.

Nelson Rockefeller had an extensive interest and background in foreign affairs, and he served a President who admitted having little expertise in the area. At the same time, Rockefeller had a very harmonious relationship with Secretary of State Kissinger.

Following his departure from the Vice Presidency, Walter Mondale engaged in a series of lectures in which he defended Carter's policies. Mondale repeatedly stressed the wisdom and necessity of the Carter human rights policy, saying, "The basic lesson of our experience and struggle to promote human rights is that the advance of our own moral concerns for humanity, democracy freedom and justice is profoundly in our national interest."**164**

Throughout the Carter-Mondale Administration, the Vice President was assigned a wide range of duties in his broader capacity as "trouble-shooter," a subject explored elsewhere in this work. Perhaps the most meaningfully utilized Vice President in American history to that point, Mondale had access to every major document received by the President.[165] Later, as a private citizen, Mondale emphasized that he was involved in every major decision during the Carter years. Regarding his access to classified materials, Mondale said, "I believe we have broken new institutional ground."[166]

Mondale's access to the President, as well as the smooth working relationship between the two men, was unparalleled in the history of the second office. As part of this relationship, Mondale enjoyed weekly luncheon business meetings with the President, an opportunity afforded to only one other person in the White House, Rosalyn Carter.[167] The weekly breakfast meetings enhanced Mondale's role in foreign policy, for the meetings were held with the administration's top foreign policy adviser. Mondale's early assignment to African relations was expanded to other issues and areas.[168]

When George H. W. Bush assumed the Vice Presidency he was the beneficiary of Mondale's advice, especially to tell the President what he thought but to disagree in private. Bush heeded this advice and ungrudgingly accepted a supporting role.

Bush saw Reagan daily for national security briefings and was the beneficiary of the Carter-Mondale weekly luncheon, a practice continued by Reagan.[169] Embracing the low profile necessary to survive in that office, Bush has been rewarded, most conspicuously by Reagan's announcement in late March 1981 that Bush would be in charge of the crisis management team, James S. Brady, Reagan's press secretary, made the announcement on March 24, saying, "The purpose of this team is to coordinate all appropriate [f]ederal resources in responding to emergency situations both foreign and domestic. The type of incident that might be involved ranges from an isolated terrorist attack upon United States territory by a hostile power." Bush would chair the team should the President be absent, and would be involved in advance planning for emergency situations, developing options to be presented to the President.**170** The assignment greatly upset Secretary of State Alexander M. Haig, Jr. Prior to Bush's appointment, Haig had already indicated that he was "not totally satisfied" with the administration's foreign policy arrangements. Initial rumors about the Bush appointment provoked Haig to suggest that it "would pose another set of problems."**171**

Unlike Bush, Haig maintained quite a visible profile, much to the consternation of many White House staffers. Perhaps the crisis management assignment for Bush was one way of getting the Secretary of State in line. Nonetheless, the assignment marked the continuing evolution of the Bush Vice-Presidency within the broader parameters of the office. Ironically just six days following Bush's new assignment, an assassination attempt was made on President Reagan's life and George Bush's behavior during the ensuing days was exemplary as he deftly and smoothly worked with the White House entourage.

In addition to being named as head of the crisis management team, Bush steadily accused foreign affairs assignments in other areas. During the campaign of 1980, Bush had made it clear that he would play a supporting role in all fields, if elected. As Director of the Central Intelligence Agency he had attended National Security Council meetings in 1975-76, where he was able to directly view Vice President Rockefeller's actions. Observed Bush, "Rockefeller gave his advice and would speak up even if he disagreed with President Ford. He was strong, and Ford was impressed." Bush promised to add his own style to the strength of convictions Rockefeller represented. Continued Bush, "If Reagan took a position that I disagreed with, I would not try to embarrass the President of the United States, but would present his views directly to the President.**172** As early as the campaign itself, Bush had a chance to act on his words and defer to the presidential prerogative. Perhaps there is no more poignant example than Bush's August 1980 restraint over a Reagan remark in which the presidential candidate had proclaimed favoring "official" relations between the United States and Taiwan. Bush's August 1980 restraint over a Reagan remark in which the presidential candidates had proclaimed favoring "official" relations between the United States and Taiwan. Bush, whose own credentials as a U. S. envoy to China (he had served as chief of the U. S. Liaison mission) certainly earned him respect in that areas of foreign policy, happened to be in China at the time of the Reagan remark. While the vice presidential candidate privately disagreed with the remark, his public stance was one of more positively reinterpreting what Reagan meant."173

Bush's former ambassadorial credentials were immeasurably useful to the administration throughout his incumbency. In a May 1982 trip to China, for example, Bush was referred to by Chinese leader Deng Xiaoping as "an old friend of China," and in this respect perhaps the Administration had nor more trustworthy spokesperson to deal with the delicate issue of the relationship between China and Taiwan.174 Similarly, Bush's travels took him to Australia, where he undertook what turned out to be a successful effort to dispel potential areas of disagreement over future trade and commerce negotiations.175 Just a year previous, in the summer of 1981, Bush had been given charge of preparations for the Canadian economic summit.

A Vice President's role as administration spokesman also involves serving as the "eyes and ears" of the President. Bush's travel to seven African states during 1982 was designed to, as Bush himself noted, "learn what key African leaders are thinking."176 So, too, would Bush attempt to get a head start on understanding the new leadership of the Soviet Union following the death of that country's leader, Leonid I. Brezhnev, in 1982. Vice Presidents are often (and erroneously) depicted as merely attending funerals abroad in place of the President. Bush did indeed attend the Brezhnev funeral (which interrupted his African tour) but he lost no time in turning that symbolic and ceremonial activity into a substantive one and made gestures of broadened cooperation toward the new Soviet leader, Yuri A. Andropov. In fact, Bush similarly met with the new Soviet leader during the Soviet Union's next two leadership successions (Bush met with Konstantin U. Chernenko following Andropov's death, and he met with Mikhail Gorbachev following Chernenko's death.) The foreign policy side of Bush's Vice Presidency was clearly an active one. As in his domestic roles, the Vice President clearly saw the advantage of being a team player, and consistently supported administration policies.

Bush's own Vice President, Dan Quayle, enjoyed a mixed experience. He had been selected as running mate because Bush needed to let the conservative wing of the Republican Party that he was serious about following the Reagan conservative thrust. But, unfortunately for Vice President Quayle, he soon suffered a largely undeserved barrage of punditry. Nonetheless, Quayle was able to champion issues championed by the right, such as the importance of family and family values. And, as Paul G. Kendor points out in a compelling article for the fall 1994 issue of *The Presidential Studies Quarterly,* Quayle was also able to serve as an administration spokesperson during the Persian Gulf crisis during 1990-1991. He also served as a shield for the administration against those who protested the United States' involvement in the Persian Gulf War.

The next incumbent of the Vice Presidency, Al Gore, served in an immensely important capacity stemming not only from his extraordinary background as a U. S. Senator, but also from the close relationship that developed between the Clintons and the Gores on the campaign trail for the 1992 presidential election. Gore was able to champion legislation on the Hill on a range of issues. Of course, the issue that had long been uppermost in Gore's heart was the environment. On this issue, Gore attempted to exert greater influence than the administration believed politically feasible given the Republican composition of the U. S. Congress. Nonetheless, Gore insisted on traveling to Kyoto to be present for discussions surrounding the Kyoto Protocol, despite the failure of the administration to present that protocol to the U. S. Senate. As argued throughout this work, the background and temperament of the President is a crucial factor in the role a Vice President plays, be it in domestic or foreign policy. This is all the more the case in the period of "the modern Presidency," with Vice Presidents during the post-WWII era being more involved in foreign policy. But certainly Dwight Eisenhower can be credited with setting a trend, one followed to a greater or lesser extent by subsequent Presidents. So Nixon was the first Vice President to sit on the National Security Council, Mondale was the first Vice President to have an office in the West Wing, virtually steps away from President Carter, President Reagan designated George H. W. Bush as chair of the new crisis-management committee.**177**

Presidential "background" was key in the role played by Mondale, who of course not only served under a President with no foreign policy experience but was also a Washington "outsider." Moreover, President Carter's staff was largely comprised of outsiders, giving Mondale the unparalleled advantage of virtually the only "insider. By contrast, while Dan Quayle played more of a role than is often perceived, President George H. W. Bush's extensive foreign policy background as ambassador to China and Director of the CIA set the scene for a lesser and less visible role for his Vice President.**178**

Contemporary wisdom would say the Vice President Dick Cheney completely transformed the office of the Vice Presidency. Nothing can be further from the truth. It is undeniable that Cheney had an extremely powerful voice in the G. W. Bush administration. Even prior to the official declaration that Bush and Cheney had captured the White House in 2000, Cheney was at work as a spokesperson. It was Cheney who was often the voice during the Bush-Gore controversy over whom should actually be President. Once in office, Cheney's broad political expertise was of immeasurable importance to the Bush Administration. He served as a vocal adviser in formulating administration policy and then in defending it, be it at home or abroad. Following the tragedy of 9/11, Cheney championed the President's actions in the Middle East, be it Afghanistan or Iraq or elsewhere.

All of this said, however, actually underscores *the very nature* of the

Vice Presidency. Cheney was powerful a powerful Vice President because George W. Bush needed and wanted him to be. Once again, the role of the Vice President is a reflection of the needs and personality of the incumbent under whom the Vice President serves.

The Cheney Vice Presidency is one that attracted and will continue to attract a great deal of commentary and that will undoubtedly become clearer as more and more documents and revelations unfold over the decades. Suffice it to say, Cheney seemed to have no hesitation in putting forth his views on policy issues, often taking positions contrary to those of President Bush, but it was the President who accepted these differences of opinion and who sometimes didn't. As Bush himself wrote, it was Secretary of State Condoleezza Rice who was told to take Cheney to task after Cheney delivered a speech on the issue of additional inspections before taking on Saddam Hussein. The Vice President's position was that there would be none, basically pushing for war.**179**

Speaking before a meeting of Veterans of Foreign Wars in August of 2002, Cheney blasted the notion of continuing inspections for nuclear weapons in Iraq, citing numerous instances of deception by Iraq. Saddam, Cheney argued, was taking full advantage of time to build up an arsenal. Sounding the alarm bell, the Vice President argued that

> Should all his ambitions be realized, the implications would be enormous for the Middle East, for the United States, and for the peace of the world. The whole range of weapons of mass destruction then would rest in the hands of a dictator who has already shown his willingness to use such weapons. . . .

> Simply stated, there is no doubt that Saddam Hussein now has weapons of mass destruction. There is no doubt his is amassing them use against friends, against our allies, and against us. . . .

In the face of such a threat, we must proceed with care, deliberation, and consultation with our allies. I know our president very well. I've worked beside him as he directed our response to the events of 9/11. I know that he will proceed cautiously and deliberately to consider all possible options to deal with the threat that an Iraq ruled by Saddam Hussein represents. . . .

To this point in his speech, Cheney played the role of administration spokesperson, a role we have seen develop for the second office. Interesting to note, however, are subsequent statements Cheney makes in the same speech. Harkening back to an earlier time in U.S. history -- appropriate for an audience of veterans from past wars -- Cheney points out that the U.S. perhaps waited too long in anticipating the coming of WWII to our shores, and notes that "To this day, historians continue to analyze that war, speculating on how we might have prevented Pearl Harbor, and asking what might have averted the tragedies that rate among the worst in human history." This is Cheney making an argument for more aggressive action. Indeed, the speech is a rhetorical masterpiece of sorts, since Cheney stakes out his own more aggressive position, while seemingly supporting the President, but then using Bush's position to support Cheney's position, noting, "as President Bush has said, time is not on our side. . . . The risks of inaction are far greater than the risk of action." Following this, Cheney laid out his very his very strident plan for the course of action he believed the U.S. should take sooner rather than later.[180]

Commenting on this speech several years later, White House Correspondent David Sanger wrote "No one has ever been more willing to set out the new domino theory than the administration's chief hawk, Mr. Cheney."[181] Indeed, the "command" taken by the Vice President in the immediacy of the 9/11 attacks more than suggest his key role in administration policy and decision-making.

But by the fall of 2006, as Sanger has argued, the Vice President found his role in the administration rather dramatically changed from the one he had played five years earlier. Referring to "a waning influence," and pointing out that "measuring the accumulation or the erosion of power is an imprecise art," Sanger's presentation of his findings over five months of confidential interviews with a vast array of Washington insiders is illuminating. Citing Republican Illinois Representative Ray LaHood, Sanger noted that "During the first term, Cheney was considered one of the smartest guys in the administration. . . . But his influence has been diminished because of the [departure of] Scooter Libby . . . and because the war in Iraq has not gone well," with the President seeking more extensive advice, and "in the second term, whether the issue was the treatment and prosecution of terror suspects or Congressional oversight of domestic spying, Cheney has been forced into an unhappy retreat.182 To the extent that there was a changed Cheney role underscores the very nature of the second office: a Vice President's role depends upon time and place and especially the President. As a President grows in the office, much as Vice President Nelson Rockefeller learned, the role of the Vice President inevitably shifts.

Similarities existed in the Obama-Biden Administration, as noted earlier regarding the vice presidential selection process. In understanding the role that emerged for Vice President Biden it is important to add some comments to what occurred during that selection process. Obama's intellectual prowess was unquestioned, reminiscent of Richard Nixon's 1960 campaign theme, "Experience Counts." It particularly counted in the area of foreign policy, when the presidential nominee would be facing the Republican Party candidacy of Senator John McCain, and a Biden Vice Presidency could contribute significantly to the role of plenipotentiary.

Biden reluctantly accepted the offer of the second spot, with one of his greatest concerns being how he might not be able to handle having someone be his "boss." If he had thought about Vice President Lyndon Johnson under the Kennedy Presidency Biden might very well have declined to offer. He was keenly aware of the vagaries involved in holding that office. As he noted in his work, <u>Promise Me, Dad: A Year of Hope, Hardship, and Purpose,</u> "There is a strange and singular elasticity to the responsibilities of a vice president. As a strictly constitutional matter, the holder of the office has very little power. . . . The actual power of the office is reflective; it depends almost entirely on the trust and confidence of the president."**183**

Towards the end of the vetting process, Biden was asked "Why do you want to be vice president?" Biden's response: "I don't want to be vice president. . . . If he wants me to do it and thinks it will help, I will."**184** I n hindsight, Biden reflected,

> I remember exactly when it became clear to me that this would be the right thing to do. Barack had me flown in secret to Minneapolis during a campaign rally. Wearing jeans, a ball cap, and sunglasses, I was sneaked into his hotel suite, where we had the single most significant conversation of our early relationship. I already knew from the presidential primary debates and from working with him on the Foreign Relations Committee that we did not have substantive differences on the issues. What differences there were, were tactical. . . . I asked him . . . if he really meant what he said: that he wanted me to help him govern, especially in foreign policy matters. He said he did. And I asked him if he meant what he said about the restoration of the middle class being a defining issue of his presidency. . . .
>
> I believed him. I was convinced he was an honest and thoroughly honorable man who kept his word. I was also convinced that he could be a really good president.**185**

As the meeting progressed, the two men discussed the role Biden would play in an Obama Administration. Biden candidly told Obama, "I want to have an impact on *all* areas. I told him I would do whatever he most needed me to do . . . and would be a vocal supporter and defender of his policies," but "I want to be the last guy in the room on every major decision."**186** This meeting was the beginning of what would become a solid relationship between the two men, both professionally and personally. On the campaign trail Biden was a feisty, loyal running mate and as Vice President he served loyally, and Obama was true to his word. "Barack Obama . . . handed me big things to run from the beginning of our first term, and once he assigned me to oversee the Recovery Act of 2009, or budget negotiations with Senator Mitch McConnell, or diplomatic relations with Iraq, he did not look over my shoulder."**187**

The Biden Vice Presidency exemplified the essence of the second office. Biden was loyal to a fault. He was active within the realm carved out for him by the President. Biden's knowledge on foreign affairs on occasion resulted in a departure from official administration policy, but with hindsight it appears that this seeming departure was in reality depicting the role of the Vice President as "administration spokesperson" who can occasionally send up "trial balloons." As Hubert Humphrey, quoted early in this work, said, "A Vice President can be an administration spokesperson, because the administration can always disavow you." Biden's longterm reputation for verbal gaffes may have come in handy in this role.

On the other hand, the vice presidential role of presidential plenipotentiary can be very useful to an administration. The was certainly the case during Vice President Biden's visit to Israel, during which Israeli Prime Minister Benjamin Netanyahu defied President Obama's position that Israeli settlements must cease to be constructed. It was a slap in the face for Obama, but delivered on the Vice President's cheek.

Biden's assignments as Vice President were perhaps best described by President Obama himself, who observed that "[Joe Biden] is like a basketball player who does a bunch of things that don't show up in the stat sheet. . . . He gets that extra rebound, takes the charge, makes the extra pass."**188** and by Chief of Staff Rahm Emmanuel, "'When there's group-think going on, the vice president tends to push the envelope in the other direction,'" . . . in conversations on a range of policy issues ranging from the advisability of health care reform to Iraq and Afghanistan."**189**

CHAOS ON THE POTOMAC:
MIKE PENCE AS PRESIDENT #46?

In the vagaries of American politics, unlike G. W. Bush in 2000 who did not have to worry about a Vice President longing to be President, even prior to his November victory Trump found himself in a position of having to look over his shoulder, questioning Pence's ambitions which he might want to advance significantly before "officially" being an heir apparent in 2024 if Trump were to win two terms for the Presidency. Pence's ambitions showed themselves early on, when, in the wake of the "Access Hollywood" revelations during the presidential campaign, Pence offered himself up to party leaders as a substitute for Trump as presidential candidate. So Pence as "administrative apologist," as he has sometimes been identified, may be balancing his public loyalty to the President while carving out his own road to the White House.**190**

The Trump-Pence Administration brought with it an unusual set of circumstances. As noted elsewhere in this where, from the outset of the Trump Presidency there was widespread concern that the billionaire businessman, while have been successful in the private sector, might not be up to the rigors of and experience for leading one of the most powerful nations in the world. For some, the presence of Vice President Pence was a reassurance; for others who disagreed with the Vice President's position on a range of issues, the prospect of a "Pence Presidency" was alarming, while embraced by others.**191**

The Vice President certainly has had governmental experience, both as a governor and as a former member of the House of Representatives, and his intellectual capabilities, often compared to the President's, are unquestioned. Beyond concern about Pence's policy views, the presidential disparagement of the Vice President puts Pence in an awkward position, as noted earlier in this work. But Pence's vision and aspirations make him willing to defer to the treatment he receives while serving as a loyal soldier in the administration, especially as an administration spokesperson in a White House that has had considerable staff turmoil. Unlike "staffers," the Vice President as an elected official who cannot be removed. Moreover, Pence's long term ambitions warrant his subjugation. In this regard, Pence has taken on Trump's enemies and responded to criticism after criticism of the administration. Much of Pence's behavior as Trump's subordinate is contrary to the views he once expressed while serving as a member of the House of Representatives. It is illuminating to re-visit at least parts of a speech Pence delivered on the floor of the House in 2010, when Barack Obama was in the White House. It is also *imperative* to do so, since this speech underlines what Vice President Mike Pence has been willing to "trade" to be the heir apparent. Entitled "The Presidency . . . Has Become Symbolic of Overreaching," Pence's comments could very well be describing the Trump White House he now defends. It is worth citing extensively.

> Isn't it amazing, given the great and momentous nature of the office, that those who seek it seldom pause to consider what they are seeking? Rather, unconstrained by principle or reflection, there is a mad rush toward something that, once its powers are seized, the new president can wield as an instrument with which to transform the nation and the people according to his highest aspirations.

> But, other than in a crisis of the house divided, the presidency is neither fit nor intended to be such an instrument. When it is made that, the country sustains a wound, and cries out justly and indignantly [and] . . . what it says quite naturally and rightly, if not always gracefully, is that we as a people are not to be ruled and not to be commanded.

It says that the president should never forget this; that he has not risen above us, but is merely one of us, chosen by ballot, dismissed after his term, tasked not to transform and work his will upon us, but to bear the weight of decision and to carry out faithfully the design laid down in the Constitution and impassioned by the Declaration of Independence.

The presidency must adhere to its definition as expressed in the Constitution, and to conduct defined over time and by tradition. While the powers of the office have enlarged . . . the framework of the government was intended to restrict abuses common to classical empires and to the regal state of the 18th century.

Without proper adherence to the role contemplated in the Constitution for the presidency, the checks and balances in the constitutional plan become weakened, *[such as]* . . . *when the three branches of government have been subject to the tutelage of a single party.* (italics added). . . .

The powers of the president are extraordinary and necessarily great, and great presidents treat them sparingly. . . . They are a potent political force when massed by the social network to which they are permanently attached. . . .

A president who slights the Constitution is like a rider who hates his horse: he will be thrown, and the nation along with him. The president solemnly swears to preserve, protect, and defend the Constitution. He does not solemnly swear to ignore, overlook, supplement, or reinterpret it. . . . [I]f he should want to hurry along the Constitution to fit his own notions or designs, he should do so my amendment rather than by adjustment, for if

he joins the powers of his office to his own willful interpretation,
he steps away from a government of laws and toward a govern-
ment of men. . . .

[I]f the politics of your own election or of your party intrude
upon your decisions for even an instant -- there are not words for
this. . . . (italics added)

The presidency, a great and complex subject upon which
I have only touched, has become symbolic of overreaching.
There have been many truths that we have been frightened to tell
or face. If we run from them, they will catch us with our backs
turned and pull us down. Better that we should not flee but
rather stop and look them in the eye. (italics added)**192**

Pence's unspoken change of position on what the Presidency is all
about fully reflects the essence of the office. As noted throughout this
work, a Vice President must be loyal almost to a fault. Pence is certainly that. It bears repeating: Pence's entire political future, as has been
the case with all of his predecessors, rests with the President..

Punditry exists on both sides of the "Pence as administration spokesperson" debate. During the second year of the Administration, the *New
York Times* put forth an image of an independent Vice President, who
played an active role vis a vis Republican candidates in the midterm
elections. The piece viewed Pence's support for candidates not backed
by Trump as evidence of this independence. But a more careful look
at Pence's behavior suggests a very clever juggling act of carving out
his own base for a future presidential run while simultaneously seemingly serving as the loyal underling. Moreover, Pence's willingness to
do party politicking is reflective of a Vice President fitting into roles in
which Presidents leave a vacuum.**193**

Recalling that the "administration spokesperson" role is often
given to a Vice President during controversies, Trump gave Pence the

difficult role of quarterback who served as a loyal "messenger" defending Trump's policies and actions.**194**

So, too, was Pence placed in this precarious position, as he took on defense of Trump's obstinate position on the southern border wall issue. The likeable Pence could serve as negotiator in a futile battle with the congressional opposition.**195** As Trump's administration became increasingly embroiled in controversy, there was endless speculation that an impeachment was not out of the question, and this speculation became Trump's reality nightmare in the wake of potential wrongdoing vis a vis policy towards Ukraine. For his part, Vice President Pence continued to play the quintessential vice presidential role of loyal servant.

The twists and turns of American politics are erratic and oxymoronic, especially as Pence continued to play Trump-defender and administration spokesperson. Pence may have never gambled in his life, but he took on the gamble of being a heartbeat away when he accepted the 2016 nomination. Pence holds a difficult job: attempting to balance his support for Trump while carving out his own potential run for the Presidency. Vice Presidents, we have seen and as Vice President Hubert Humphrey pointed out, "walk a tightrope" and "with two left feet." This balancing act is difficult enough without carrying the weight of the most divisive Presidency this country has probably ever seen. Yet Pence persists is staying as close to the President's side as possible, even under extreme circumstances. By way of example, following Trump's lukewarm remarks in the wake of the Charlottesville, VA clash between neo-Nazis and white supremacists, in which the President said, "There are good people on both sides," Pence compared Trump to President Teddy Roosevelt, who, Pence claimed, said "white people [are] the forward race."**196** Pence gave only the mildest of "rebukes" to Trump on the campaign trail when Trump made egregiously disparaging and sexually lewd remarks about women, simply saying, "As a husband and father, I was offended by the words and actions described by Donald Trump in the eleven-year-old video released yesterday. I do not condone his remarks and cannot defend them. . . . I am grateful that he has expressed remorse and apologized to the American people. We pray for his family and look forward to the opportunity he has to show what is in his heart when he goes before the nation tomorrow night."**197**

So what does this bode for Mike Pence? Will the Vice Presidency be a steppingstone or a stumbling block? Unless Pence succeeds Trump *prior to* 2020, the cards would suggest a vice presidential replacement, especially if Trump sees his Vice President as less than loyal to a fault. Should Trump survive a full term and move on to a second term, what will Mike Pence's life be like in 2024, after eight years shackled to a controversial President and a set of confusing and misdirected policies? Under the best of circumstances, Vice Presidents have to defend the administration record, no matter how good that record might have been. During the period of the modern Vice Presidency, only one Vice President – George H. W. Bush in 1988 – was able to do so, only to be relegated to but one term in office. And even with a four year hiatus between the Carter-Mondale Administration and Mondale's own run for the Presidency, the former Vice President found himself still defending the Carter record. Vice President Pence's candidacy and incumbency give a significant nuance to what has elsewhere in this work been referred to as an "administrative spokesperson." That nuance is that "spokesperson" should be replaced by the word "echo." There used to be a joke about how tight a control President Lyndon Johnson had over his Vice President, Hubert Humphrey. "Hubert," the joke began, 'did I hear you belch?" "No, Mr. President. Did you want me to?" This might aptly be applied to the Trump-Pence relationship. Vice Presidents, as we have seen, are expected to be loyal to the President under whom they serve, but at what expense? Humphrey was forced to remain silent about his disagreement with Johnson's policies in Southeast Asia, even though every bone in his liberal body was in fervent disagreement. That silence cost him the Presidency in 1968.

So a question now is, what does Mike Pence really believe and how far is he willing to go to advance his own political career? Certainly, as the "most conservative" and probably the most "religious" Vice President in fifty years, Pence has a constituency of his own that enhances Trump's appeal to some audiences. But the contradiction between Pence's moral views and his willingness to stand behind Trump, seemingly regardless of what the President says and does is at least puzzling if not hypocritical. As the Trump Presidency pushes towards an autocracy, the Pence Vice-Presidency's undercurrent is a theocracy. To what extent is Mike Pence willing to sublimate his seemingly profound religious and ethical beliefs to achieve the Presidency? Or is Pence more clever than one might think?

Brian Beutler, writing for *The New Republic,* wrote a compelling piece in August 2017, that reflects that potential cleverness. In reflecting on the vice presidential selection during the 2016 campaign, Beutler observes the dilemma faced by those who might have been selected. "Among up-and-coming Republicans, Trump was still an object of derision and scorn: vulgar, ignorant, embarrassing, and destined to lose to Hillary Clinton. Hitching one's wagon to Trump would entail enormous, potentially career-ending risks, with only far-fetched upsides. Trump's optimistic or desperate supplicants had to hope that Trump would shape up and lose in a somewhat dignified manner; or that he'd win unexpectedly and (just as unexpectedly) govern well; or that he'd win unexpected and then self-destruct so thoroughly that the vice president would enjoy a short cut to history."**198** What is curious, in some ways, is that the Vice President has so fully embroiled himself in his "loyalty" to Trump that whatever gains he might get from being a heartbeat, resignation, impeachment away would be bittersweet. And then, at least briefly during the several investigations into Trump's activities, there was raised the possibility that the Vice President himself had intentionally or inadvertently been involved in wrongdoing. 199 Ron Klain, former chief of staff to two Vice Presidents (Gore and Biden) observed about Pence: "Overall, I would say that whenever Mike Pence runs for office in the future, the liability he will carry from this period is not how he distanced himself from Trump, but, rather, how he deepened his ties to the President."**199**

Beyond this, the alleged presidential disparagement of the Vice President puts Pence in an awkward position, such as at the last Cabinet meeting in 2017, in which The President asked his Vice President to say some words about the extraordinary Trump accomplishments. Pence's hyperbolic remarks were just what Trump expected. The Vice President gave laudatory praise to what Trump had achieved in restoring the U.S.' image around the world and at home. He talked about his own gratitude at being the Vice President to such an extraordinary man.**200**

Pence's servitude towards Trump far exceeds the often humiliating experiences suffered by LBJ.s Vice President, Humbert Humphrey, who knew his fate and future rested in the President's hands. As Vice President Hubert Humphrey observed, "The Vice President is potentially everything, yet nothing."**201** Reportedly, Trump often publicly disparages his Vice President. As one report observed "A staff member from Trump's campaign recalls him mocking Pence's religiosity. He said that when people met with Trump after stopping by Pence's office, Trump would ask them, 'Did Mike make you pray?'" And on another occasion when the subjects of gay rights as well as legalized abortion came up when Trump and Pence were with a "legal scholar," Trump purportedly told Pence that he was "wasting his time" on the issue of abortion. And then Trump, in discussing gay rights at the same meeting said, "Don't ask [Pence] – he wants to hang them all."**202** And Pence subjugates his own views and political positions. So Pence puts up with the image he has of being Trump's "First Toady." As Ed Kilgore noted, "This willingness to serve as First Toady was evident in Pence's initial interview – on a Trump golf course," and Pence even sought Kellyanne Conway's advice regarding how to behave at this meeting. The advice: don't talk about politics and show how much he wanted to learn from Trump. At the end of the game, Pence reported to the media that Trump "beat me like a drum."**203** Kilgore reported that Ms. Conway later said, "Mike Pence is someone whose faith allows him to subvert his ego to the greater good."**204** Pence, much like Humphrey had been, is a survivor and has been willing to defer to the treatment he receives while serving as a loyal soldier in the administration, especially as an administration spokesperson in a White House that has had considerable staff turmoil.

A Vice President can be effective in areas a President needs. Vacuums tend to get filled, Perhaps there is no better area demonstrating that a Vice President's duties are a product of the particular President's needs than the foreign policy vacuum being filled by Pence.**205** As Josh Rogin noted in an early Washington Post commentary, Pence's foreign policy role was one area in which the Vice President skillfully deviated from the President's positions. The skill came in Pence's ability to "navigate complex internal politics while service a president who has an unconventional view of foreign policy and the United States' role in the world. Pence, a traditional hawk influenced by his Christian faith, is carefully and deliberately assuming a stance that fits within the president's agenda while respecting the prerogatives of other senior White House aides."**206** And here is a classic example of a Vice President able to finesse a position in a policy area because of a President's deficiencies in that area. So early on Pence began to serve as an intermediary of sorts with U. S. allies concerned about a Trump Presidency.**207**

Punditry exists on both sides of the "Pence as administration spokesperson" debate.

During the second year of the Administration, the New York Times put forth an image of an independent Vice President, who played an active role vis a vis Republican candidates in the midterm elections. The piece viewed Pence's support for candidates not backed by Trump as evidence of this independence. But a more careful look at Pence's behavior suggests a very clever juggling act of carving out his own base for a future presidential run while simultaneously seemingly serving as the loyal underling. Moreover, Pence's willingness to do party politicking is reflective of a Vice President fitting into roles in which Presidents leave a vacuum.**208**

Recalling that the "administration spokesperson" role is often given to a Vice President during controversies, Trump gave Pence the difficult role of quarterback who served as a loyal "messenger" defending Trump's policies and actions.**209**

So, too, was Pence placed in this precarious position, as he took on defense of Trump's obstinate position on the southern border wall issue. The likeable Pence could serve as negotiator in a futile battle with the congressional opposition.**210** As Trump's administration became increasingly embroiled in controversy, there was endless speculation that an impeachment was not out of the question, and this speculation became Trump's reality nightmare in the wake of potential wrongdoing vis a vis policy towards Ukraine. For his part, Vice President Pence continued to play the quintessential vice presidential role of loyal servant, undoubtedly looking ahead to 2024, if not sooner.**211** But for Pence this is a two-edged sword, since his unswerving loyalty to Trumps is so disparate from what Pence at least formerly believed, that it cannot help but leave commentators to question the dangers of a potential Pence Presidency. Pence's political future is also tied to the Trump-Pence 2020 reelection campaign. Much as Walter Mondale learned after the Carter-Mondale 1980 defeat, even a hiatus of four years keeps a former Vice President tied to the administration under which s/he served.

THE IMPACT OF WHITE HOUSE STAFF

Some years ago, the then Vice President George H. W. Bush wrote an unsolicited note to this author. Bush had just read my article "Perspectives on the Vice Presidency," published in *The Presidential Studies Quarterly*.**212** The purpose of the article was to give an overview of the second office. This was certainly a topic that was covered in other articles and in the first and second editions of <u>American Prince, American Pauper: The Contemporary Vice Presidency and Presidential</u>

- Vice Presidential Relations**213** but not in the piece read by Vice President Bush, which was all for the better, since his remarks were not prompted any commentary in the article regarding staff. In his note of 11-26-82 to me, he wrote, "Dear Professor Natoli, I read with interest your article on the Vice-Presidency. It was good. One area that needs exploring is the relationship of the VP to the President's staff. This is a major thing. For me, it's working well. Well done. George Bush"**214**

In many ways, the vice presidential staff are akin to a "shadow" government, with only a heartbeat, impeachment, or resignation away from becoming the "first string." Vice President Bush's comments in his kind note were echoed by the late Vice President Hubert H. Humphrey's sister, Frances Humphrey Howard, when I coincidentally but fortuitously sat next to her at a Center for the Study of the Presidency conference luncheon in Minneapolis. In talking about the frustrations her brother met as Vice President, Mrs. Howard told me how difficult the Johnson White House staff made life for Humphrey. This had been earlier said by her brother during my 1973 interview with him.**215**

Observing the role of the Vice Presidency in foreign policy, political scientist Paul Kengor has justifiably noted that one additional wrinkle faced by a Vice President on the foreign policy side of involvement is "The Secretary of State Factor," pointing out that Vice President Nixon was able to be active in foreign affairs not only because of President Eisenhower's flexibility but because Secretary of State John Foster Dulles did not stand in Nixon's way, and indeed, "Dulles encouraged and aided it." Similarly President Clinton's Secretary of State Warren Christopher was supportive of Vice President Gore playing a large role in the foreign policy arena.**216** By contrast, Quayle suffered from Bush's Secretary of State Jim Baker's blocking Quayle from particular foreign policy areas, allegedly stemming from ideological differences between the two.**217** This contemptuous relationship is discussed by Quayle during his post vice presidential years in his work Standing Firm.**218**

Chapter 6

———✲✲✲———

THE VICE PRESIDENCY: THE IMPACT OF EVENTS AND PERSONALITIES

Being vice president is comparable to "a man in a cataleptic fit; he cannot speak; he cannot move; he suffers no pain; he is perfectly conscious of all that goes on, but has no part in it."

WOODROW WILSON'S VICE President, Thomas Marshall, would un-doubtedly be very surprised to view how the second office has changed since he made this observation. Many of the changes have come about, as noted in the "Preface" to this work, because of the growth of the "modern" Presidency's roles and dominance in U. S. politics and gov-ernment, with the second office growing correspondingly. And three of the nine unscheduled successions from the Vice Presidency to the Presidency occurred during the "modern" Presidency, as detailed in

Chapter 3 of this work, underscoring the need to have the person a heartbeat away fully prepared in the event of the circumstances beyond anyone's control. While there is no inevitability for a particular Vice President's stature, the office has reacted, too, to the combination of presidential and vice presidential personalities, changing demands, and often unanticipated events, as this chapter explores.

WATERGATE

The series of events that collectively became known as "Watergate" was far reaching in both origin and effects. These events must be analyzed thoroughly here, for they profoundly contributed to the shape of the contemporary Vice Presidency.

At the same time that the 1972 Democratic presidential candidate, Senator George McGovern, was lambasting the Nixon Administration as the "most corrupt administration in history," the "Eagleton" scenario was unfolding and lessening the credibility of the populist presidential candidate. Nixon scored a landslide victory, but, ironically, that landslide victory coincided with the emergence of Watergate, both the break-in at Democratic National Headquarters in 1972 and the series of events following the break-in and continuing over a period of two years into 1974.

While not directly or literally connected to the Watergate break-in and cover-up, the 1973 Agnew scandal nonetheless emerged as part of the total picture of an administration that was indeed perhaps "the most corrupt in history." As noted elsewhere in this work, once the disclosure of Vice President Spiro T. Agnew's indiscretions as Baltimore County executive had been made, the White House hoped that Agnew's problems would take the heat off the President. As the history of the Vice Presidency has demonstrated, the Vice President must always be expendable to the President. The Agnew resignation provided President Nixon the opportunity to at least symbolically forge a "new beginning," and thus the appointment of Gerald Ford as Agnew's successor.

The period of time from 1972 to 1973 established a new frame-work within which the Vice Presidency would be viewed. Symbolically, the Ford vice presidential confirmation hearings, following President Nixon's use of the Twenty-Fifth Amendment for the first time since its 1967 ratification, emphasized the need for a thorough scrutiny of vice presidential candidates. (It should be recalled here that the Eagleton Affair and the Agnew resignation were the backdrops against which the Ford hearings were conducted.) The need for a thorough investigation of the candidate was further emphasized by the very real awareness that this particular Vice President could well become President within a matter of months. It was widely expected that Nixon would be im-peached and convicted, or resign.

Thus, Gerald Ford received an unprecedented screening for the job, focusing on an issue that the Vice Presidency is really all about: the Presidency. This formed the essence of the vice presidential selection process from 1972 on; the Ford hearings simply gave greater intensity to this new concern. The hearings also help focus increased public and political attention on the second office – not only in terms of succes-sion to the Presidency (as, indeed, events since 1963 had already done), but also in terms of the functions of the second office itself.

Following his confirmation and inauguration as Vice President, Ford was in the public eye almost incessantly, for he was so likely to succeed Nixon. Thus, the Ford Vice Presidency brought even greater awareness of the already visible Vice Presidency. In a Nixon White House besieged by doubt and uncertainty, however, the duties assigned to Ford did not reflect any real change in the office.

By the time the Twenty-Fifth Amendment was used again to fill a vice presidential vacancy, the nation had become far more aware of the importance of the second office. Following the Nixon resigna-tion, Ford became the first unelected President in American history. Since he carried no national mandate, he had to be extremely cautious about his own choice of Vice President. He had to select someone who would give his "caretaker" administration as much credibility as possible. Thus, it was no accident that a figure as renowned as Nelson A. Rockefeller was selected. When the President first mentioned the office to Rockefeller in 1974, he did so with the heavy burden of having to establish legitimacy.

Rockefeller's prominence in national and international affairs gave the Ford Administration the tone of dignity and competence it needed. While some might have questioned Ford's credentials for the Presidency, none would challenge his credentials for the Vice Presidency.1 Moreover, Rockefeller's reputation for attracting talented people was of enormous value to a President who had to rid himself of the past President's entourage. But by the time Rockefeller finally received congressional confirmation in December, circumstances had changed rather dramatically, and the picture of the Vice Presidency Ford had drawn for Rockefeller only in August took on a different image and reality.

While Vice President Rockefeller did enjoy a policymaking position in the Ford White House, the duties he had expected to perform following his August conversation with the President never materialized. By December 19, the day Rockefeller assumed the Vice Presidency, a very different President Ford and White House organization existed. Part of what had happened, of course, was that between August and December President Ford had become familiar and comfortable with the Presidency. Thus, what he needed in a Vice President had changed. Specifically, in August President Ford had promised Rockefeller a domestic policy directorship with decision-making power. But while Rockefeller was responsible for the activities of the Domestic Council – the domestic counterpart of the National Security Council – his potential for utilizing the council as an implement of policymaking was not what he had expected it would be. This unanticipated difficulty arose precisely because of the changes that had occurred between August and December of 1974. Although Rockefeller's role as Vice President needed redefinition, Ford never quite did so. Neither did the President tell his staff what relationship he thought Rockefeller would have with both the President and the staff.2

By the time Rockefeller came to office, the Ford staff had been operative for several months; Rockefeller appeared somewhat as an afterthought, but as one who expected to be a vital part of the policy making process in domestic affairs, as Secretary of State Kissinger was in foreign affairs. Apparently, the Ford staff was unaware of the agreement (i.e., that the Vice President would serve as a domestic policy director) that Ford and Rockefeller had reached during the summer.3

While the domestic policy role he came to play did not meet his initial expectations, Rockefeller was able to exert significant influence in this area. Rockefeller was so committed that he bluntly referred to himself as a "staff assistant" to the Preident,4 causing the President's staff considerable irritation. They correctly judged that, while it would be difficult for *any* Vice-President to fulfill the role of a staff assistant – because the Vice President is a constitutionally elected official – Rockefeller in particular would not be able to subjugate himself in that role.

To those staff people who jealously guarded the perquisites of the Presidency, A Nelson Rockefeller would be considered dangerous. In fact, the President himself had pondered whether a Rockefeller Vice Presidency would upstage him.5 Ford need not have worried about being overshadowed, for no President is ever secondary to his Vice President.

One of the early controversies of the Ford-Rockefeller Administration centered around the Domestic Council. Rockefeller eventually agreed to abandon the idea of personal leadership of the council and to vest such leadership in council staff directors, selected by the Vice President himself. Rockefeller took this compromise directly to Ford, making clear that he intended to maintain a strong and active role in policymaking.6

Rockefeller was able to carve out a role for himself because of both his political savvy and his personal relationship with the President. In this regard, too, the President's own personality played a key role. Rockefeller immediately insisted that he hold weekly meetings with the

President. The President agreed, thereby strengthening their relationship and, more importantly, creating an environment in which that close relationship would be sustained.

The second agreement between Ford and Rockefeller concerned the Vice President's insistence that he be able to disagree publicly with the President. Rockefeller actually did so only once – on the issue of the New York City fiscal crisis – but the important point is that both men knew that open and honest disagreement was part of the ongoing relationship. Both demands demonstrate Rockefeller's basic approach to the Vice Presidency: he was determined to be active and to seek out areas of policymaking. The achievements of his relatively short tenure in office are testimony to his initiative. In addition to his work with the Domestic Council, Rockefeller initiated proposals leading to the creation of a federal energy development finance corporation and gave Ford input for domestic policy options in the State of the Union address. In addition, of course, Rockefeller inherited all of the statutory and ceremonial duties of the Vice Presidency.

While short-lived, the Rockefeller Vice Presidency was thus very active, but only because the Vice President was conscious of forging a role for himself and because the President under whom he served gave him such latitude. Thus, personality and circumstances are key in understanding the relationship between the two offices. As has been amply demonstrated in this book, the Vice President is subject almost entirely to presidential good favor and presidential needs. What happened to Rockefeller Ford's July 1975 announcement that he intended to run for the Presidency in his own right in 1976 is a prime example of this. Ford's announcement immediately intensified liberal-conservative tensions within the Republican Party, which now focused on whether Rockefeller would be Ford's running mate. In his initial statement, Ford expressed "great admiration" for Rockefeller and his confidence that "both of us can convince the delegates that individually and as a team, we should be nominated." Shortly thereafter, the President's campaign manager, Howard Callaway, declared that

Ford and Rockefeller would not run as a team.**7** Callaway said Ford approved of Rockefeller's performance, but in his words, "These are separate campaigns. Between now and the conventions next summer, I am not asking delegates if they will vote for Ford for President and Rockefeller for Vice President. I am asking them to vote for Ford for President, period."**8**

Why President Ford's *volte face* with regard to his future running mate? Ford was apparently concerned that Republican conservatives might abandon him and try to win the nomination for former California Governor Ronald Reagan. Shortly thereafter, Rockefeller indicated that he agreed with Callaway; he said disarmingly that "the nomination is for the President. When he's nominated, he decides who he wants to be his Vice President." Rockefeller went on to say that he was "not a candidates" and facetiously asked, "Have you ever heard of anyone running for Vice President?"**9** Ultimately, even Nelson Rockefeller was beaten by the nature of the second office.

CARTER-MONDALE: A MODEL FOR
THE VICE PRESIDENCY

The Carter-Mondale Administration further demonstrates this point. To the extent that Walter Mondale was a viable part of the administration, it was because one man – President Jimmy Carter – wanted him to be. The Mondale incumbency has served as a model for future administrations.

Mondale was a viable, though not visible, part of the administration from its outset – viable because of Carter's personality and political needs, and invisible because of Mondale's keen grasp of the Vice Presidency and his own personality.

In the post-Watergate era and the Agnew and Nixon resignations from office, candidate Carter was acutely aware of the importance of conducting a careful vice presidential search and of maintaining an open administration.

The circumstances of the Mondale selection clearly foretold the role he would play in the administration. As essentially the only Washington "insider" in the Carter camp, Mondale had knowledge that experience that Carter desperately needed, Mondale also possessed links interest and constituency groups that the President and his Georgia entourage lacked. As the protégé of the much-respected Hubert Humphrey, Walter Mondale added" legitimacy" to the relatively unknown administration. Of course, as the administration progressed, the President's needs inevitably changed, much as President Fords needs changed vis-à-vis Rockefeller. As was true of all of his predecessors, Mondale sometimes suffered the "ebb and flow" of the Vice Presidency, as Hubert Humphrey had termed it.[10]

Jimmy Carter was not unique when he promised an active role for his Vice President; all Presidents since Harry Truman have at least paid lip service to the need for a more active role for the Vice President. On one occasion during the campaign, Carter discussed the prospective role of his Vice President.

I have to be frank in telling you that the relative duties that would be accepted by me and by Senator Mondale if we are elected will have to be evolved   as we get to know one another better and as we discern each other's particular strengths and weaknesses and particular interests in matters of public importance.

I am determined, beyond was ever been done in this country, to put major
responsibilities on the Vice President if I'm elected.

I can't give you now any better analysis that that, but I have discussed it enough with him to know that he and I will be for searching for a way to let the Vice President be completely involved in our nation's affairs.[11]

Meanwhile, Mondale provided Carter with a very specific memo delineating his own expectations of what his role in a potential Carter Administration would be. Mondale informed Carter that he had consulted with former Vice Presidents Hubert Humphrey and Nelson Rockefeller and their staffs in an effort to gain perspective on the second office and the best role to carve out for himself. This resulted in a lengthy memo delineating a "set of relationships, functions and assignments" Mondale thought would be appropriate and useful in his service as Vice President under Carter. His first suggestion was that he not take on any specific area but rather serve as a "general adviser" so that the President would be "exposed to independent analysis not conditioned by what it is thought he wants to hear or often what others want him to hear. To achieve this role, Mondale noted the need for "frequent and comprehensive briefings from the CIA and other intelligence agencies" that reported to the President and "advance warnings of issues to be discussed at critical meetings." And here Humphrey's mentorship was central, with Mondale noting in the memorandum that "Senator Humphrey emphasized the importance of this point to me repeatedly. He was not given adequate briefings and was, therefore, unable to participate effectively on the National Security Council or in this general area of foreign and defense policy. Mondale also asked that he receive information from "key administrative officials who provide information to the President," that he "participate in Cabinet meetings, discussions with the Congressional leadership, meetings of the National Security Council, Domestic Council, and the economic policy group" as well as being provided a "staff representative of his own" for these Councils as well as having one of his own staffers participate in White House staff meetings. And Mondale listed a key point –indicated as such by the asterisk with which he marked it: "Access to you," via at least a weekly meeting and general ongoing access 12 Ryan Lizza of *The New Yorker* reported that "Joe Biden had . . . studied this memo."13 It can truly be said that the Mondale legacy set the office of the Vice Presidency on a new trajectory.

The streets of Washington, D. C. were still littered with the confetti of the inauguration when Carter announced his intention to send Mondale on an important trip to Western Europe to discuss issues of Middle West policy, economic policy toward the United States, and nuclear industrial technology with heads of government.14 Mondale described this task as "unprecedented for a Vice President, going to the major allies and opening up own new relationship, discussing sensitive issues, laying the groundwork for the summit and many, many other concerns."15 From the outset, however, Mondale worked quietly and behind the scenes.

While Mondale had learned much from his talks with his predecessors Rockefeller and Humphrey, he chose to reject one bit of advice: to identify himself with one particular area of interest and responsibility. Instead, he chose to involve himself in a wide range of issues. White not becoming Carter's "chief staff person," whom President-elect Carter had claimed Mondale would be, 16 the Vice President took on a general trouble-shooter role. As noted more extensively elsewhere in this work, Mondale his role as that of the President's "adviser on critical, broad issues affecting government; to be the bearer of bad news."17

As a generalist in the Carter White House, Mondale was free to attend any meeting he chose. Statutorily, of course, Vice Presidents are members of certain bodies, such as the National Security Council. Mere attendance at such meetings, however, does not mean that a Vice President has a policymaking role. What was different, however, about the Mondale role was that he attended *working* meetings of the National Security Council. With his senatorial background as the second-ranking Democrat on the Church Committee (investigating intelligence abuses), Mondale thus had the qualifications necessary to oversee the President's intelligence operations study. In addition, Mondale had a role in reviewing major foreign policy positions, and he seemed to enjoy a good working relationship with national security affairs adviser Zbigniew Brezinski.18

As in all presidential-vice president interactions, personalities played a crucial role in shaping the Carter-Mondale White House. President Carter was comfortable with his Vice President and seemed to enjoy the closes personal contact they shared. Indeed, much Mondale's time was spent with the President, and the move of his office from the Executive Office Building to the West Wing of the White House, within a few steps of the Oval Office, illustrated the role of the Vice President in this administration.

Mondale's easygoing, back-stage manner fit the vice presidential job description well. Indeed, early on it had been conjectured that Mondale's cautiousness, willingness to accommodate, and reticence would round out the liberalism Carter so desperately needed. Mondale knew when to speak out and when to be silent. He did not disappoint the early spectators. Mondale himself noted, "I think I'm a discreet person. In other words, when I have something I feel deeply I go to the President, and I don't go out and talk about it."[19] Mondale preferred to limit himself to private disagreement, which Presidents have increasingly demanded. He also limited himself to the private influencing of policies and issues, a strategy that his mentor, Hubert Humphrey, had found most effective. Mondale pointed out that he found the wisest route was to say little at White House meetings. "If I speak up," said the Vice President, "it kills discussion. A lot of people think I must be talking for the President. Second, if the President says something with which I disagree, I don't like to argue, in front of others. I'll go and tell him. Many times I've been very silent at these meetings and I'll go right in afterwards and tell him what I think."[20] His restrained public role has made it difficult to assess Mondale's full impact on the Carter White House. Through his trouble-shooter role, Mondale was able to engage in a myriad of activities beyond that of the roving ambassador begun early in his incumbency. Often serving as an administration spokesperson he served as a vital link to business groups.[21] He took on the steel industry for the Carter Administration, criticizing U. S. Steel in March 1978 for its price increase,[22] he vigorously defended the administration's SALT Treaty; and he severely criticized "the shameless attacks on people who voted their conscience on the Panama Canal issue.**23** As had other Vice Presidents, Mondale often substituted for the President when the White House needed to lend credibility to an issue or an area but did not want to have the President himself make an appearance. For example, Mondale was asked to address the May 19978 United Nations special session on disarmament in Carter's place. Because Carter and Secretary of State Cyrus Vance were to deal with Soviet Foreign Minister Andrei Gromyko one week after the session, neither could politically make the address Mondale could.**24**

Mondale was well regarded within the Democratic Party. This was increasingly important to the President as his own popularity sagged and plummeted until the Iranian and Afghanistan crises temporarily resurrected him both in public opinion polls and among fellow Democrats. In the interim, Mondale took to the political hustings and pursued the administration's party responsibilities. As one Democratic member of the House of Representatives put it, "Whatever people feel about Carter, they don't transfer it to Mondale. He knows how to campaign, he helps raise money, and he is also very popular here in the Midwest."**25** Mondale's extensive experience with this kind of politicking took enormous pressure off the President and a party worried that their titular leader might be an albatross. As the party and the administration approached the 1978 congressional elections, one vice presidential adviser summed up the state of affairs. "Mondale is clearly going to be the one to do the party's work this year. Because of the problems Carter is having – and also because Fritz is simply better at this party stuff – he will have to be the main one trying to save . . . congressional seats. This year, Mondale is Carter's point man."**26**

As Mondale campaigned for congressional candidates in 1978, he coupled his party role with his role as administration spokesman and hinted at the administration's 1979-1980 presidential campaign strategy. Speaking in Dubuque, Iowa, in April 1978, Mondale faced head-on the criticisms of the Carter Presidency and the administration's record. Carter, said his Vice-President, was having difficulties because he is willing to face hard issues and refused to "duck and run." Said Mondale, "I predict before this is over that Jimmy Carter is going to be one of the most respected and popular Presidents in American history because he was man enough to do his job."27 Once the Iran and Afghanistan crises intervened, Mondale quite effectively campaigned for the President in the 1980 re-nomination campaign, while Carter tended to the affairs of the world. The President rode to a comfortable victory in the early 1980 Iowa caucus.

During Carter's administration, when the President became too preoccupied with a trouble area, Mondale was asked to oversee much of the President's "normal" business. Such was the case during the fall of 1978 when Carter, engrossed in the campaign David talks with Egypt's Anwar Sadat and Israel Menachem Begin, asked Mondale to handle most domestic business while the three executives were secluded at Camp David.28 As presidential Press Secretary Jody Powell commented, "The President's attitude is that he wishes the Vice President, in essence, to assume the responsibility for virtually all other activities of government and leave him free to the maximum extent possible to concentrate on his work at Camp David."29 In addition, since Mondale's background in the Middle East was more extensive than that of the President. Mondale shuttled to Camp David to attend some of the sessions. Similarly, he took over many presidential burdens during the long hostage ordeal in Iran and the subsequent invasion of Afghanistan by the Soviet Union.

With regard to the thorn of presidential staff, the Mondale experience was no exception. While both Carter and Mondale worked hard to lessen the inevitable tensions, nonetheless problems arose. As noted elsewhere in this study, the White House staff even used the Vice President as a sacrificial lamb when the President's popularity plummeted during the summer of 1979. They suggested that Mondale was lazy, and they hinted that he might be dropped from the 1980 ticket.

But Carter ended all speculation with the announcement that Mondale would indeed be his running mate. As the President's popularity in the polls climbed during the ensuing Iran and Afghanistan crises, Mondale assumed many commitments and activities the President had to forego, especially on the presidential campaign trail. Throughout his vice presidential incumbency, Mondale also had a forum from which to serve as administration spokesperson in a number of other areas. For example, he forcefully picked up on what the President had merely hinted at in his January 1980 remarks to the nation regarding the Soviet invasion of Afghanistan. Whereas the President had only hinted at a U. S. boycott of the summer Moscow Olympics, his Vice President openly called for moving the games. This was a controversial point, but Mondale had heretofore taken on other controversial subjects in the name of the administration, such as in the natural gas filibuster, as well as in his public defense of the SALT Treaty, an area in which Mondale had contributed substantively.**30**

All of Mondale's assignments were, of course, dependent entirely on what Jimmy carter wanted. Mondale was acutely aware of this fact. "My future public life . . . depends upon the success of the Carter Presidency,"**31** Mondale said early in his incumbency. These words were indeed prophetic, for four full years following the defeat of the 1980 Carter-Mondale ticket, the Carter legacy followed 1984 presidential candidate Mondale.

TEAMWORK:
THE REAGAN-BUSH ADMINISTRATION

George Bush's early years in the White House witnessed the continuation of at least the symbolic changed brought by the carter-Mondale White House. The Vice President's office remained in the White House, exactly where Mondale's was. With regard to the matter of the Vice President's visibility, Bush remarked, "It might work for awhile. But the President's staff will look at you differently. I have a good relationship with the President's staff and my staff does, too. . . . If I'm out there with a high profile, holding press conferences, putting my spin on whatever it is, I won't have a [good] relationship with the President."**32**

Vice President Bush met with President Reagan virtually daily, when he attended national security briefings. And the two had a weekly luncheon to discuss "a range of issues."**33** Shortly following the 1980 electoral victory, the new Vice President had correctly speculated that he would have a role in foreign affairs and on the Hill, but he added, "I'm not going to be a lobbyist. I'll be talking to members of the Congress from time to time and on a selective basis."**34**

Regarding the role of his predecessor, Bush remarked, "Mondale had the best relationship with the President of any vice-president in history. . . . Mondale set a pattern – a mold – that I think is very good. It helped us to start off – President Reagan and me – on what I hope will be for him a constructive way to go. Clearly it is constructive for me. Mondale persevered. The general feeling is that he was a useful vice president."**35**

Bush observed that he could best fulfill his growth potential as Vice President if he remembered the cardinal rule regarding viability and visibility. In all the statements he made, Bush consistently defended the President and spoke forcefully in support of administration policies.**36** For example, Bush, who as a candidate in the 1980 Republican primaries had opposed Ronald Reagan and labeled Reagan's economic program "voodoo economics," as Vice President embraced that same program. In fact, Bush became a staunch spokesman for it. Indeed, Bush began to play down his differences with Reagan as soon as he received the 1980 vice-presidential nomination. Shortly after the beginning of the new administration, in a March 1981 interview with Godfrey Sperling, Jr. of the *Christian Science Monitor*, Bush was asked, "When you called the Reagan program 'voodoo economics,' what did you have in mind?" Bush responded, "That's not worth discussing anymore. . . . If I start pointing out even in a substantive way present differences (which there are none at this point) – well, that's not my concept of how you something in my job—make something good happen." Then, in the same interview, Bush offered a defense of the program. "Whenever you chart an economic course in troubled economic seas like these, there is a certain amount of inexactitude in the science of prediction. But having said that, I think that the need for acceptance of this program which is threefold – spending constraints, tax relief, and regulatory relief – is unarguable."**37**

Similarly, as President Reagan came under Democrat's charges – especially during the congressional campaigns of 1982 – that he lacked compassion for the poor and less fortunate in America, his Vice President took on a forceful defense of the President. In an appearance on the "Good Morning, America" show, Bush charged the Democrats with conducting a propaganda campaign, adding, "For these demagogues to accuse the President of having ice water in his blood" – Bush was referring to a remark made by House Speaker Thomas P. "Tip") O'Neill in a televised interview – 'it gets my bile really moving."**38**

Bush's defense of the Reagan economic program and its effects upon various segments of Americans continued throughout his incumbency and it logically became a part of his role in the 1984 Reagan-Bush reelection campaign.**39** In his acceptance speech at the 1984 Republican Convention, Bushed label the Democrats the part of "tax and spend, tax and spend." Said Bush, "Mr. Mondale calls [his] promise to raise taxes an act of courage. But it wasn't courage, it was just habit." Drawing a contrast between the Democratic and Republican conventions, Bush suggested the former was the "temple of doom," while he characterized his own party's message as "the American people want less spending and less regulation, not more taxes."**40**

Bush's defense of and deference and dedication to Ronald Reagan paid off. Reagan, who initially had misgivings over giving Bush the second place on the 1980 ticket, later frequently referred to Bush as the "best" Vice President in history. Reagan said so throughout the 1984 campaign, and repeated this during the televised presidential debates with Walter Mondale (whom himself had been quite an extraordinary and active Vice President). Meanwhile, Bush even won the respect of some members on the Republican Party's right; in 1980, the right had been enraged by the Bush selection. In a 1984 *Dallas Morning News* Republican delegate poll, Bush received 48 percent support; Congressman Jack Kemp received 26 percent; former Senate Majority Leader Howard Baker received 16 percent. As 1988 neared, other Republicans eyed the presidential nomination, but Bush's proven abilities and loyalty combined with Ronald Reagan's adulation of his Vice President placed Bush in the advantageous position as heir apparent. Riding on what the Democratic vice presidential nominee labeled "the illusion of prosperity," George Bush became the first Vice President since Martin Van Buren in 1936 to win election to the Presidency directly from the Vice Presidency.

THE IMPACT OF PERSONALITY OR RESPONDING TO CIRCUMSTANCES?

DICK CHENEY AND THE "IMPERIAL" VICE PRESIDENCY?

References to Dick Cheney as "President Cheney" or as "Co-President," or among some commentators as "the Imperial Vice President" surrounded the Bush-Cheney Administration throughout its tenure and even following it. While Cheney's role was indeed powerful, it is a misrepresentation to assert that Cheney's incumbency in the second office demarcated the beginning of "The Imperial Vice Presidency."41

While the Cheney selection was appealing to Bush partially because Cheney had no presidential ambitions of his own, "official" ambitions bely the ultimate emergence of ultimate fruitions, and many a commentator has commented on the "Cheney Presidency," or "The Cheney White House," or quite specifically, Shirley Anne Warshaw's excellent work, The Co-Presidency of Bush and Cheney.42 Importantly, Warshaw points out that "Cheney's emergence as co-president was hardly scripted or anticipated by the campaign staff or by

George W. Bush when he brought Cheney onto the presidential ticket in July. Bush and Cheney, unlike Reagan and Ford twenty years earlier, never discussed sharing power in a co-presidency. Cheney's unprecedented role in the administration resulted, instead, from a confluence of factors that restructured the traditional relationship between president and vice president," which included the expansion of the Vice President's role, with Cheney having an ongoing role in issues across the board.43

So while this did not seem to be the vision as the two set out for campaign 2000. Ironically, however, the ins and outs of that campaign may very well have put Cheney in a far more advantageous position than either he or Bush might have imagined.

As election night came to a crawl of a close, it was unclear what the outcome would be. Some media had declared Al Gore the winner of Florida's electoral votes; others claimed it for Bush. And the outcome of the election by that point depended entirely upon Florida. With neither Bush nor Gore as President-elect, the drama began and continued for weeks. Nonetheless, Dick Cheney hit the ground running, even before the presidential nominee convinced him to serve on the ticket.

That drama put Dick Cheney in the position of "administration spokesperson" even before there was an administration. Indeed, one of the first actions having but a slim majority in the Senate with only fifty votes and the incoming Vice President being the tie-breaker, moderate Republicans wanted the administration to tone down its conservativism. But, "Cheney disabused them of this notion straightaway. He was polite but blunt: We got elected, and we're not going to moderate out positions. Full speed ahead."44

Enter 9/11 – with a still neophyte President and a very experienced Vice President. The 9/11 attacks set the scene for a very involved Vice President. And Cheney was more than willing to be that. But for the combination of these two factors the Cheney incumbency might not have turned out to be potentially the most powerful Vice President in the history of the office to date. "9/11" has to be seen as extending far beyond a day to remember; rather, it is better described as a major demarcation point in U. S. history, politics, and culture and Dick Cheney became a key player in that new era.

With President Bush out of Washington, D.C. for a brief visit to a second grade class, and Vice President Cheney at the White House, Cheney took charge. In fairness to the Vice President, the utter chaos demanded his calm composure. Meanwhile, the chaos included telecommunications problems, with President Bush apparently having difficulty establishing contact with the White House. Later analyses reveal that there was a communications overload, largely generated by White House personnel with the President. Still controversial is an order by the Vice President to shoot down unidentified planes. While both Bush and Cheney claim the President had given Cheney authorization to do so, critics argue that there is no record of such a communication. As noted by Washington Post Staff writer Dana Millbank, "Cheney's comment, which were soon proved erroneous, were detailed in a report issued . . .by the commission investigating terrorist attacks. The comments are part of the considerable confusion that surrounded top government officials as the tense drama unfolded."**45** As it turned out, the military ignored Cheney's order. One issue of concern is that the Vice President is not in the military chain of command. That said, this author would argue that, with the Vice President a "heartbeat away" from the Presidency, it would seem that this an area in need of reform to have the Vice President immediately follow the President in the military chain of command.

Dick Cheney's extensive foreign policy experience – and views – harkened back to a different era. Coupled with his confident and persistent demeanor – one Republican Senator, moderate Lincoln Chafee, questioning the wisdom of the administration's aggressive moves across the board noted of Cheney, "What really unnerved me was his attitude. He welcomed conflict."**46** Cheney was instrumental in gaining congressional support for U.S. military action in Iraq, including wearing down House Majority Leader Dick Armey, who had not been persuaded by numerous intelligence briefings in the White House. But then the Vice President "paid a call and summoned Armey to his office in the West Wing. 'When you hear the whole story, you'll agree with me. . . . The VP wasted none of the time on rosy talk of ridding Iraqis of their dictator or of installing a fountainhead of democracy in the Middle East. He was all about imminent threat" and although Armey still had doubts he finally succumbed, because "Dick Cheney had credibility with him."47

The Cheney Vice Presidency has typically been depicted as a major surge of power for the second office. This view detracts from understanding the essence of the second office. There is no denying that Vice President Dick Cheney played a very powerful role in the administration of George W. Bush, but that role was unique to that administration and did not completely transform the *office* of the Vice Presidency. His extensive domestic and foreign policy would have been valued additions to any administration and were especially so for the neophyte Bush. Even prior to the official declaration that Bush and Cheney had captured the White House in 2000, Cheney was at work as a spokesperson. It was Cheney who was often the voice during the controversy over whom actually should be President. Once in office, Cheney's broad political expertise was of immeasurable importance to the Bush Administration. As the noteworthy scholar Shirley Anne Warshaw quite correctly observed, "Cheney's power permeated the administration," beginning even prior to the official beginning of the Bush-Cheney years when Cheney was in charge of the transition team.48 He served as a vocal adviser in formulating administration policy and then in defending it, be it at home or abroad. Following the tragedy of 9/11, Cheney championed the President's actions in the Middle East, be it in Afghanistan or Iraq or elsewhere.

Rather than seeing a transformation of the second office at the hands of Dick Cheney, it is crucial to keep in mind that the Cheney

Vice Presidency in reality underscores the very *nature* of the Vice Presidency. Cheney was a powerful Vice President only because George W. Bush needed and wanted him to be. Once again, the role of the Vice President is a reflection of the needs and personality of the incumbent under whom the Vice President serves.

THE IMPACT OF PRESIDENTIAL AND VICE PRESIDENTIAL PERSONALITIES:

The OBAMA-BIDEN "BROMANCE"

Joe Biden's Vice Presidency demonstrates the essence of the second office. Biden was loyal to a fault. He was active within the realm carved out for him by the President. Biden's knowledge of foreign policy on occasion resulted in a departure from official administration policy, but it is indeed conceivable that that seeming departure was in reality depicting the Vice President in the role of "administration spokesperson" who can occasionally send up "trial balloons." As Hubert Humphrey, quoted earlier in this work, said, "A Vice President can be an administration spokesperson, because the administration can always disavow you." Biden's long-time reputation for verbal gaffes may have come in handy in this role. On the other hand, the vice presidential role of presidential plenipotentiary can be very useful to an administration. This was certainly the case during Vice President Biden's visit to Israel, during which Israeli Prime Minister Benjamin Netanyahu flagrantly defied President Obama's position that Israeli settlements must cease to be constructed. It was slap in the face for Obama, but delivered on the Vice President's cheek.

From the outset, indeed, when presidential nominee Obama asked Biden to join him on the ticket, as journalist Jules Witcover has noted, "Biden . . . made clear he had no interest in being an ornament, and Obama had made it similarly clear that he had no interest or intention of making him one. Biden's own job description as adviser in chief to the president without specific portfolio squared with what Obama said he wanted in his vice president."**49**

Biden's meetings with several of his predecessors in the Vice Presidency – Mondale, George W. H. Bush and Al Gore – helped shape the views he held of what his own role should be as the heir apparent, with Walter Mondale's memo to Carter being harmonious with what both Biden and Obama envisioned. Moreover, much as had Carter and Mondale, the presidential and vice presidential staffs "had a degree of intertwining and overlap."**50**

Early in the Obama Administration, Vice President Biden's "official" jobs placed him in the thick of the many inherited problems facing the administration. Biden's long service in the Senate allowed him to serve as an administrative liaison, albeit, as Hubert Humphrey noted, for the most part quietly and behind the scenes. And Biden's long service in the U. S. Senate served him well in assisting the administration in foreign policy matters regarding Iraq and Afghanistan as well as pre-inaugural trips to the two countries as well as Pakistan.**51**

President Obama certainly underscored his concern for economic recovery by naming his Vice President to oversee infrastructure spending under Obama's stimulus package. And Biden's assignments did not stop there. As Mark Leibovitch reported for the New York Times in March of 2009, the President himself observed of his Vice President that Joe Biden is like a basketball player "who does a bunch of things that don't show up in the stat sheet. . . . He gets that extra rebound, takes the charge, makes that extra pass." Leibovitch further underscored a key role that Biden was allowed to play. Quoting Obama's Chief of Staff Rahm Emmanuel, Leibovitch observed, "When there's group-think going on, the vice president tends to push the envelope in the other direction."**52** During his incumbency in the second office, Biden certainly did so in conversations on a range of policy issues, both domestic and international, ranging from the advisability of health care reform to Iraq and Afghanistan. But this is what President Barack Obama wanted and needed in a Vice President. By the time the

2012 re-election bid arose, President Barack Obama clearly knew the strength of his teamwork with Biden.

The Obama-Biden relationship reflects an interesting phenomenon. While at the outset, Obama realized he needed Biden to balance personal background, the personal relationship between President and Vice President was an evolutionary one. As the years went on, the two development deeper respect and even affection for each other, to the point where their friendship made for a very powerful twosome. The genuine affection the two had for each other was clearly obvious, perhaps no more poignantly than when Biden's son, Beau, was diagnosed with a terminal brain tumor. Obama was there for his Vice President, not as a political leader, but as a friend. At one point, Biden talked about the possible need to sell his home to help pay for Beau's medical expenses. The story is well-known by now, but worth repeating. Obama insisted he not do that, and offered to give Biden the money. And when Beau Biden lost his battle to cancer, it was Obama who the Biden family asked to deliver the eulogy. Obama did so from the heart and with tears in his eyes. Afterwards, the two friends gave each other a long, supportive hug.

A TURBULENT PRESIDENCY, A HOPEFUL VICE PRESIDENT?

DONALD TRUMP AND MIKE PENCE

Just a little over six months into the Trump Presidency, *The New Republic* asked a chilling question in a piece of the same title: "Is Mike Pence the 'Deep State' That Trump Fears?"**53** The journal's commentary is an insightful piece into the potential inner workings of a deeply divided White House and Republican Party and cites the reactions of both to a *New York Times* article that claimed developing opposition to Trump in 2020 -- indeed, a "shadow campaign," a claim that Pence vehemently denied and called "disgraceful and offensive to me, my family, and our team."**54**

The Trump-Pence ticket seemed like a "match made in Heaven," which some observers have commented is the way Mike Pence actually saw it – the path to the place God meant him to be – has resulted in the quintessential model of the question of whether the Vice Presidency is a steppingstone or a stumbling block to the Presidency. As has been noted above, Trump needed the pure "holy man" to appeal to evangelicals. Pence, whose gubernatorial reelection prospects in Indiana seemed dim, needed to be propelled on a new path. Could Pence have even remotely anticipated just how controversial a Presidency Donald Trump would have? The answer matters little, since things are what they are. Both Trump and Pence are in the race for reelection together, with an administration record that will need a lot of explaining on the campaign trail: ghosts of the alleged Russian involved in the 2016 U. S. elections; the continuing firings of presidential advisers who raised any opposition to Trump; the lingering questions of the role played by the Trump family; the divisiveness created by the Trump rallies and rhetoric; the impeachment that would always be associated with the Trump Presidency; the lack of leadership at the presidential level during the COVID 19 pandemic. And even if the Trump-Pence ticket wins reelection and there is more of the same in the Trump Presidency, where would that leave Pence in 2024? If the ticket loses, and Pence finds himself in the position Walter Mondale was in in 1984 – with a hiatus from his association with the Trump Administration but stuck with a legacy to explain, Mike Pence's future will face more obstacles than any Vice President in the history of the office.

EPILOGUE: SUGGESTIONS FOR RESTRUCTURING THE SECOND OFFICE: A CONCLUDING NOTE

The Founding Fathers provided for the presidential succession with the least possible delay to avoid hiatus in the functioning of government. The shocking and tragic assassination of President John F.

Kennedy in Dallas underscores having had a Vice President available and ready to assume the reins of government. Perhaps at no single moment before or since has the awesome importance of the Vice President been so apparent.

A different situation occurred with Watergate. As Watergate enveloped President Nixon, the need to fill the Vice Presidency vacated by the resignation of Spiro Agnew became urgent. The extended period of time required to select candidates and to secure the necessary congressional confirmation of the appointee did not reassure the public of uninterrupted presidential leadership.

Critics of the vice presidential office correctly maintain that it is not necessarily a training ground for the Presidency. Even though Vice Presidents may be well versed in critical government areas and problems, there is only one executive upon whom responsibility falls. Increasingly, however, the Vice-President has held promise for the development of the office in both domestic and foreign affairs. Walter Mondale's function as adviser to the President, albeit with a low profile, marked the continuing preparation of an individual who had been considered for the Presidency when tapped for the number two spot. George Bush, who had been a contender for the 1980 Republican presidential nomination before accepting second place, masterfully dealt with the crisis imposed by the March 1981 assassination attempt on the President and would have been prepared to assume the presidential reins. Vice President Dan Quayle, many felt, was a throwback to a different era of the Vice Presidency and often the object of political pundits' jokes. History didn't give Quayle to tell us one way or the other. Vice President Al Gore was fully in the loop in the Clinton White House, as has been Vice President Richard ("Dick") Cheney. Both men, regardless of dramatically divergent ideological positions, are certainly of presidential caliber. Indeed, Vice President Al Gore won the popular vote for election to the Presidency in 2000, but George Walker Bush captured the electoral vote.

One approach to changing the structure of the Vice Presidency would be to require Presidents to designate specific powers to the Vice

President. Such a change would require a constitutional amendment, as those engaged in the 1980 Republican vice presidential talks with former President Gerald Ford were reminded. In that case, presidential candidate Reagan was severely criticized for not understanding the indivisibility of presidential power, and Ford's request for considerable presidential power in exchange for running on the Reagan ticket was abandoned.

Perhaps Ford's suggestions, made several months later, should be given careful consideration. In offering a commentary on the Presidency itself, Ford noted the frustration of disregarded orders. As a possible source of aid in this regard, the former President suggested "using the Vice President as a real Chief of Staff, both to control the administrative bureaucracy and to see that Administration relations with the Congress really mesh. Having been the Vice President and having been the President, I know that there has to be a better delegation of responsibility between the two offices. . . . The President has always relied much more upon his own people. I believe you have got to take an elected official, a Vice President, and move him right into the West Wing of the White House as the Chief of Staff of the whole Administration."55

It can nonetheless be argued that an informal understanding that a President will assign his Vice President major roles in either domestic or foreign affairs is both constitutionally feasible and a flexible enough mandate so as not to unduly harness a President. Any Vice President incapable either intellectually or politically of being given such assignments should not be in line of presidential succession. Such an understanding would force presidential candidates to give even greater thought to the qualifications of the individual chosen as a vice presidential running mate.

These suggestions are aimed at strengthening rather than abolishing the Vice Presidency. The recent history of the office has demonstrated that it can encompass significant functions. To abolish the Vice Presidency and create a system of succession whereby a member of the legislature would act as President until a presidential election could be held, as suggested by the late historian Arthur Schlesinger, Jr., would only create new problems. Under such a plan, control of the White House might shift from one party to another abruptly. The public must have an understudy prepared and waiting in the wings; this individual must be someone chosen in the previous election rather than a member of the Congress who may be a relatively unknown figure and unprepared to assume the highest office in the land, no matter for however a short period of time.

Perhaps much of the dissatisfaction and confusion concerning the office of the Vice Presidency is misplaced and derives from the egregious flaws and ramifications of the Twenty-Fifth Amendment. Its repeal or amendment is highly y desirable. The need for such action should action should not be equated with abolishing the Vice Presidency. Two separate issues are involved.

The Ford-Rockefeller Administration was an aberration that departed widely from a basic principle of American government, that is, that the President is elected by and represents all of the people. Such a deviation is not to be repeated. If the Twenty-Fifth Amendment is to remain an operative part of the Constitution, it should be qualified by a further amendment providing for a special national election in the event an *unelected* Vice President should succeed to the Presidency for a remainder of a presidential term exceeding two years. This would provide stability of succession via the Vice Presidency and minimize the length of time a President by succession (who had not been elected to the Vice Presidency) would be apt to serve as the only national leader of the United States.

In his critique of the office, Schlesinger contended that the only function of the Vice Presidency is as a jumping ground to the Presidency, or at least to the presidential nomination. While this is obviously true, what Schlesinger perceives as a negative may be viewed alternatively as an already evolving solution to the challenging problem of the position of the Vice Presidency: individuals capable of being President are indeed willing to spend several years in the second office, virtually at the mercy of the President's whim. Precisely because the Vice Presidency provides a built-in advantage, the office has appealed to individuals of the stature of Hubert Humphrey, Nelson Rockefeller, Walter Mondale, George Bush, and Dick Cheney, to cite just several. Politicians of high caliber who show interest in the Vice Presidency today are aware that the office has fare more public interest and potential than it had several decades ago. Those who come to occupy the second-highest office, even though perhaps not destined to succeed to the Presidency, are much less likely to be the type of political figures that characterized the office in the past.

Whatever formal changes may be made by constitutional, statutory elaboration, presidential order and personalities, the evolution of the Vice Presidency has been, and will continue to be, also conditioned by the opportunities and challenges of future events. It may be said with some certainty that such developments as are likely to occur in the foreseeable future will continue to depend in large measure on the person who occupies the Presidency and on what that person is willing to share with and assign to the Vice President.

The contemporary Vice Presidency has evolved considerably since Harry Truman struggled to overcome his inadequate preparation in that office. Public awareness of the office has increased both because of the strength of its incumbents and because of several disabilities and successions during that period. Since 1952 Presidents have made much better use of the more prestigious incumbents, and these Vice Presidents have become serious presidential contenders. The Vice Presidency is no longer a "superfluous Excellency." It is indeed a unique institution: it may be everything, as Hubert Humphrey pointed out, or it may be nothing. Which it is depends on both the President and the Vice President, their likes and dislikes, their personalities and temperaments, and their understanding of the political realities facing the executive branch and the nation. It is an office, Humphrey once said, that is ultimately "filled with all the uncertainties of human emotions."**56** Indeed, it is both a prince and a pauper.

APPENDIX A
"CIVIL RIGHTS AND RIOTING"

(A statement delivered by Governor Spiro Agnew, July 1967)

Our country is as much threatened by the lawless rioting in our streets as it is by our enemies abroad. In such a serious time, the people of a State are entitled to a clear and direct statement of their Governor's position. This is such a statement.

In the first place, it is evident that there is ample cause for unrest in our cities. There is still discrimination and, in too many cases, there are deplorable slum conditions. Our Negro citizens have not received, and in many cases are not receiving, equal educational, job and housing opportunities, The gains recently made, while good, are not enough.

I believe that responsible militants within the Negro leadership should use every means available to place legitimate pressure on those in authority to break the senseless and artificial barriers of racial discrimination. But legitimate pressure — the power of the vote, the power of organized political, economic and social action — does not give any person or group a license to commit crimes.

Burning, looting, and sniping, even under the banner of civil rights, are still arson, larceny and murder. There are established penalties for such felonies, and we cannot change the punishment simply because the crime occurred during a riot. The laws must be consistently enforced to protect all our people. If any angry man burns his neighbor's house, loots his neighbor's store, or guns his neighbor down, no reason for his anger will be enough of an excuse.

In Maryland, rioting or inciting to riot, no matter what wrong is said to be the cause, will not be tolerated. There are proper ways to protest and they must be used. It shall now be the policy in this State to immediately arrest any person inciting to riot and to not allow that person to finish his vicious speech. All lawbreakers will be vigorously and promptly prosecuted.

Acts of violence will not be later forgiven just because the criminal after a while adopts a more reasonable attitude. The violent cannot be allowed to sneak unnoticed from the war dance to the problem solving meeting. No, the problem-solving conference must be reserved for those who shun lawlessness, who win their places at the conference table by leadership that builds rather than destroys.

The problem-solving must be done by constructive militants such as the Wilkinses, Kings, Youngs and Randolphs—not by the Carmichaels, Joneses and Browns. But it should include the younger responsible leadership as well as older, more established leaders. Responsibility is the yardstick.

It shall continue to be my firm policy to do everything possible to provide jobs, good housing and better educational opportunities for the poor and underprivileged, both Negro and white, in Maryland. I will meet with any responsible leaders to discuss the problems that confront us. I will not meet with those who engage in or urge riots or other criminal acts as weapons to obtain power.

In conclusion, I commend the citizens of both races who have continued to conduct themselves with intelligent restraint in spite of great pressure. I share the sorrow of those who have suffered and who continue to suffer from the reckless acts of a few.

For the confused and weak who seek to excuse, appease and rationalize for the criminals who threaten our society, I have only pity.

Appendix B

(A statement delivered by Governor Spiro Agnew, April 11, 1967)

I did not ask you here to recount previous deprivations, nor to hear me enumerate prior attempts to correct them. I did not request your presence to bid for peace with public dollars.

Look around you and you will notice that everyone here is a leader – and that each leader present has worked his way to the top. If you'll observe, the ready-mix, instantaneous type of leader is not present. The circuit-riding, Hanoi-visiting type of leader is missing from the assembly. The caterwauling, riot-inciting, burn-America-down type of leader is conspicuous by his absence. That is no accident, ladies and gentlemen, it is just good planning. And in the vernacular of today – "that's what it's all about, baby."

Several weeks ago a reckless stranger to this city, carrying the credentials of a well-known civil rights organization, characterized the Baltimore police as "enemies of the Black man." Some of you here, to your eternal credit, quickly condemned this demagogic proclamation. You condemned it because you recognized immediately that it was an attempt to undermine lawful authority- the authority under which you hold your leadership position. You spoke out against it because you knew it was false and was uttered to attract attention and inflame.

When you, who courageously slapped hard at irresponsibility, acted, you did more for civil rights than you realize. But when white leaders openly complimented you for your objective, courageous action, you immediately encountered a storm of censure from parts of the Negro community. The criticism was born of a perverted concept of race loyalty and inflamed by the type of leader whom I earlier mentioned is not here today.

And you ran. You met in secret with that demagogue and others like him- and you agreed, according to your published reports that have not been denied, that you would not openly criticize any black spokesman, regardless of the content of his remarks. You were beguiled by the rationalization of unity; you were intimidated by veiled threats; you were stung by insinuations that you were Mr. Charlie's boy, by epithets like "Uncle Tom." God knows I cannot fault you who spoke out for breaking and running in the face of what appeared to be overwhelming opinion in the Negro community. But actually it was only the opinion of those who depend on chaos and turmoil for leadership- those who deliberately were not invited today. It was the opinion of a few, distorted and magnified by the silence of most of you here today.

CHAPTER NOTES

Introduction

1. Louis Clinton Hatch, <u>History of the Vice-Presidency of the United States</u>, revised by Earl L. Shoup (Westport, Ct.:Greenwood Press, 1934, 1970), p. 157.

2. Ibid., pp.5-6.

3. Ibid., pp, 45, 47.

4. Ibid.,p. 9.

5. Marcus Cunliffe, <u>American Presidents and the Presidency</u> (McGraw-Hill, 1968, 1972), pp. 213-14.

6. Wilfred E. Binkley, <u>The Man in the White House: His Powers and Duties</u> (Baltimore: Johns Hopkins University Press, 1958), p. 268.

Chapter 1.

1. Louis Clinton Hatch, <u>History of the Vice-Presidency of the United States</u>, revised by Earl L. Shoup (Westport, Conn.: Greenwood Press, 1934, 1970), p. 67.

2. Ibid., p. 68.

3. Ibid., p. 85.

4. Ibid., p. 419.

5. Bill Welch, Interview held at his Washington, D.C., office, March 1974.

6. "A New Kind of Vice President?" U.S. News 66 (March 16, 1969) : 32-34; "A look Inside the Nixon Administration," U.S. News 67 (October 6, 1969): 32-38.

7. Rowland Evans and Robert D. Novak, <u>Nixon in the White House</u> (New York: Random House, 1971), p. 311.

8. Lee Jordan in correspondence with author, December 10, 1973.

9. Evans and Novak, pp. 311-12.

10. "Spiro Speaks," *Economist* 33 (November 1, 1969): 50.

11. Ibid.

12. Whitney M. Young, Oral History Interview, Lyndon B. Johnson Library, Austin, Texas.

13. Arthur M. Schlesinger, Jr., <u>A Thousand Days </u>(Boston: Houghton Mifflin, 1965), p. 706 .

14. George Christian Interview held at his Austin, Texas, office, April 1973; see also "Apprentice President," *Economist* 213 (December 26, 1964): 1423.

15. Senator Gale McGee, Interview held at his U.S. office, Washington, D.C., March 1974.

16. Ibid.

17. Christian, Interview.

18. Walter Jenkins, Interview Held at his Austin, Texas, office, April 1973. See also Hale Boggs, Oral History Interview, John F. Kennedy Library, Columbia Point, Massachusetts, pp. 17-18.

19. Schlesinger, p. 706.

20. Ibid., pp. 706-707.

21. Charles Daly, Oral History Interview, John F. Kennedy Library, Columbia Point, Massachusetts, pp. 34-35.

22. Norbert Schlei, Oral History Interview, John F. Kennedy Library, Columbia Point, Massachusetts, p. 44ff.; Clarence Mitchell, Oral History Interview, Lyndon B. Johnson Library, Austin, Texas, pp. 22-34; Roy Wilkins, Oral History Interview, Lyndon B. Johnson , p. 1ff.; Robert C. Weaver, Oral History Interview, Lyndon B. Johnson Library, Austin, Texas, pp. 1-4; George Reedy papers, (AF) Container 6, Civil Rights, Lyndon B. Johnson Library, Austin, Texas; VP Papers Box 5, Container: Civil Rights, July 13-July 31, 1963, Lyndon B. Johnson Library, Austin, Texas.

23. Hubert Humphrey, Interview held at a U.S. Senate reception room, Washington, D.C., March 1974.

24. Ibid.

25. Harry S Truman, Years of Decisions (Garden City, N.Y.: Doubleday, 1955), pp. 57, 196ff.; Senator John Sparkman, Interview held at his U.S. Senate office, Washington, D.C., March 1974.

26. Alben W. Barkley, "The Vice Presidency," Speech File 63M143. Box XXII. 1952, pp. 1-2. Alben W. Barkley Papers, University of Kentucky Library, Lexington, Kentucky. See also Truman, *Years of Decision*, p. 57.

27. Donald R. Matthews, *U.S. Senators and Their World* (New York: Vintage Books, 1960), p. 101ff.

28. Ibid., Chapter 5 in its entirety; Christian, Interview. Senator Gale McGee has indicated that the high degree of "clubbishness" during the Kennedy-Johnson Senate days has lessened; McGee, Interview.

29. Senator Herman Talmadge, Interview held at his U.S. Senate office, Washington, D.C., March 1974.

30. Humphrey, Interview.

31. James MacGregor Burns, John Kennedy: A Political Profile (New York: Harcourt, Brace, & World, 1961), p. 14.

32. Welch, Interview.

33. "I Enjoy It," *Newsweek* 65 (March 15, 1965): 28-29.

34. Albert Eisele, Almost to the Presidency (Blue Earth, Minnesota: Piper Co., 1972), p. 235ff.; Louis W. Koenig, The Chief Executive (New York: Harcourt, Brace & World, 1964, 1968), p. 162; Welch, Interview; Humphrey, Interview; "The Humphreys: Right Image for '68?," *U.S. News* 65 (September 9, 1968): 379ff; and Allan H. Ryskind, *Hubert* (New York; Arlington House 1968), p. 320.

35. See also "Vice President of Many Causes?"; "The Bright Spirit,; *Time* 87 (April 1, 1966): 21-25; "I Enjoy It"; "Happy Understudy," *Saturday Review* 48 (May 8, 1965): 16-17.

36. "Happy Understudy."

37. Humphrey, Interview.

38. McGee, Interview.

39. Richard H. Rovere, <u>The Eisenhower Years</u> (New York: Mentor books, 1960, 1956), p. 297.

40. "Nixon's Own Story of 7 Years in the Vice Presidency," *U.S. News* 48 (May 16, 1960): 98-106. See also Rovere, <u>The Eisenhower Years</u>, pp. 298-99. For more on Nixon in the legislature, see Ralph DeToledano, <u>One Man Alone: Richard Nixon</u> (New York: Funk & Wagnalls, 1969), p. 163ff.

41. Time (February 24, 1975): 15.

42. New York Times, October 1, 1977.

43. Ibid., October 5, 1977.

44. Ibid.

45. Marie D. Natoli, "Vice Presidency: Walter Mondale in the Lion's Den," *Presidential Studies Quarterly* (Winter 1978): 100-102

46. Ibid.

47. "Walter Mondale," the MacNeil/Lehrer Report, February 1977 (WNET/13, New York City).

48. Finlay Lewis, <u>Mondale: Portrait of an America Politician</u> (New York: Harper & Row, 1980), p. 247.

49. Ibid., p. 247.

50. Humphrey, Interview.

51. Vice President Thomas Marshall refused to pick up the constitutionally ambiguous gauntlet of the gap in the Presidency; the result was a period of no leadership while President Woodrow Wilson lay incapacitated. Earlier, Vice-President Arthur had behaved similarly, assuming the Presidency's powers (and, of course, the office) only when he was certain Garfield had breathed his last breath. And Richard Nixon was the epitome of discretion during the Eisenhower illnesses, even going as far as to symbolize, by presiding from his own chair and not from that of the President, that he was acting in his capacity as Vice-President in carrying out the chores of heading cabinet and National Security Council meetings, tasks given to him by **Eisenhower** during his illness.

52. Hatch, <u>History of the Vice-Presidency</u>, p. 413.

53. Whitney M. Young, Oral History Interview, Lyndon B. Johnson Library, Austin, Texas.

54. Arthur M. Schlesinger, Jr., <u>A Thousand Days </u>(Boston: Houghton Mifflin, 1965), p. 706 .

55. George Christian Interview held at his Austin, Texas, office, April 1973; see also "Apprentice President," *Economist* 213 (December 26, 1964): 1423.

56. Senator Gale McGee, Interview held at his U.S. office, Washington, D.C., March 1974.

57. Ibid.

58. Christian, Interview.

59. Walter Jenkins, Interview Held at his Austin, Texas, office, April 1973. See also Hale Boggs, Oral History Interview,

John F. Kennedy Library, Columbia Point, Massachusetts, pp. 17-18.

60. Schlesinger, p. 706.

61. Ibid., pp. 706-707.

62. Charles Daly, Oral History Interview, John F. Kennedy Library, Columbia Point, Massachusetts, pp. 34-35.

63. Norbert Schlei, Oral History Interview, John F. Kennedy Library, Columbia Point, Massachusetts, p. 44ff.; Clarence Mitchell, Oral History Interview, Lyndon B. Johnson Library, Austin, Texas, pp. 22-34; Roy Wilkins, Oral History Interview, Lyndon B. Johnson , p. 1ff.; Robert C. Weaver, Oral History Interview, Lyndon B. Johnson Library, Austin, Texas, pp. 1-4; George Reedy papers, (AF) Container 6, Civil Rights, Lyndon B. Johnson Library, Austin, Texas; VP Papers Box 5, Container: Civil Rights, July 13-July 31, 1963, Lyndon B. Johnson Library, Austin, Texas.

64. Hubert Humphrey, Interview held at a U.S. Senate reception room, Washington, D.C., March 1974.

65. Ibid.

66. Harry S Truman, Years of Decisions (Garden City, N.Y.: Doubleday, 1955), pp. 57, 196ff.; Senator John Sparkman, Interview held at his U.S. Senate office, Washington, D.C., March 1974.

67. Alben W. Barkley, "The Vice Presidency," Speech File 63M143. Box XXII. 1952, pp. 1-2. Alben W. Barkley Papers, University of Kentucky Library, Lexington, Kentucky. See also Truman, *Years of Decision*, p. 57.

68. Donald R. Matthews, *U.S. Senators and Their World* (New York: Vintage Books, 1960), p. 101ff.

69. Ibid., Chapter 5 in its entirety; Christian, Interview. Senator Gale McGee has indicated that the high degree of "clubbishness" during the Kennedy-Johnson Senate days has lessened; McGee, Interview.

70. Senator Herman Talmadge, Interview held at his U.S. Senate office, Washington, D.C., March 1974.

71. Humphrey, Interview.

72. James MacGregor Burns, John Kennedy: A Political Profile (New York: Harcourt, Brace, & World, 1961), p. 14.

73. Welch, Interview.

74. "I Enjoy It," *Newsweek* 65 (March 15, 1965): 28-29.

75. Albert Eisele, Almost to the Presidency (Blue Earth, Minnesota: Piper Co., 1972), p. 235ff.; Louis W. Koenig, The Chief Executive (New York: Harcourt, Brace & World, 1964, 1968), p. 162; Welch, Interview; Humphrey, Interview; "The Humphreys: Right Image for '68?," *U.S. News* 65 (September 9, 1968): 379ff; and Allan H. Ryskind, *Hubert* (New York; Arlington House 1968), p. 320.

76. See also "Vice President of Many Causes?"; "The Bright Spirit,; *Time* 87 (April 1, 1966): 21-25; "I Enjoy It"; "Happy Understudy," *Saturday Review* 48 (May 8, 1965): 16-17.

77. "Happy Understudy."

78. Humphrey, Interview.

79. McGee, Interview.

80. Richard H. Rovere, <u>The Eisenhower Years</u> (New York: Mentor books, 1960, 1956), p. 297.

81. "Nixon's Own Story of 7 Years in the Vice Presidency," *U.S. News* 48 (May 16, 1960): 98-106. See also Rovere, <u>The Eisenhower Years</u>, pp. 298-99. For more on Nixon in the legislature, see Ralph DeToledano, <u>One Man Alone: Richard Nixon</u> (New York: Funk & Wagnalls, 1969), p. 163ff.

82. *Time* (February 24, 1975): 15.

83. *New York Times,* October 1, 1977.

84. Ibid., October 5, 1977.

85. Ibid.

86. Marie D. Natoli, "Vice Presidency: Walter Mondale in the Lion's Den," *Presidential Studies Quarterly* (Winter 1978): 100-102

87. Ibid.

88. "Walter Mondale," the MacNeil/Lehrer Report, February 1977 (WNET/13, New York City).

89. Finlay Lewis, <u>Mondale: Portrait of an America Politician</u> (New York: Harper & Row, 1980), p. 247.

90. Ibid., p. 247.

91. Humphrey, Interview.

92. Vice President Thomas Marshall refused to pick up the constitutionally ambiguous gauntlet of the gap in the Presidency; the result was a period of no leadership while President Woodrow Wilson lay incapacitated. Earlier,

Vice-President Arthur had behaved similarly, assuming the Presidency's powers (and, of course, the office) only when he was certain Garfield had breathed his last breath. And Richard Nixon was the epitome of discretion during the Eisenhower illnesses, even going as far as to symbolize, by presiding from his own chair and not from that of the President, that he was acting in his capacity as Vice-President in carrying out the chores of heading cabinet and National Security Council meetings, tasks given to him by Eisenhower during his illness.

93. Hatch, <u>History of the Vice-Presidency</u>, p. 413.

Chapter 2.

1. Gerald M. Pomper, <u>Nominating the President: The Politics of Convention Choice</u> (New York: W. W. Norton, 1966), p. 158ff.

2. Patrick Anderson, <u>The President's Men</u> (Garden City, N.Y.: Doubleday, 1968), p. 63; James MacGregor Burns. <u>The Lion and the Fox</u> (New York: Harcourt, Brace & Co., 1956), pp. 428-39; Pomper, <u>Nominating the President</u>, p. 164.

3. For example, see Charles Roberts, Oral History Interview, John F. Kennedy Library, Columbia Point, Massachusetts; Hale Boggs, Oral History Interview, John F. Kennedy Library, Columbia Point, Massachusetts; Pierre Salinger, <u>With Kennedy</u> (Garden City, N.Y.: Doubleday, 1966), p. 40ff.; Arthur M. Schlesinger, Jr., <u>A Thousand Days</u> (Boston: Houghton Mifflin, 1965), p. 50ff.; Theodore Sorensen, <u>Kennedy</u> (New York: Harper & Row, 1965), p. 162ff.

4. Somewhat of a parallel is the selection of Lyndon Johnson as

John Kennedy's running mate in 1960. All of the Kennedy team's efforts had been devoted to getting the presidential nomination; little if any attention had been paid to what would happen once that nomination had been secured. The goal of capturing the presidential nomination causes the vice presidential nomination to become an afterthought.

5. Regarding the "Dump Johnson" question, see, for example, Tom Wicker, JFK and LBJ (New York: Morrow, 1968), p. 158; Boggs, Oral History Interview, John F. Kennedy Library, Columbia Point, Massachusetts, p. 18; G. Gould Lincoln, Oral History Interview, John F. Kennedy Library, Columbia Point, Massachusetts, pp. 22-23; Lyndon B. Johnson, The Vantage Point: Perspectives on the Presidency (New York: Holt, Rinehart and Winston, 1971), p. 2; Michael Dorman, The Second Man (New York: Delacorte Press, 1968), p. 261; "A Conversation with the Vice President," Interview, ABC News, March 26, 1963, Vice-Presidential Statements, Container 43, Lyndon B. Johnson Library, Austin, Texas, p. 11; George E. Reedy to Lyndon B. Johnson, in the folder for ABC Interview (Reedy, in his briefing to Johnson regarding remarks about his political future, cautions Johnson not to mention 1964 so as not to express any doubt); "Bobby Kennedy on LBJ's '64 Ticket?" U.S. News 56 (March 23, 1964): 44; Kenneth P. O'Donnell, telephone interview, February 1974; Hobart Taylor, Jr., Interview held at his Washington, D.C., law firm March 1974.

6. Harry S Truman, Years of Decisions (Garden City, N.Y.: Doubleday, 1955), p. 191.

7. Milton S. Eisenhower, Oral History Interview, Eisenhower Administration Oral History Collection, Columbia University, New York, New York, p. 48; Sherman Adams,

Oral History Interview, Eisenhower Administration Oral History Collection, Columbia University, New York, New York, pp. 230-34.

8. Herbert S. Parmet, <u>Eisenhower and the American Crusades</u> (New York: Macmillan, 1972), p. 173.

9. Ibid., p. 434.

10. Truman, <u>Years of Decisions</u>, p. 190ff.; Dorman, <u>Second Man</u>, p. 156ff.; Papers of Henry A. Wallace, Franklin D. Roosevelt Library, Hyde Park, New York; manuscript of <u>This I Remember</u>, chap. 13, p. 196, Eleanor Roosevelt Papers, Franklin D. Roosevelt Library, Hyde Park, New York. See George Allen, Oral History Interview, Harry S Truman Library.

11. FDR Statement re: Wallace Trip, May 20, 1944, Official File 12, April 17, 1944, Vice-President, Franklin D. Roosevelt Papers, Franklin D. Roosevelt Library, Hyde Park, New York. Official File 12, April 17, 1944, Vice-President, Franklin D. Roosevelt Papers, Franklin D. Roosevelt Library, Hyde Park, New York.

12. George W. Bush, <u>Decision Points</u>, p. 49 (New York: Crown Publishers, 2010).

    Peter Baker, "Bush Considered Dropping Cheney From 2004 Ticket," NYT, Nov. 2, 2010, discusses this issue as well.

13. Pomper, <u>Nominating the President</u>, p. 164; John Morton Blum, <u>Years of War, 1941-45</u> (from the Morgenthau Diaries) (Boston: Houghton Mifflin, 1967), pp. 280-81.

14. John Morton Blum, <u>Years of War</u>, pp. 280-81; Cabell

Phillips, <u>The Truman Presidency: The History of a Triumphant Succession</u> (New York: Macmillan, 1966), p. 38; Mrs. Hannegan to Rosenman, undated, Rosenman 25 MS 62-4, Papers of Samuel Rosenman, Franklin D. Roosevelt Library, Hyde Park, New York.

15. CBS Broadcast, 1955, Official File 339-99B, Papers of Dwight D. Eisenhower, Dwight D. Eisenhower Library, Abilene, Kansas, p. 17.

16. Sherman Adams, Oral History Interview; Parmet, <u>Eisenhower and the American Crusades</u>, p. 100ff.; Sherman Adams, <u>Firsthand Report</u> (New York: Harper & Brothers, 1961), p. 34ff

17. In 1960, Nixon, now the presidential candidate, selected a vice-president running mate who epitomized the central issue Nixon wanted to emphasize-international affairs and the maturity to deal with them. Henry Cabot Lodge, former U.S. ambassador to the United Nations, well exemplified this criterion.

18. Richard M. Scammon and Ben J. Wattenberg, <u>The Real Majority </u>(New York: Coward, McCann & Geoghegan, 1970), pp. 43-44.

19. See Appendix A.

20. *U.S. News* 67 (October 6, 1969):32-38

21. Jules Witcover, <u>White Knight: The Rise of Spiro Agnew</u> (New York: Random House 1972), p. 268.

22. Robert Curran, <u>Spiro Agnew: Spokesman for America</u> (New York: Lancer Books, 1970), p. 39.

23. See Appendix B.

24. As quoted in Curran, <u>Spiro Agnew</u>, p. 54.

25. Sorensen, <u>Kennedy</u>, p. 163.

26. Edwin Guthman, <u>We Band of Brothers</u> (New York: Harper & Row, 1971), p. 78.

27. Johnson, <u>The Vantage Point</u>, p. 78.

28. Lyndon B. Johnson, Press Conference, Chicago Airport, July 7, 1960, Container 39, July 7, 1960, Vice-Presidential Statements, Lyndon B. Johnson Library, Austin, Texas.

29. Lyndon B. Johnson, "Meet the Press," July 10, 1960, Container 3, July 10, 1960, Vice-President Papers, Lyndon B. Johnson Library, Austin, Texas.

30. Hugh Sidney Oral History Interview John F. Kennedy Library, Columbia Point, Massachusetts, p. 45ff.; Sorensen, <u>Kennedy</u> p. 165.

31. Salinger, <u>With Kennedy</u>, p. 44ff.; Johnson, <u>The Vantage Point</u>, p. 92.

32. Johnson, Ibid.

33. Guthman, <u>We Band of Brothers</u>, p. 77.

34. Walter Jenkins, Interview held at his Austin, Texas, office, March 173.

35. For more on this point, see Schlesinger, <u>A Thousand Days</u>, p. 46ff.

36. Hodding Carter, Jr., Oral History Interview, Lyndon B. Johnson Library, Austin, Texas; Allen J. Ellender, Oral

History Interview, Lyndon B. Johnson Library, Austin, Texas, p. 8ff.; Schlesinger, <u>A Thousand Days</u>, p. 46ff.; Bill Welch, Interview held at his Washington, D.C., office, March 1974.

37. Ellender, Oral History Interview, p. 8.

38. Ibid., p. 9ff., Bill Welch, Interview.

39. Hobart Taylor, Jr., Interview.

40. Ibid.

41. Boggs, Oral History Interview, pp. 22-23; George Christian, <u>The President Steps Down</u> (New York: Macmillan, 1970), p. 154.

42. Johnson, <u>The Vantage Point</u>, p. 90.

43. Christian, Interview.

44. Liz Carpenter, Interview held at her Washington D.C., office, March 1974.

45. Robert Troutman, Jr., Telephone Interview, Atlanta, Georgia, May 1973.

46. For additional material on the reaction of the Robert Kennedy and JFK aids, see Leonard Baker, <u>The Journal Ellipse: The President's Vice Presidency</u> (New York: Macmillan, 1966), pp. 182-86; Salinger, <u>With Kennedy</u>, p. 46; Kenneth P. O'Donnell, Telephone Interview, February 1974. O'Donnell claims Bobby Kennedy was "almost neutral" to Johnson's selection by JFK. See also "Bobby Kennedy on LBJ's '64 Ticket?"

47. Dorman, <u>Second Man</u>, pp. 249-50; Guthman, <u>We Band of</u>

Brothers, p. 252; see Salinger, With Kennedy, p. 46, for a contrary view. Salinger claims that it was just "a semantic misunderstanding"; Sorensen, Kennedy, p. 166, claims that Bobby Kennedy, in offering the alternative of the Democratic National Committee chairmanship, was acting on the orders of his brother Jack, and not on his own initiative.

48. Schlesinger, A Thousand Days, p. 50.

49. Walter Jenkins to Lyndon B. Johnson, Remarks, Joint Session of Congress, November 27, 1963, *Vice-Presidential Statements*, Container 5. Lyndon B. Johnson Library, Austin, Texas.

50. See Vice-Presidential Papers on Civil Rights, Lyndon B. Johnson Library, Austin, Texas: Frances Keppel, Oral History Interview, Lyndon B. Johnson Library, Austin, Texas; Fred Lazarus, Jr., Oral History Interview, Dwight D. Eisenhower Library (part of the Columbia University Oral History Project), Abilene, Kansas.

51. Johnson, The Vantage Point, Along these lines, Harry McPherson's memorandum of February 18, 1963, is interesting. He wrote:

> Yesterday, Berl Bernhard, staff director of the Civil Rights Commission, was at my home. Berl is young, very able, and I think more interested in progress in civil rights than in the politics connected with it.
>
> He talked about the Equal Employment Committee. He said that according to his information you were about to be the target of terrific abuse on the matter. It will come from Republicans, and from some Democrats; it may have help from within the White House. In

general it will attack the record of the committee, and its personnel. Its purpose will be to make you look foolish and insincere in your claims of effectiveness for the committee.

Berl said he regards this as "wretched stuff; because it hits somebody I think responds a great deal more sincerely and basically to the underdog than the President does."

He is in my opinion genuinely concerned about this attack, which he says will come in early 1964 (with a prologue in *Newsweek* this week.) Container 7, Civil Rights: Labor-President's Committee on Equal employment Opportunity, Vice-Presidential Papers, Lyndon B Johnson, Austin, Texas.

52. Johnson, The Vantage Point, p. 18.

53. Albert Eisele, Almost to the Presidency (Blue Earth, Minnesota: Piper Co., 1972), p. 205.

54. To a large extent, the characteristics Carter was seeking in a running mate paralleled those sought by Johnson in 1964.

55. Ibid.

56. *Time,* July 12, 1976.

57. *New York Times*, July 16, 1976.

58. Inexplicable, incidentally, was Ronald Regan's announcement that, if nominated in 1976, Pennsylvania Senator Richard Schweiker, a staunch liberal, would be his running mate. Perhaps this was in part attributable to the realistic appraisal of the necessities of ticket balancing,

especially if one candidate is clearly identified, as was Reagan, with an extreme ideological position.

59. *New York Times,* July 17, 1980.

60. Ibid.

61. Ibid.

62. Ibid., July 22, 1980.

63. Ibid.

64. Ibid.

65. Ibid., July 18, 1980.

66. Ibid.

67. Ibid.

68. Parmet, <u>Eisenhower and the American Crusades</u>, pp. 91-94.

69. Sidney Warren, <u>The Battle for the Presidency</u> (Philadelphia: Lippincott, 1969), p. 363; see also *News Statesman* 68 (August 21, 1964): 237+ .

70. Johnson, <u>The Vantage Point</u>, p. 159

71. Eisele, <u>Almost to the Presidency</u>, p. 225.

72. Dean Rusk, Interview held at his Athens, Georgia, office, May 1973.

73. Bill Welch, Interview, March 1974.

74. Eisele, <u>Almost to the Presidency</u>, pp. 206-12.

75. Jules Witcover, <u>The Resurrection of Richard Nixon</u> (New York: Putnam, 1970), p. 350.

76. Jules Witcover, <u>White Knight: The Rise of Spiro</u> Agnew (New York: Random House, 1972) p. 219.

77. Witcover, <u>The Resurrection of the Richard Nixon</u>, p. 351.

78. *Time*, July 12, 1976.

79. As cited in Congress, House of Representatives, Committee of House Administration, The Presidential Campaign, 1976, Vol. 1, Jimmy Carter, 2d Session, 1978, p. 317.

80. *Time*, July 12, 1976.

81. *New York Times*, July 15, 1976.

82. Ibid.

83. Ibid., July 26, 1980.

84. "Mondale's Demanding Suitors," *Time* 124:12-17 (July 9, 1984).

85. "Filling the Democratic Pipeline," *Time* 123:28-29 (June 18, 19840).

86. "Mondale's Demanding Suitors."

87. "Ferraro the Campaigner," *New York Times Magazine*, September 30, 1984.

88. Ibid.

89. Ibid.

90. Stephen F. Hayes. <u>Cheney: The Untold Story of America's</u>

Most Powerful and Controversial Vice President (New York" HarperCollins, 2009), p. 280, interview with George W. Bush, Dec. 11, 2006.

91. Ibid., p. 279, interview, with Dick Cheney, Aug. 22, 2006.

92. Barton Gellman., <u>Angler: The Cheney Vice Presidency</u> (New York: Penguin Press, 2009), passim.

93. Ibid.

94. Ibid, passim.

95. Ibid., p. 16.

96. Hayes, p. 281.

97. George W. Bush, <u>Decision Points</u> (New York: Crown Publishing Group, 2010), p. 68.

98. Ibid., p. 65.

99. Richard Cheney, <u>In My Time</u> (New York: Threshold Editions, 2011), passim.

100. Joseph Biden, <u>Promise Me, Dad: A Year of Hope, Hardship, and Purpose</u> (New York:Flatiron Books, 2017), passim.

101. Jane Mayer, "The Dangers of A President Pence," *The New Yorker,* October 23, 2017.

102. McKay Coppin, "God's Plan for Mike Pence, *The Atlantic,* October 7, 2016, passim.

103. Jennifer Harper, "American Conservative Union: 'Mike Pence Is the Most Conservative VP in 50 Years,'" *The Washington Times,* Oct. 3, 2016.

104. Mike Pence, Address delivered at the Republican National Convention, Cleveland, Ohio, July 6, 2016.

105. Kate Brower. <u>First In Line: Presidents, Vice Presidents, and the Pursuit of Power,</u> (New York: HarperCollins, 2018), pp. 1 – 2.

106. *Statement of Senator Birch Bayh Before the Senate Committee on Rules and Administration Regarding the Nomination of the Hon. Gerald Ford as Vice-President of the United States.*

107. Ibid.

108. Biden-Sanders Democratic presidential primary debate, Washington, D.C., March 15, 2020. 109. Pomper, <u>Nominating the President</u>, pp. 174-75.

110. Ibid., pp. 175-176; Sidney Hyman, *The American President* (New York: Harper, 1954), pp.

111. Vice President Gerald R. Ford made this suggestion, during an interview with this author at his Senatorial office, March, 1974.

Some of the views held by past Vice Presidents regarding the vice presidential selection process are expressed below.

Barkley:

I would adopt the same method for nominating a candidate for Vice President that I would favor for President, and that is nominating them by the people, let the people vote on whom they want to nominate. But, as long as the convention system prevails it is difficult to visualize any reform in the method of nominating a Vice President different from that which now prevails. ...

No convention would want to nominate a candidate for Vice President who was offensive to the nominee for President, or out of harmony with him.

Barkley admitted, however, that "it does result in the people themselves having practically no voice in the selection of a Vice President." Sidney Shalett, Interviews with Alben W. Barkley, Harry S Truman Library, Independence, Missouri; Franklin D. Roosevelt, Hyde Park, New York, reel 12, side 2, pp.1-2. Barkley expressed similar views in a 1955 CBS Broadcast with Edward R. Murrow, in which Barkley, Eisenhower, Truman, and Wallace participated. Official File 339, 99B, 1955 CBS Broadcast, Papers of Dwight D. Eisenhower, Dwight D. Eisenhower Library, Abilene, Kansas, pp. 16-21.

Truman:

The direct primary is an ideal situation for selecting public officials, but there isn't a man in the world with money enough in the world to put on a direct primary for President and then run for President. It would require an immense amount of money in each one of the States, and I am not so sure that it would obtain the results that we think about. (CBS Broadcast 1955.)

Chapter 3.

1. Hubert Humphrey, Interview held at the U.S. Senate, Washington, D.C., March 1974

2. Harry S Truman, <u>Years of Decisions</u> (New York: Doubleday, 1955), p. 5. Frank McNaughton, commenting on Roosevelt's appearance before Congress on March 2, 1945, described at length the marked changes that had taken place in the President.

> The President was jovial enough, but one impression struck forcibly on those who chatted with him in the Speaker's office: He wasn't the Roosevelt of two years ago.
>
> When he was wheeled into the chamber, there was a shocked hush for an instant before Congress and the galleries applauded. It seemed unreal, almost fantastic to see Franklin D. Roosevelt rolled into the chamber on a wheel chair. Never before had he uncloaked his infirmity so openly, so frankly, before so many people...
>
> Everybody knew that Roosevelt couldn't walk without steel braces; it was something else to see him wheeled in a char, admitting his physical disabilities.
>
> The President was dressed in a blue suit that hung slackly on his shoulders. It accentuated a marked loss of weight, and his wrists seemed to have lost their beefy, rugged marks of strength. They were slender, markedly slender. ... The skin of his face was a good color but it had one greatly distinguished quality: it seemed to droop in the folds along the neck, at the collar line, and from the point of the chin to the Adam's apple it was stretched in a loose thin line that is the mark of advanced age.
>
> The body did not have the buoyancy of yesteryears. When he sat in the chair, his shoulders and body seemed slightly hunched-not markedly but

perceptibly. There was a good deal of evidence of strain in the face. ...

The tremble in the hands-always noticeable over the past years- was plainly accentuated....

His voice was weak; it did not have the pitch and timber of Roosevelt's voice....

The President spoke immediately of the wild rumors, and did a good, witty job by remarking that he had been ill only when he got back to Washington and heard rumors about his health.

But the impression stuck, even as he spoke-this was more than a public appearance on Yalta; it was also to convince Congress that Franklin D. Roosevelt is still a well man, full of faculties and reason, albeit deathly tired and worn.

He was talking through congress and over it to the millions at fireside radios... and he was demonstrating that Roosevelt is still at the throttle in domestic and world affairs.

Frank McNaughton to Don Permingham, March 2, 1945, The Pepers of Frank McNaughton, Harry S Truman Library, Independence, Missouri; see also Frank McNaughton, This Man Truman (New York: McGraw-Hill, 1945), p. 200.

John Gunther, Roosevelt in Retrospect (New York: Harper, 1950) p. 345, wrote:

Age clamped down on him. If one looks at photographs taken month by month it seems that he became white-haired almost overnight. But in some respects nobody could accuse him of losing grip; in fact as he grew older he held the reigns of power even more tightly, as if to compensate for fatigue and growing weakness. Nothing was going to budge him from the driver's seat except death. Soon, death did.

Roosevelt's press secretary, Jonathan Daniels, in an oral history interview for the Truman Library, p. 26, has admitted being part of the "protective mechanism" in portraying Roosevelt as healthy and able to carry on his work

> I remember that when the pictures came back from Yalta, the only photographs that were made by the Signals Corps, and all the pictures from Yalta came back to my desk. And I had to select the pictures to be released. Some of them were appalling. I must admit that I picked only those pictures which seemed to me to be the best ones of Franklin Roosevelt. Now I am subject to criticism for that, but I figured that was my duty at the time.

3. Gunther, Roosevelt in Retrospect, p. 352.

4. The Papers of Harry Hopkins, Box 95, Unpublished Gallup Poll, July 5, 1944, Franklin D. Roosevelt Library, Hyde Park, New York.

5. Truman, p.193.

6. Ibid.

7. Ibid., p. 194.

8. *Time*, April 23, 1945, p. 23.

9. Truman, p. 19; see also Alben Barkley, That Reminds Me (New York: Doubleday, 1954), p. 196ff.

10. Truman, p. 199.

11. Ibid., p. 14.

12. Ibid., pp. 10-11.

13. Ibid.

14. Ibid., p. 56.

15. Harry H. Vaughan, Oral History Interview, Harry S Truman Library, Independence, Missouri, p. 36.

16.

Roosevelt's negligence of his Vice President has been recalled by General Vaughan:

> Mr. Roosevelt, even though he must have known that his health was not good, probably took the same attitude Mr. Truman did, just didn't want to think of it-if you don't think about it it won't happen. He had never talked to Mr. Trumann a minute on what happened at Teheran, and what happened at Yalta, and what happened at Casablanca, so Truman was not prepared at all. He didn't know of any of the commitments we had made to Russia or to France or to Great Britain, and so... all the sudden he had to do a terrific lot of reading and research.

As Vaughan points out, Truman did precisely that:

> He talked to everybody that had been to Yalta; everybody that had been to Teheran and everybody that had been to Casablanca, to any of these conferences; he talked to Mrs. Roosevelt and even talked to Anna

Roosevelt, the President's daughter, because she had accompanied the President. I'm sure she wasn't in on any of the conferences but he thought that might give him some pointers. It was a terrific job to try to prepare him because the Potsdam Conference was scheduled.... I can recall meetings at the Potsdam Conference when some item would could up and Mr. Churchill said, "Now, Mr. Roosevelt promised me he would do so-and-so." Well, you don't want to doubt Mr. Churchill's word, but Mr. Churchill is a man who is dedicated to do everything possible [sic] in the interests of the British Empire. I'm sure he demonstrated that sufficiently. Mr. Joe Stalin would say, "Now the President Roosevelt [sic] promised that he would...." Everyone within the sound of his voice suspected that it was a lie from start to finish but how could you prove it?

17. Truman, pp. 54-55.

18. Ibid., p. 53; see also Herman Finer, <u>The Presidency: Crisis and Regeneration</u> (Chicago: University of Chicago Press, 1960), p. 210; *New York Times Magazine*, June 24, 1973.

19. Newsweek, April 23, 1945, p. 23.

20. Truman, p. 283.

21. Ibid., p. 257ff.

22. Ibid., pp. 367-68.

23. Ibid., p. 31.

24. Ibid., p. 22.

Truman, intent on forging the sense of tranquility

and unity which the country so desperately needed, advanced this effort in another direction and was even willing to soothe the ruffled feathers of Byrnes, who had expected to receive the 1944 vice-presidential nomination. Byrnes was a bitter man; now it was painfully apparent to him that he might have been President of the United States. Truman decided to make a conciliatory gesture, inviting Byrnes back to Washington to help ease the transition as well as to offer him the position of Secretary of State, which Byrnes eagerly accepted.

Johnathan Daniels, The Man of Independence (Philadelphia: Lippincott, 1950), pp. 264-65; see also Sidney Shalett, Interviews with Alben Barkley, reel 7, side 2, page 1, Harry s Truman Library, Independence, Missouri; Franklin D. Roosevelt Library, Hyde Park, New York.

25. Daniels,p. 266.

26. Vaughan, Oral History Interview, p. 40.

27. *New York Times,* April 23, 1945; April 17, 1945.

28. Ibid., May 2, 1945.

29. Truman, p. 19.

Truman reflected,

> I pledged myself to carry out the war and peace policies of Franklin Roosevelt, and I made it clear that I would work for the peace and security of the world. I asked for public support for a strong and lasting United Nations organization. I called upon all Americans to help me keep our nation united in

defense of those ideals which had been so eloquently proclaimed by Roosevelt.

I reaffirm our demand for unconditional surrender and expressed my full confidence in the grand strategy of the United States and our allies. I expressed, as well, my confidence in the ability of Admirals Leahy, King and Nimitz, and Generals Marshall, Arnold, Eisenhower, and MacArthur to carry out the task assigned to them, and left no doubt that this direction would remain unchanged an unhampered. (Truman, p. 42.)

Truman appealed to the Congress for its support in this way:

You, the members of Congress, surely know how I feel. Only with your help can I hope to complete one of the greatest tasks ever assigned to a public servant. With divine guidance, and your help, we will find the new passage to a far better world, a kindly and friendly place, with just and lasting peace. (*Public Papers of the Presidents of the United States: Harry S Truman*, April 12 to December 3, 1945, pp. 5-6.)

30. Truman, pp. 17, 272, 291.

31. Committee for Economic Development, "Presidential Succession and Inability," A Statement on National Policy by the Research and Policy Committee of the CED, January 1965, p. 13; hereafter cited as CED, "Presidential Succession and Inability."

32. Speech before a Joint Session of Congress, November 26, 1963.

33. See Marcus Cunliffe, <u>American Presidents and the Presidency</u> (New York: McGraw-Hill, 1968, 1972), p. 68, for more on Tyler's succession; Louis Clinton Hatch, <u>History of the Vice-Presidency of the United States</u>, revised by Earl L. Shoup (Westport, Conn.: Greenwood Press, 1934, 1970), p. 57ff.

34. Truman, p. 111.

35. Lyndon B. Johnson, <u>The Vantage Point</u> (New York: Holt, Rinehart & Winston, 1971), chap. 2.

36. Hatch, p. 413.

37. Johnson, p. 27.

38. Ibid., p. 15.

39. Louis Heren, <u>No Hail, No Farewell</u> (New York: Harper & Row, 1970), p. 16.

Truman noted in this memoirs, <u>Years of Decisions</u>, p. 87:

> From the moment I first sat down in the President's chair I found myself part of an immense administrative operation. There had been a change of executives, but the machinery kept going on in its customary routine manor and properly so. It would have been sheer nonsense to expect anything else.

40. Hubert H. Humphrey, Interview held at a U.S. Senate reception room, March 1974.

41. Gerald R. Ford, Interview conducted at his U.S. Senate office, March 1974.

42. Johnson, p. 18.

43. Ibid.

44. Ibid., p. 73.

45. Ibid., p. 19.

46. Ibid., p. 95.

47. Tom Wicker, <u>JFK and LBJ</u> (New York: Morrow, 1968), p. 195.

48. *Time*, November 12, 1973, p. 37.

49. Ibid.

50. *New York Times*, October 14, 1973, p. 1.

51. Ibid., pp. 1, 4.

52. Ibid., p. 1.

53. *New York Times*, March 10, 1974, p. 51.

54. Ibid.

55. *New York Times*, March 17, 1974, p. 14.

56. Ibid.; Ford, Interview, March 1974.

57. *New York Times*, May 12, 1974, p. 2.

58. As quoted by the *New York Times*, October 14, 1973, p. 1.

59. *Public Papers of the Presidents of the United States*: Gerald R. Ford, August 9, 1974, p. 1.

60. See *Christian Science Monitor*, August 9, 1974, for more on this point.

61. *Boston Globe,* August 9, 1974, p. 49.

62. Boston Globe., August 11, 1974, p. 1ff.

63. *New York Times,* August 11, 1974, p. 1; *Boston Globe,* August 11, 1974.

64. *Boston Globe,* August 11, 1974, p. 16.

65. *Newsweek,* August 19, 1974, p. 25.

66. *New York Times,* August 11, 1974, p. 1; *Boston Globe,* August 11, 1974, p. 17.

67. Birch Bayh, <u>One Heartbeat Away</u> (New York: Bobbs-Merrill, 1968) provides a useful discussion of the formulation of the Twenty-Fifth Amendment, as does the Report of the Subcommittee on Constitutional Amendments to the Committee on the Judiciary. "Selected Materials on the Twenty-Fifth Amendment." 93d Congress, 1st Session (Washington, D.C.: U.S. Government Printing Office, 1973), hereafter referred to as "Subcommittee Report."

68. "Subcommittee Report," p. 49ff. See also CED, "Presidential Succession and Inability."

69. "Subcommittee Report," p. 51.

70. Dwight D. Eisenhower, *Mandate For Change* (New York: Doubleday, 1963), pp. 545-46. See John C. Kirby, Jr., "A Breakthrough on Presidential Inability: The ABA Conference Consensus," *The Vanderbilt Law Review*, 18, No. 12 (March 1964) p. 47ff. for a discussion of the renewed attention on the issue of disability.

71. See American Bar Association, "Supplemental Report of the Standing Committee on Jurisprudence and Law

Reform: Presidential Inability and Succession," 1964, pp. 4ff., 201ff., for a review of presidential-vice-presidential agreements on disability.

72. CED, "Presidential Succession and Inability," p. 13.

73. See also George Reedy's memo to LBJ, March 21, 1963, Re: ABC Program. Vice-Presidential Statements, Box 43, Papers of Lyndon B. Johnson, Lyndon B. Johnson Library, Austin, Texas. See OF 339. 99B, CBS Broadcast, pp. 16-21; Papers of Harry S Truman, Harry S Truman Library, Independence, Missouri. See also "The Vice Presidency," Speech File 63M143, Box XXII, Papers of Alben W. Barkley, University of Kentucky Library, Lexington, Kentucky.

74. CED, "Presidential Succession and Inability," p. 13.

75. "Nixon's Own Story," *U.S. News* 48 (May 16, 1960): 98-106.

76. On this point, see Howard K. Smith, Oral History Interview, Eisenhower Administration Oral History Collection, Columbia University, New York, New York, p. 45, who suggests Eisenhower's possible annoyance that Nixon had been building up what he was doing as Vice-President in order to enhance his position in the presidential campaign. Nevertheless, noted Smith, Nixon did grow in the Vice-Presidency, and "he became a very good traveling ambassador. I followed him through Africa, and I think he did a good job in many respects" (p. 28ff). See also Ralph DeToledano, One Man Alone: Richard Nixon (New York: Funk & Wagnalls, 1969), p. 170ff., for material on Nixon's Asian trip as Vice-President.

77. Max Farrand, ed., The Records of the Federal Convention,

vol. 2 (New Haven: Yale University Press, 1937, 1966), p. 427.

78. See Hansen to Merriman Smith, September 5, 1961, Richard Hansen Microfilms, Harry S Truman Library, Independence, Missouri. Smith apparently noted that Eisenhower's openness with the press was in pointed contrast to the handling of John F. Kennedy's not very serious illness in the early 1961. Hansen, in an August 10, 1961, letter to Richard Nixon noted: "Disability is not... a series of isolated illnesses or instances, but actually concerns the whole problem of the president's general health.... Legislation should be adopted to insure public disclosure of the president's condition during serious illness."

79. Eisenhower, Mandate for Change, p. 540.

80. Ibid., p. 538.

Regarding the first Cabinet meeting decisions under Vice President Nixon, Eisenhower (Mandate for Change, p. 540) noted:

1. On actions which Cabinet members would normally take without consulting either the Cabinet or the President, there would be no change in procedure from the normal.
2. Questions which would normally be brought before the Cabinet for discussion before decision should continue to be discussed there.
3. *Decisions* which would require consultation with me shouldgo first to the Cabinet or the National Security council for thorough discussion and

possible recommendation and then go to Denver for my consideration.

4. The proper channel for the submission to me of matters requiring presidential decisions should go to General Persons in the White House and then through Governor Adams to me in Denver.

5. The Vice President had emphasized that any important new administration policies should be set only by me.

See also Roscoe Drummond, Oral History Interview, Eisenhower Administration Oral History Collection, Columbia University, New York, New York, p. 19.

1. Eisenhower, p. 542.

2. Sherman Adams, Firsthand Report (New York: Harper, 1961), p. 181.

3. Herbert Brownell, Oral History Interview, Eisenhower Administration Oral History Collection, Columbia University, New York, New York, p. 241; see also Adams, *Firsthand Report*, p. 181.

4. Eisenhower, p. 545.ann

Eisenhower further reflected:

I could not have selected a better time... to have a heart attack... The economy was booming, Congress was not in session. I had been able to handle with Foster the major foreign-policy problems, and at the moment there was no new crisis pending in the world. This it was not necessary to consult daily with members of the Council of Economic Advisers, or to approve or veto bills passed by the Congress, or to send messages recommending courses to that body. Probably most important was the fact that I was not required to make any immediate operation decisions involving the use of the armed forces of the United States.... *However had a situation arise such as occurred in 1958 in which I was eventually sent troops ashore in Lebanon, the concentration, the weighing of pros and cons, and the final determination would have represented a burden,* during the first week of my illness, which the doctor would likely have found unacceptable for a new cardiac patient to bear. [Italics added]

5. "Presidential Inability Study Raises Problems," *Washington Evening Star*, February 10, 1956.

6. Adams, p. 192.

7. Ibid., pp. 185-86. See also "A Reminder from Mr. Adams," *St. Louis Post-Dispatch*, May 29-June 24, 1961, Hansen Microfilms, Harry S Truman Library, Independence, Missouri.

8. Richard Rover, <u>The Eisenhower Years </u>(New York: Farrar, Straus & Cudahy, 1956), p. 322.

9. Richard M. Nixon, <u>Six Crises</u> (New York: Doubleday, 1962), p. 144.

10. Adams, , p. 186ff.

11. Ibid.

12. Ibid., p. 193.

13. Herbert S. Parmet, <u>Eisenhower and the American Crusades</u> (New York: Macmillan, 1972), p. 516.

Chapter 4.

1. *America* 113 (October 2, 1965): 363

2. Robert Finch, who had been with Nixon when Nixon served as Vice President, said:

> I came aboard with the clear understanding that he was going to be a Presidential candidate, so that the major thrust of my activity was along that line. That is, first of all, assessing his time in terms of what needed to be done, what had to be done to strengthen, prepare us right away for the nomination; the places he had to go, the people he had to see.

> Robert Finch, Oral History Interview, Eisenhower Administration Oral History Collection, Columbia University, New York, New York, p. 28.

3. For additional material on Alben Barkley's 1952 availability, see Alben Barkley, <u>That Reminds Me</u> (Garden City, N.Y.: Doubleday, 1954), chap. 17; Cabell Phillips, <u>The Truman Presidency</u> (New York: Macmillan, 1966), p. 420ff.; The Papers of Alben Barkley, University of Kentucky, Lexington, Kentucky; Sidney Shallet, *Interviews with Alben Barkley*, Harry S Truman Library, Independence, Missouri, and Franklin D. Roosevelt Library, Hyde Park, New York,

passim; *New York Times*, July 19, 1952; Michael Dorman, The Second Man (New York: Delacorte Press, 1968), p. 196ff.; Harry S Truman, Years of Trial and Hope (New York: Doubleday, 1956); The Papers of Harry S Truman, Harry S Truman Library, Independence, Missouri; the oral history interviews of Joseph G. Feeney and Donald Hansen, Harry S Truman Library, Independence, Missouri.

4. Earl Mazo and Stephen Hess, Nixon: A Political Portrait (New York: Harper and Row, 1968), p. 220ff.

5. Leverett Saltonstall, Oral History Interview, Eisenhower Administration Oral History Collection, Columbia University, New York, New York, p. 146.

6. Emmet John Hughes, The Ordeal of Power (New York: Ahteneum, 1963), p. 29

7. Herbert S. Parmet, Eisenhower and the American Crusades (New York: Macmillan, 1972), p. 527ff.

8. *New York Times*, May 4, 1960. Herman Finer, The Presidency: Crisis and Regeneration (Chicago: University of Chicago Press, 1960), p. 295, points out that, while the Vice-President is the potential successor, it is more likely that an incumbent President would avoid naming him publicly.

9. Sidney Warren, The Battle for the Presidency (Philadelphia: Lippincott, 1968), p. 301.

10. For more on the delegation of political duties to the Vice President, see Richard Rovere, Oral History Interview, Eisenhower Administration Oral History Collection, Columbia University, New York, New York, pp. 35-36.

11. Dorman, <u>The Second Man,</u> p. 240.

12. Kenneth Keating, Oral History Interview, Eisenhower Administration Oral History Collection, Columbia University, New York, New York, p. 13ff

13. Hughes, <u>The Ordeal of Power,</u> pp. 323; 200.

14. Several observers have pointed out Nixon's views on the party platform. The presidential candidate, he felt, should have the strongest say. Accordingly, Nixon had "insisted upon some revisions," noted Prescott Bush in an Oral History Interview for the Eisenhower Administration Oral History Collection, Columbia University, New York, New York, pp. 13-14.

15. Ibid.

16. In a memo from Max Rabb to James Hagerty, dated June 20, 1965, the message was transmitted: "Nixon wants publicity for work of Committee on Government Contracts" (Official File 101-I-2 Box 441, Dwight D. Eisenhower Papers, Dwight D. Eisenhower Library, Abilene, Kansas).

17. Finch, in his Oral History Interview for the Eisenhower Administration Oral History Collection, noted the importance of civil rights legislation to the impending 1960 campaign. Thus, he and William P. Rogers worked on civil rights legislation. See p. 34ff. for more on this point. See pp. 35-36 for Nixon's work with the National Urban League/NAACP.

Finch also discusses the usefulness of Nixon's foreign travel to the 1960 campaign strategy, p. 65ff.

Milton S. Eisenhower points out that, although Nixon

suffered indignity during his Latin American trip, it gained him sympathy. Oral History Interview, Eisenhower Administration Oral History Collection, Columbia University, New York, New York, p. 94.

18. Donald Paarlberg, Interview held at his Washington, D.C., office, March 1974.

19. Mazo and Hess, Nixon, p. 238.

20. Howard K. Smith, Oral History Interview, Eisenhower Administration Oral History Collection, Columbia University, New York, New York, p. 44.

21. Mazo and Hess, Nixon, p. 238. "It was just a mistake," according to Roscoe Drummond, although it was, he continued, "a bumbling answer," "awkward," and "embarrassing" to Nixon." Oral History Interview, Eisenhower Administration Oral History Collection, Columbia University, New York, New York, p. 20.

Prescott Bush suggests that it was because Eisenhower was "a rather fuzzy-minded man. Also, he didn't have the facts at his disposal a good part of the time, unlike Truman, and Kennedy and Johnson." Rovere also observes, "He probably didn't know really what Nixon had been doing. Whereas Johnson knows from minute to minute what Humphrey's doing." Oral History Interview, p. 28.

Regarding the remark, Nixon said:

It was to plague me the rest of the campaign.... Eisenhower had called me on the phone and expressed chagrin at the way this exchange had been handled by the press. He pointed out that he was simply being facetious and yet they played it straight and wrote it seriously....I am sure that to millions of unsophisticated televiewers, this question had been most effective in raising a doubt in their minds with regard to one of my strongest campaign themes and assets-my experience as Vice-President. (Richard M. Nixon, <u>Six Crises</u> [New York: Doubleday, 1962], p. 339.

22. William F. Knowland, Oral History Interview, Eisenhower Administration Oral History Collection, Columbia University, New York, New York, pp. 83-84.

23. Howard K. Smith, Oral History Interview, p. 44.

24. Mazo and Hess, <u>Nixon</u>, p. 234ff. See also Parmet, <u>Eisenhower and the American Crusades,</u> Edward McCabe in his oral history interview for the Dwight D. Eisenhower Library, pointed out that during the debates Nixon had to watch his Ps and Qs every step, and Kennedy...was in a position to take a gamble, if he could look good, or take the chance of looking good....That's the difference between the fellow in office and the fellow seeking office. It'll always be that way, I suspect (p. 76).

25. Hughes, <u>The Ordeal of Power</u>, p. 323.

The "couple of telephone calls" referred to relate to the incident of the arrest of civil rights leader Martin Luther King, Jr. in Atlanta. John Kennedy telephoned a Georgia judge to intercede on King's behalf. See Arthur M. Schlesinger, Jr., <u>A Thousand Days</u> (Boston: Houghton Mifflin, 1965), p. 74.

King himself remarked of the action: "I am deeply indebted to Senator Kennedy, who served as a great force in making my release possible. It took a lot of courage for Senator Kennedy to do this, especially in Georgia."

Kennedy received a huge percentage of the Negro vote in the election; see Schlesinger, A Thousand Days, pp. 929-30.

Nixon, meanwhile, was trying to work via the resources he thought were at his disposal, and, as Finch observes, "Dick tried to reach Bill Rogers, or tried to reach someone at the White House to intercede, on King's behalf. But some hang-up occurred someplace. In the meantime, Kennedy had made the call and the damage was done." Oral History Interview, p. 54. See also Harris Wofford, Oral History Interview, John F. Kennedy Library, Columbia Point, Massachusetts, p. 23.

Nixon's greater accessibility to power and influence had backfired.

26. Nixon, Six Crises, p. 357.

27. Edward McCabe remarked that the timing of the unfortunate incident did

> "a great deal of damage to the Nixon candidacy. It set the stage...for a downgrading of the administration, its handling of foreign affairs. It set in motion...a feeling of great public annoyance, irritation, dissatisfaction... an undefinable kind of reaction that things weren't going well." (Oral History Interview, p. 74)

Nixon found himself with no alternative but to defend the administration, as he did on a May 1960 television show with David Susskind; see McCabe, Oral History Interview, p. 103. See also Hughes, The Ordeal of Power, p. 314.

28. *Minneapolis Sunday Tribune*, December 22, 1957.

29. Apparently, Nixon and several others in the administration had wanted a tax cut in order to give the economy a lift, but it was turned down. Agnes Waldron, Interview at her Washington, D.C., office, March 1974.

This is a clear indication of the bottleneck the incumbent Vice President is in. His candidacy is often jeopardized by circumstances, yet he has little or no decision-making power to ameliorate those circumstances. See Mazo and Hess, Nixon, p. 243

30. Finch, Oral History Interview, pp. 43-44, 50. Finch also reports that by 1959 a great deal of Nixon's time was spent in anticipation that Rockefeller would be his most critical opponent within the party; p. 50ff.

31. "Nixon's Way to the Top," *The New Republic* (June 9, 1973): 15ff.

32. Mazo and Hess, Nixon, p. 232ff.

33. Waldron, Interview, March 1974.

34. William Lawrence, Oral History Interview, John F. Kennedy Library, Columbia Point, Massachusetts, p. 13.

35. Vice-President's remarks re: farm policy June 21, 1960, Box No. 9, The Papers of Donald Paarlberg, Dwight D. Eisenhower Library, Abilene, Kansas.

36. Lawrence, Oral History Interview, p. 13.

Finch, in his Oral History Interview, pp. 59-60, comments:

The ultimate problem...was that he was

essentially defending an administration; an eight-year administration. So he was on the defensive, to that extent, and Kennedy could bring the attack to him, and did.

I recall he [Nixon] kept referring to the Eisenhower years as "the best years of our lives," and he was sensitive about his role in it....I think on balance, he felt that it had been a good administration and he was doing his best to defend it. But obviously there had accumulated ills that build up against any incumbent administration that's been in for eight years, and those were the things that Kennedy played on very well.

Hughes, The Ordeal of Power, p. 316, commenting on Nixon's "oddly mixed retorts" to Kennedy's accusations, concluded:

There was a tone to many of these...that strongly suggested the extravagance of a man angrily defying his own private doubts as much as those of the public. And the fact was that, for many months in Washington, there had been -not for the first time, his critics who would have insisted-two Richard Nixons occupying the office of the vice presidency. The first, the public Nixon, acclaimed Eisenhower as a savior of world peace, a statesman of rare acumen, and a national hero whom a thankful electorate would not dare to slight by a vote for the Democratic Party. The second, the private Nixon, patiently explained to visitors and journalists, in the off-the-record conversations or over intimate dinners, his dismay with White House leadership, his dissent from decisions in the field of national defense and foreign policy, and his anxiety to offer the nation a more youthful, more vigorous, and more coherent presidency-in the person of himself.

37. Parmet, <u>Eisenhower and the American Crusades</u>, p. 562; James David Barber, <u>The Presidential Character</u> (Englewood Cliffs, N.J.: Prentice-Hall, 1972), pp. 364ff.; 322. See also George Smathers, Oral History Interview, John F. Kennedy Library, Columbia Point, Massachusetts, p. 4.

38. Barber, <u>The Presidential Character</u>, p. 322.

39. Mazo and Hess point out that a Republican candidate has the added burden of dissociating himself from his party in order to capture Democratic votes. See *Nixon,* p. 321.

40. Hauge, Oral History Interview, p. 118.

41. Parmet, <u>Eisenhower and the American Crusades</u>, p. 517.

42. Hughes, <u>The Ordeal of Power</u>, pp. 320; 315ff.

43. Several observers noted Eisenhower's regret at not having participated in the campaign at an earlier stage. See Milton S. Eisenhower, Oral History Interview, p. 45; Howard K. Smith, Oral History Interview, p. 30.

Howard K. Smith maintains that the President was annoyed by the decision that he would not be needed in the 1960 campaign, a decision he felt was a mistake.

Sherman Adams claims Eisenhower was disappointed that the party had not been able to convert the younger independent vote. See <u>Firsthand Report</u> (New York: Harper, 1961), pp. 48-49.

44. Sigmund Larmon, an adviser from the business community, maintains that Eisenhower called Nixon and

volunteered his help, which the Vice-President accepted. Eisenhower reportedly kept saying, "Mr. Nixon has never asked me. He's never asked me. I've always been available." Following the bad results in the polls, Larmon and two other advisers, A. Alton Jones and Len Hall, decided that Eisenhower should make a television appearance for Nixon.

Oral History Interview, Eisenhower Administration Oral History Collection, Columbia University, New York, New York, pp. 82; 31.

Milton S. Eisenhower contends the Nixon people had not sought President Eisenhower's help earlier because they felt it would create the impression that Dick Nixon was "riding on the coattails of President Eisenhower." The President's brother also notes that Eisenhower thought the President of the United States should "represent all the people and not be partisan." However, he adds, the President did not participate when the tides turned against Nixon, and although he was disappointed by Nixon's defeat, he did not regard that defeat as a rejection of the administration. Oral History Interview, pp. 40; 44. See also Chalmers Roberts, Oral History Interview, Eisenhower Administration Oral History Collection, Columbia University, New York, New York, pp. 26-28 and 38, for more on the President's role in the 1960 campaign.

Larmon responds to one theory that Nixon had rejected large-scale politicking by Eisenhower because of concern over the President's health; see for example, Mazo and Hess, Nixon, pp. 26-27. Larmon does not believe that this was a primary consideration in Nixon's decision not to enlist the President's aid. Oral History Interview, pp. 33-34.

45. Paarlberg, Interview, March 1974. Paarlberg also noted that this was "a misguided effort and may have cost Nixon the election."

46. McCabe, Oral History Interview, p. 73. See also Drummond, Oral History Interview, pp. 26-27; James R. Shepley, Oral History Interview, Eisenhower Administration Oral History Collection, Columbia University, New York, New York, p. 31; and Charles Halleck, Oral History Interview, John F. Kennedy Library, Columbia Point, Massachusetts, p. 34.

   McCabe also noted that Nixon had been labeled "the hand-picked candidate who was going to continue the Eisenhower Administration."

47. Finch, Oral History Interview, p. 50.

48. George Christian, The President Steps Down (New York: Macmillan, 1970), pp. 148-49.

   Christian further notes:

   > On war policy Humphrey was left pretty much to his own devices. He sat on the National Security Council, but this body dealt mostly with broad policies other than Vietnam. The critical decisions on the war were made at the "Tuesday lunch" and supplemental meeting, especially in the last two years of the Johnson Administration. Humphrey was only rarely a participant in these sessions. Most of his insight into the President's deeper feelings about Vietnam came from private conversations with Johnson and from the routine flow of war information. As Vice President he participated in a few Vietnam decisions-such as the decision to bomb the North Vietnamese depots in 1966-but only a few.

50. Dean Rusk, Interview held at his Athens, Georgia, office, May 1973.

51. Walter Jenkins, Interview held at his Austin, Texas, office, April 1973.

52. Kenneth P. O'Connell, Telephone Interview, Boston, Massachusetts, February 1974.

During the 1968 campaign, Humphrey was vulnerable on the very issue of loyalty, regarding which vice presidential candidate Spiro Agnew said,

The Vice President must become convinced of the logic of the President's position. If it does such violence with his theory and his philosophy, I guess he has nothing left to do but to resign if he was really seriously concerned about his disagreement with the President.

Agnew's opponent for the Vice Presidency, Humphrey's running mate, Ed Muskie, agreed, saying, "I don't believe I could in any public office endorse a policy that violated my conscience." See "If a President and a 'Veep' Disagree," *U.S. News* 65 (September 16, 1968): 14.

53. Allan H. Ryskind, Hubert (New York: Arlington House, 1968), p. 319. See also Jules Wiitcover, The Resurrection of Richard Nixon (New York: Putnam, 1970), p. 323.

54. Ryskind, Hubert, p. 319; see also pp. 174-75.

55. Ibid., p. 176.

56. *Saturday Review* 48 (May 8, 1965): 16-17.

57. "The Bright Spirit," *Time* 87 (April 1, 1966): 21-25. Ryskind, Hubert, pp. 321-22 observed:

Humphrey has received some sharp criticism for his loyalty to the Johnson Administration, particularly from his old left-wing friends who cannot understand why their long-time ally is supporting the war effort. Yet his friends ignore the practical realities of politics. Assuming Humphrey desperately wishes to succeed to the Presidency-which, of course, no one doubts-he must be at least loyal to the crown.

His extravagant eulogizing of the President may be entirely in earnest, yet it is also the surest road to the White House. If Johnson were unhappy with the Vice President's performance, one can be certain that Lyndon would be making plans to unload Humphrey in 1968. Furthermore, Humphrey is well aware that his popular appeal is less than over-whelming, and that his most likely chance of succeeding to the Presidency is either through Lyndon Johnson's death, or by becoming LBJ's hand-picked successor after the Texan retires. Whatever Humphrey actually believes, his future welfare rests with what voters think about the Johnson Administration. Thus, it is clearly to his advantage to be the Saint Paul of the Great Society, the total defender of the faith.

58. David W. Abbott and Edward R. Rogowsky, Political Parties: Leadership Organization, Linkage (New York: Rand McNally, 1971), p. 254ff.: see also *"Politics Without Joy-On the Road with Hubert Humphrey"* U.S. News 65 (August 12, 1968): 30-31; Senator Herman Talmadge, Interview held at his Washington, D.C., Senate office, March 1974.

"His basic problem," wrote Albert Eisele, "...was that too many Americans regarded him as Lyndon Johnson without the Texas accent." *Almost to the Presidency* (Minnesota:

Piper Co., 1972), p. 334.

> Said another observer, "He had won the nomination because he had accepted the loss of his own identity.... He had availed himself of the President's piggyback to the nomination." Lewis Chester et al., <u>An American Melodrama: The Presidential Campaign of 1968</u> (New York: Viking Press, 1968), p. 577.

59. As cited by Eisele, <u>Almost to the Presidency</u>, p. 372.

60. Richard M. Scammon and Ben J. Wattenberg, <u>The Real Majority</u> (New York: Coward, McCann & Geoghegan, 1970), p. 119.

61. Christian, <u>The President Steps Down</u>, p. 157.

62. Chester, et al., <u>An American Melodrama</u>, p. 718.

63. Ibid.

64. "Chicago: The Assumptions About Nixon and Humphrey," *New York Times*, September 1, 1968.

65. *Wall Street Journal*, August 30, 1968.

66. *New York Times*, September 1, 1968.

67. See Eisele, <u>Almost to the Presidency</u>, p. 344ff., for a discussion of Humphrey's difficult position on the plank. The plank read: "We strongly support the Paris talks and applaud the initiative of President Johnson which brought North Vietnam to the peace table."

> *"Promises the Democrats Make: Promises for 1968,"* U.S. News 65 (September 9, 1968): 50-52. See New York Times, September 1, 1968, "Planks to Run On-Or Away From"

for a comparison of the Democratic and Republican 1968 platforms, both very similar in content.

68. Lyndon B. Johnson, <u>The Vantage Point: Perspectives of the Presidency</u> (New York: Holt, Rinehart & Winston, 1971), p. 432.

Johnson claims to have informed Humphrey of his decision the previous year and to have suggested that the Vice-President begin to ready himself for a campaign. See pp. 541ff. regarding Johnson's account of his conversation with Robert F. Kennedy.

69. See "Candidates Sure That Johnson Is Calling Signals on Convention," *New York Times*, August 15, 1968.

70. Eisele, <u>Almost to the Presidency</u>, pp. 347-48.

71. *"L.B.J., Nixon and the Campaign," U.S. News* 65 (September 9, 1968): 17-18.

72. Gerald R. Ford, Interview held at his Washington, D.C. office, March 1974; Dean Rusk, Interview, May 1973.

Ford, in response to a question asking him to comment on the suspicion that arises between the President and his Vice-President, pointed out that, in the Johnson-Humphrey case, even though Johnson had said he would not run, there was always the expectation that he might. Vice-President Ford went on to say that that certainly was not the case in his relationship with President Nixon, since Nixon was ineligible for reelection and he (Ford) had "no intention of running...so the competition isn't there."

73. Bill Welch, Interview held at his Washington, D.C. office, March 1974; Christian, <u>The President Steps Down</u>, p. 157

74. Hubert H. Humphrey, Interview held in a U.S. Senate reception room, Washington, D.C., March 1974.

75. Jenkins, Interview, March 1973.

76. Scammon and Wattenberg, *The Real Majority*, p. 170.

77. "Humphrey vs. Nixon vs. Wallace," *U.S. News* 65 (September 9. 1968): 31-33. For more on the Republican party's seeming unity, see Chester et al., <u>An American Melodrama,</u> p. 451ff.

78. As cited *"Nixon Looks to November: Here's His Strategy,"* in U.S. News 65 (July 29, 1968): 28.

79. Scammon and Wattenberg, <u>The Real Majority</u>, pp. 206-209. The authors add, "Perhaps the clearest indication Nixon gave that he understood these factors...was his choice of Spiro Agnew as Vice-President. It may be said, in fact, that Agnewism as a social thought won the election for Nixon, while Agnew, the individual, almost lost it for him."

80. See Eisele, <u>Almost to the Presidency</u>, p. 333ff.; Rusk, Interview, May 1973; *New York Times*, September 1, 1968; Chicago Daily News, August 14, 1968.

81. Johnson, <u>The Vantage Point</u>, p. 517.

82. Eisele, <u>Almost to the Presidency</u>, pp. 378-79.

83. *Vital Speeches* 35 (1968/9): 8-11.

84. Ibid.

85. Eisele, <u>Almost to the Presidency</u>, p. 377.

86. Ibid., pp. 377-78.

87. For more on Johnson's role, see Christian, <u>The President Steps Down</u>, pp. 153-54; 165ff.; 381ff.

Stephen A. Mitchell noted in a September 4, 1968, "Memo to Political File" that in a conversation with Humphrey,

We talked about the possibility of helping his ticket in Texas; that I had some standing among the liberal elements here and we would need all the help we could get, and he said "I know that very well and I realize that the leaders there have been making it very hard for me." (The reference was clearly to L.B.J.) He also said, "Yes, and the governor, too, had made it very hard for me." (Papers of Stephen A. Mitchell, Harry S Truman Library, Independence, Missouri.)

88. Johnson, <u>The Vantage Point</u>, pp. 513, 517. Johnson noted in his memoirs: "An election is a difficult time to try and carry out an objective foreign policy-or a domestic policy… .I had deliberately taken myself out of political contention in order to devote all my energy to the urgent tasks that remained." See Johnson, pp. 513, 548-50, for his views regarding Vice-President Humphrey's Salt Lake City speech and its potential impact on the ongoing peace talks with Hanoi.

89. Witcover, <u>The Resurrection of Richard Nixon</u>, p. 407

90. As cited by ibid., p. 420.

91. Ibid., pp. 429-30.

92. Ibid., p. 432.

93. Eisele, <u>Almost to the Presidency</u>, p. 350.

94. Ibid., p. 332.

95. Scammon and Wattenberg, <u>The Real Majority</u>, pp. 175ff..

96. Eisele, <u>Almost to the Presidency</u>, p. 357.

97. Scammon and Wattenberg, <u>The Real Majority</u>, pp. 144, 201.

Regarding the relative ability to perform effectively on law and order, the September Gallup poll indicated the following breakdown, as cited by Scammon and Wattenberg.

Nixon   36%

Wallace   26%

Humphrey   23%

Not sure   15%

98. *"Promises the Democrats Make: Platform for 1968,"* *U.S. News* 65 (September 9, 1968): 50-52.

99. Johnson, <u>The Vantage Point</u>, p. 424; David Halberstam, <u>The Unfinished Odyssey of Robert Kennedy</u> (New York: Random House, 1968), p. 113ff.; Chester et al., <u>An American Melodrama</u>, pp. 6-7.

100. Jack Newfield, *Robert Kennedy: A Memoir* (New York: E.P. Dutton, 1969), p. 218.

Newfield reports of Kennedy's hesitation that Kennedy had said,

My own brother suggested Lyndon Johnson to be the Vice President of the United States. All that is involved inside me. To break with the party that made my brother the President isn't a simple thing for me to do....I keep thinking that I represent something more than just myself, or my own ambition (Ibid., p. 224).

101. Eisele, <u>Almost to the Presidency</u>, p. 331. See also "Hubert Recycled," *Economist* 235: (June 13, 1970): 54+; Newfield, *Robert Kennedy*, p. 274ff., for Kennedy's attacks on Humphrey; "McCarthy's Win Strategy-Act II-Confrontation with Robert Kennedy," *New Republic* (April 23, 1968); and Chester et al., <u>An American Melodrama</u>, p. 310. Chester, et al., p. 738, also cite a summary of the situation by one of McCarthy's aides: "I thought the United States could only get out of the war if we cleared out everybody who had been locked into Johnson's policies. And that meant getting rid of Humphrey."

102. Newfield, <u>Robert Kennedy</u>, 169ff.

103. See "Era of Democrats Ending? A Shattered Strategy," *U.S. News* 65 (September 16, 1968): 29ff.; "Politics Without Joy-On the Road with Humphrey," U.S. News 65 (August 12, 1968): 30-31; *Los Angeles Times*, August 28, 1968, for Joseph Kraft's views in "The Democrats in Transition"; *New York Times*, Part II-5, March 5, 1968, for James Reston's expansion of this point in "Washington: The Decline of Party Politics."

104. See Chester et al., <u>An American Ordeal</u>, p. 343; p. 742, for more on McCarthy's reaction to the speech, as well as Eisele, <u>Almost to the Presidency</u>, p. 382ff.

105. Halberstam, <u>The Unfinished Odyssey of Robert Kennedy</u>, p. 48.

106. As quoted by Chester, et al., <u>An American Ordeal</u>, p. 424.

107. See Johnson, pp. 548ff., for his insightful analysis on the growing resentment toward the Democratic party on domestic issues and the war in Vietnam, and its effect on Humphrey's bid for the Presidency.

108. Robert Curran, <u>Spiro Agnew: Spokesman for America</u> (New York: Lancer Books, 1970), p. 143ff.

109. *New York Times Magazine*, pp. 38; 11.

110. Ibid.

111. According to a confidential source, Agnew's popularity in general, but especially his "Mr. Clean" image after the Watergate scandal broke, had resulted in bitterness within the White House, a bitterness that reportedly turned to glee once Agnew's own problems were disclosed.

112. *New York Times Magazine*, pp. 38; 11.

113. Ibid., p. 10ff.

114. Ibid., p. 11.

115. This is just the reverse of what Humphrey had said in 1968, and for precisely the same reason. Johnson's foreign policy was in serious trouble, while his domestic policy was well received. For Nixon, the problems were reverse. Each Vice-President, respectively, struck a note of independence only within the area of his President's trouble spots.

116. *Time*, July 2, 1973, p. 17.

117. *New York Times Magazine*, June 24, 1973, p. 11.

118. *Time*, July 2, 1973, p. 17.

119. Gerald R. Ford, Interview held at his U.S. Senate office, March 1974.

120. For a fuller account of the Nixon resignation, see *New York Times*, August 5, 6, 7, 8, 9, 1974.

121. In addition, under the provisions of the Twenty-Fifth Amendment, Ford was called upon to name his own successor to the Vice Presidency. The confirmation process through which he had been scrutinized just ten months earlier would begin anew, and Congress would find its impeachment proceedings against President Richard Nixon replaced by hearings on a new Vice President. Nelson A. Rockefeller, confirmed as Vice President in November 1974, was to be the second candidate within a matter of months to experience the close scrutiny of the Congress as a presidential appointee to the second highest office.

122. Jane Mayer, "The Dangers of President Pence," *The New Yorker*, October 23, 2017.

123. McKay Coppins, "God's Plan for Mike Pence," *The Atlantic Monthly*, January/February 2018, is a brilliant analysis of Pence's background, motivation, and behavior.

124. Carol E. Lee, Fristen Welker, Stephen Ruhle, Lafna Linzer, "Tillerson's Fury at Trump Required Intervention from Pence," NBCNews, October 4, 2017.

125. Niall Stanage, "Vice President Pence's Power in Trump White House," *The Hill*, 02/16/17.

126. Brian Beutler, "Is Mike Pence the 'Deep State' That Pence Fears?" *The New Republic*, August 10, 2017.

127. Nick Gass, "He Reminds Me of Ronald Reagan," POLITICO, July 9, 2016.

128. Kate Brower, <u>First in Line: Presidents, Vice Presidents, and the Pursuit of Power</u>, New York: Harper Collins, 2018), passim.

Chapter 5.

1. Hubert H. Humphrey, Interview held in a U.S. Senate reception room, March 1974.

2. Joseph Ernest Kallenbach, <u>The American Chief Executive</u> (New York: Harper & Row, 1966), pp. 232-33.

3. Speech File 63M143, Box XXII, 1952, The Papers of Alben W. Barkley, University of Kentucky Library, Lexington, Kentucky.

4. Ibid.

5. Kallenbach, <u>The American Chief Executive</u>, pp. 232-33. See also Sidney Hyman, <u>The American President</u> (New York: Harper, 1954), pp. 315-16; Michael Dorman, <u>The Second Man</u> (New York: Delacorte Press, 1968), p. 193; Harry S Truman, <u>Years of Decisions</u> (New York: Doubleday, 1955) p. 196.

6. Vice-President Statements, Container 3, Folder July 10, 1960, "Meet the Press," The Papers of Lyndon B. Johnson, Lyndon B. Johnson Library, Austin, Texas. See also "A Conversation with the Vice President," Vice-President Statements, Box 43, Interview, ABC News, March 26, 1963, Lyndon B. Johnson Library, Austin, Texas; Whitney M. Young, Jr., Oral History Interview, Lyndon B. Johnson

Library, Austin, Texas, pp. 1-11, for a review of Johnson's views of the historical view of the office.

7. "Apprentice President," *Economist* 213 (December 26, 1964): 1423.

8. "A Conversation with the President."

9. "Apprentice President," p. 1423.

10. Ohio State University Speech, Vice-President Statements, Container 3, Folder: September 29, 1960, Lyndon B. Johnson Papers, Lyndon B. Johnson, Library, Austin, Texas. See also "Apprentice President," p. 1423; Lyndon B. Johnson, <u>The Vantage Point: Perspectives on the Presidency</u> (New York: Holt, Rinehart & Winston, 1971), p. 2; Kenneth P. O'Donnell, Telephone Interview, Boston, Massachusetts, February 1974.

11. Albert Eisele, <u>Almost to the Presidency</u> (Blue Earth, Minnesota: Piper Co., 1972), p. 226.

12. As quoted by Rowland Evans and Robert D. Novak, <u>Nixon in the White House</u> (New York: Random House, 1971), p. 310.

13. President's Press Conference, May 31, 1955, Box 10 (SF) Fox, Folder: Vice-President. President's Press Conference May 31, 1955, Dwight D. Eisenhower Papers, Dwight D. Eisenhower Library, Abilene, Kansas. See also Michael Dorman, <u>The Second Man</u>, p. 209.

14. Joseph Albright, What Makes Spiro Run: The Life and Times of Spiro Agnew (New York: Dodd, Mead, 1972), p. 227.

15. Dorman. <u>The Second Man</u>, p. 224.

16. "Nixon's Own Story of Seven Years in the Vice Presidency," U.S. News 48 (May 16, 1960): 98-106.

17. Birch Bayh, <u>One Heartbeat Away</u> (New York: Bobbs-Merrill, 1968), p. 87.

18. Ibid.

19. As cited by Evans and Novak, Nixon in the White House, p. 168; Vice President Agnew concurred with this view; see "A New Kind of Vice President?" U.S. News 66 (March 17, 1969): 32-34.

20. Bayh, <u>One Heartbeat Away</u>, p. 87.

21. *Time* (July 2, 1973): 17.

22. *New York Daily News*, August 3, 1975.

23. *Time* (January 20, 1975).

24. "Walter Mondale," MacNeil/Lehrer Report, February 22, 1977.

25. Ibid.

26. *Christian Science Monitor* (March 3, 1981).

27. Hubert H. Humphrey, Interview, March 1974.

28. Vice-President Throttlebottom, a fictional character in the musical satire on the Presidency during the Franklin D. Roosevelt era entitled "Of Thee I Sing" was a nonentity who could not even obtain a library card because he lacked the requisite two references.

29. Harry S. Truman, <u>Years of Decisions</u>, p. 195ff. See also Frank McNaughton, <u>This Man Truman</u> (New York: McGraw-Hill, 1945), p. 191ff.; "Our Imaginary Vice," American Scholar 39 (Summer 1970): 387-94; Grant McConnell, <u>The Modern Presidency</u> (New York: St. Martin's Press, 1967), p. 59.

30. Alben W. Barkley, <u>That Reminds Me</u> (Garden City, N.Y.: Doubleday, 1954), p. 208.

31. Sidney Shalett, Interviews with Alben W. Barkley, Reel 6, side 1 (pp. 14-15; 18-23), Harry S. Truman Library, Independence, Missouri. Also on file at the Franklin D. Roosevelt Library, Hyde Park, New York. See also Barkley, That Reminds Me, pp. 105-14.

32. Dorman, <u>The Second Man</u>, p. 193ff.

33. For more on the Truman-Barkley relationship, see Barkley, <u>That Reminds Me</u>; pp. 105-14, Shalett Interviews, passim, Susan M. Hartmann, Truman and the 80th Congress (Missouri: University of Missouri Press, 1971), p. 17; Jonathan Daniels, Oral History Interview, Harry S Truman Library, Independence, Missouri, p. 49ff.

34. For more on this point, see Patrick Anderson, <u>The President's Men</u> (Garden City, N.Y.: Doubleday, 1968), passim, who also notes the trend toward greater reliance on staff, especially at the expense of Cabinet officials who, claims Anderson, have been the victims of a "centrifugal force.pulling them away from the presidential orbit, making them prisoners of their bureaucracies, giving them priorities and loyalties that may not be identical with the President's." See also Kallenbach, <u>The American Chief Executive</u>, p. 256; Truman, <u>Years of Decisions</u>, p. 330.

Anderson adds that the White House staff has increasingly come to displace the influence and advice of so-called Distinguished Outsiders, the wise men of the party and business community who had traditionally been sources of advice (p. 2).

See also James Gaither, Oral History Interview, Lyndon B. Johnson Library, Austin, Texas, p. 8, for his account of the duties and responsibilities the presidential staff must assume because the President cannot possibly handle them. For more on the Johnson staff, see Louis Heren, No Hail, No Farewell (New York: Harper & Row, 1970), passim.

35. Anderson, The President's Men, p. 10.

36. Ibid., p. 6.

37. Humphrey, Interview, March 1974.

38. Anderson, The President's Men, p. 9.

39. Ibid. See also McConnell, The Modern Presidency, p. 59ff.; Louis Clinton Hatch, A History of the Vice-Presidency of the United States (revised by Earl L. Shoup) (Westport, Conn.: Greenwood Press, 1934, 1970), p. 419.

40. "Nixon's Own Story."

41. Truman, Years of Decisions, p. 54, Herman Finer, The Presidency: Crisis and Regeneration (Chicago: University of Chicago Press, 1960), p. 294ff. echoed this, pointing out that a President can only give his Vice President a small amount of executive responsibilities, Jonathan Daniels, Oral History Interview, Harry S. Truman Library, Independence, Missouri, p. 50, talks of a President's heavy reliance on his

personal staff, rather than on a Cabinet official or the Vice President, because of political considerations.

42. Anderson, <u>The President's Men</u>, p. 7ff. See also Arthur Krock, Oral History Interview, John F. Kennedy Library, Columbia Point, Massachusetts, Part 1, p. 28ff.

43. James David Barber, <u>The Presidential Character</u> (Englewood, N.J.: Prentice-Hall, 1972), pp. 93-95; 129-40; 78-87; 347-442; 446-48.

44. Johnson, <u>The Vantage Point</u>, p. 2 Walter Jenkins said the same. Interview held at his Austin, Texas, office, April 1973.

45. "Apprentice President," p. 1423; see "Happy Understudy," Saturday Review 48 (May 8, 1965); 16-17, for additional material on Johnson's frustration in the Vice Presidency. This point was made by former Secretary of State Dean Rusk. Interview held at his Athens, Georgia, office, May 1973.

46. Barber, <u>The Presidential Character</u>, p. 79ff.

47. Francis Keppel, Oral History Interview, Lyndon B. Johnson Library, Austin, Texas, p. 28.

48. Walter Jenkins, Interview, May 1973.

49. Dean Rusk, Interview, May 1973.

50. Hubert H. Humphrey, Interview, March 1974.

51. Ibid. See also Allan H. Ryskind, <u>Hubert</u> (New York: Arlington House, 1968), p. 177ff. Bill Welch, in an interview held at his Washington, D.C., office in March 1974, talked about the lack of the Vice

President's follow up power, no matter what his constituencies may be.

52. Eisele, <u>Almost to the Presidency</u>, pp. 251; 236.

53. Ibid., pp. 237-38; see also "Happy Understudy."

54. Ryskind, <u>Hubert</u>, p. 323ff.; Johnson, <u>The Vantage Point</u>, p. 342; Walter Jenkins, Interview, April 1973.

55. Humphrey demonstrated the wisdom Truman had regarding the Vice Presidency, Truman had said that it is difficult for a President to always be open with his Vice President:

    A possible leak. every President realizes, need not be the result of an intentional act on the part of the Vice President. But an unintentional leak can be as harmful as an intentional one, and, conceivably, might upset the whole program on which a President is working. (Truman, <u>Years of Decisions</u>, p. 54.)

56. Barber, <u>The Presidential Character</u>, p. 83.

57. "I Enjoy It," *Newsweek* 65 (March 15, 1965): 28-29; Ryskind, <u>Hubert</u>, p. 320.

58. "The Bright Spirit," *Time* 87 (April 1, 1966): 21-25. See also "Foreign Policy--A New Strategy for Peace," *Vital Speeches* 35 (1968-69): 8-11 -- the much compromised speech in which presidential candidate Hubert Humphrey tried to sever his link with the administration's Vietnam policy.

59. Eisele, <u>Almost to the Presidency</u>, p. 231ff.

60. Ibid., p. 322.

61. George Christian, <u>The President Steps Down</u> (New York: Macmillan, 1970), pp. 148ff.; see also "Happy Understudy," for more on the question of Humphrey's role in Vietnam decision-making.

62. Eisele, <u>Almost to the Presidency</u>, p. 233ff.

63. Hubert Humphrey, Interview, March 1974.

64. Eisele, <u>Almost to the Presidency</u>, pp. 251; 237.

65. Ibid. See also "The Humphreys: Right Image for '68?" *U.S. News* 65 (September 9, 1968): 17-18; and "The Bright Spirit."

67. Robert Wood, Oral History Interview, Lyndon B. Johnson Library, Austin, Texas, p. 10. For more on Humphrey's other areas of expertise, see Christian, <u>The President Steps Down</u>, p. 148ff.; Dorman, <u>The Second Man</u>, pp. 165-83; Eisele, Almost to the Presidency, p. 226ff.; Ryskind, <u>Hubert</u>, p. 320; "I Enjoy It"; and "Apprentice President."

68. "The Bright Spirit."

69. William V. Shannon, <u>The Heir Apparent</u> (New York: Macmillan, 1967), p. 285.

70. Ryskind, <u>Hubert</u>, pp. 319-320.

71. Eisele, <u>Almost to the Presidency</u>, p. 240; "I Enjoy It."

72. Richard Rovere, <u>The Eisenhower Years</u> (New York: Farrar, Straus & Cudahy, 1956), p. 15ff.; 195.; Ralph DeToledano, <u>One Man Alone: Richard Nixon</u> (New York: Funk & Wagnalls, 1969), p. 163ff.; Richard Rovere, Oral History Interview, Eisenhower Administration Oral History Collection, Columbia University, New York, New York,

pp. 28-30, 35-36, 43; Sigmund S. Larmon, Oral History Interview, Eisenhower Administration Oral History Collection, Columbia University, New York, New York, p. 87; Robert Finch, Oral History Interview, Eisenhower Administration Oral History Collection, Columbia University, New York, New York, for a glimpse of Nixon's views on Eisenhower's lack of partisanship.

73. Jacob Javits, Oral History Interview, Eisenhower Administration Oral History Collection, Columbia University, New York, New York, p. 5.

74. Confidential interview with former member of the Eisenhower staff. The "Checkers debacle" referred to the Nixon difficulties during the 1952 campaign, during which he had to defend himself against charges of a questionable "slush" fund established by California businessmen. Nixon addressed the nation on television, during which speech he referred to his acceptance of only one gift in his political career, his dog Checkers. The speech has become widely known as the "Checkers" speech.

75. Rovere, The Eisenhower Years, p. 34.

76. "Washington's Rival Regents," *Economist* 185 December 21, 1957): 1049-50.

77. Javits, Oral History Interview, pp. 3-4.

78. Kenneth Keating, Oral History Interview, Eisenhower Administration Oral History Collection, Columbia University, New York, New York, p. 14.

79. See Rovere, The Eisenhower Years, p. 122, for more on this point.

80. See "Washington's Rival Regents" for a word on Nixon's party popularity, especially in comparison to Sherman Adams. DeToledano, <u>One Man Alone</u>, p. 162, takes the view that Eisenhower, contrary to the general characterization of a "bumbling refugee from the military life," was in reality "a consummate politician., who respected Nixon's ability to grasp and synthesize issues-and he used that ability to the maximum. He was keenly conscious of Nixon's expertise, his knowledge of the nitty-gritty of day-to-day politics." Nevertheless, Nixon was still afforded the opportunity to expand the role and functioning of the Vice Presidency. Laurin Henry, <u>Presidential Transitions</u> (Washington, D.C.: Brookings Institution, 1960), p. 490, feels that Eisenhower would have made good his campaign talk of an increased role for Vice President Nixon and would have given Nixon an even heavier assignment but that he had never forgotten or forgiven the 1952 slush fund scandal.

81. "Nixon's Own Story."

82. DeToledano, <u>One Man Alone</u>, p. 162ff.; OF 656 114-N, Folder: Cabinet Committee on Price Stability, Dwight D. Eisenhower Papers, Dwight D. Eisenhower Library, Abilene, Kansas; Frank McNaughton and Walter Hehmeyer, <u>Harry Truman, President</u> (New York:Whittlesey House, 1948), p. 215ff.; Box 31 (SF) Rogers, Folder: Nixon-VP. Correspondence Nixon to Jones, January 21, 1960, Dwight D. Eisenhower Papers, Dwight D. Eisenhower Library, Abilene, Kansas; Fred Lazarus, Jr., Oral History Interview, Eisenhower Administration Oral History Collection, New York, New York, p. 910.

83. Leverett Saltonstall, Oral History Interview, Eisenhower Administration Oral History Collection, Columbia University, New York, New York, pp. 140-41.

84. DeToledano, <u>One Man Alone</u>, p. 164. See also Rovere, <u>The Eisenhower Years</u>, pp. 296-97; Henry R. McPhee, Oral History Interview, Eisenhower Administration Oral History Collection, Columbia University, New York, New York, pp. 47-48.

85. DeToledano, <u>One Man Alone</u>, p. 164.

86. Mansfield D. Sprague, Oral History Interview, Eisenhower Administration Oral History Collection, Columbia University, New York, New York, pp. 47-48.

87. DeToledano, <u>One Man Alone</u>, p. 164.

88. Ibid., pp. 182-83; see also James R. Shepley, Oral History Interview, Eisenhower Administration Oral History Collection, Columbia University, New York, New York, pp. 29-30; OF 99B, Box 339, for an example of the Vice President's speeches on communism; Earl Mazo and Stephen Hess, <u>Nixon: A Political Portrait</u> (New York: Harper & Row, 1968), p. 209, regarding Nixon and Fidel Castro, p. 333ff. Prescott Bush, Oral History Interview, Eisenhower Administration Oral History Collection, Columbia University, New York, New York, pp. 328-37; 145-46; Emmet John Hughes, <u>The Ordeal of Power</u> (New York: Atheneum, 1963), p. 83ff., for more on Nixon and Joseph McCarthy; Jerry Voorhis, <u>The Strange Case of Richard Milhous Nixon</u> (New York: Paul S. Eriksson, 1972), pp. 17-18.

89. DeToledano, <u>One Man Alone</u>, pp. 183ff.

90. Ibid., pp. 186-87; see also Herbert S. Parmet, <u>Eisenhower and the American Crusades</u> (New York: Macmillan, 1972), pp. 347ff.

91. Ibid., p. 186ff., provides more on this point.

92. As cited by DeToledano, <u>One Man Alone</u>, p. 183; 190.

In a memorandum to DeToledano, Nixon said,

> My theory as far as relations with McCarthy are concerned is that while the President would undoubtedly win in any head-on clash with McCarthy, he could not help but be hurt in the process. A controversy would cause a very decided split among Republicans and could well lead to defeat for us in the 1954 elections. There may be a time when as a matter of principle the President may have to become involved in such a fight. But I think it is the responsibility of all of us to avoid it as long as we possibly can. It will give aid and comfort to no one but the Democrats. It is interesting to note that many of the columnists who have been taking the President to task for not attacking McCarthy are neither friends of McCarthy nor of the President.

> Nixon's leitmotif seemed to be the unity of the Republican party, above and beyond all else and for as long as possible. The memorandum to DeToledano explains the position he ultimately took in regard to McCarthy.

> McCarthy and I broke when he attacked the Administration. I did my best to avoid this break, not only because I felt it would be harmful to the party and the Administration, but because I felt it would be harmful to the cause of those who had been engaged in the anti-communist fight. McCarthy's intentions were right, but his tactics were, frankly, so inept at times that he eventually did our cause more harm than good.

93. Parmet, <u>Eisenhower and the American Crusades</u>, p. 431; "Address of Vice President of U.S. Before Global Syndicate Press Awards Dinner," New York City, June 24, 1955, OF 339 99B, Dwight D. Eisenhower Papers, Dwight D. Eisenhower Library, Abilene, Kansas; "Washington's Rival Regents"; (SF) Hagerty Papers, Folder: Nixon -- VP, Press Conference, June 30, 1954; "Responsibility for Delay in the Missile Program," Congressional Record, January 14, 1959, which includes Nixon's defense of the administration record; see William Knowland, Oral History Interview, Eisenhower Administration Oral History Collections, Columbia University, New York, New York, p. 9ff. See Parmet, Eisenhower and the American Crusades, p. 328ff., for a description of Nixon's role in relationship to labor and his delivery of presidential messages.

94. DeToledano, <u>One Man Alone</u>, p. 167.

95. Voorhis, <u>The Strange Case of Richard Milhous Nixon</u>, pp. 17-18, See Hughes, The Ordeal of Power, p. 83ff, for more on Nixon's role and Eisenhower's behavior in the struggle with Joseph McCarthy. See also Dwight D. Eisenhower, <u>Mandate for Change</u> (New York: Doubleday, 1963), chap. 13; DeToledano, <u>One Man Alone</u>, pp. 176-93; Henry, <u>Presidential Transitions</u>, p. 600ff.; Rovere, <u>The Eisenhower Years</u>, p. 297.; Bush, Oral History Interview, pp. 328-37.

96. Hubert W. Humphrey, Interview, March 1974.

97. Rovere, <u>The Eisenhower Years</u>, p. 319ff., provides more on this point.

98. This was underscored by President-elect Kennedy's November 14, 1960, visit to Nixon for the purpose of

discussion, Paul T. David et al., <u>The Presidential Election and Transition, 1960-61</u> (Washington, D.C.: Brookings Institution, 1961), p. 326ff.

99. Tom Wicker, <u>JFK and LBJ</u> (New York: Morrow, 1968), p. 172.

100. Lyndon Johnson, Interview with Walter Cronkite, CBS News, December 12, 1972, Lyndon B. Johnson Papers, Lyndon B. Johnson Library, Austin, Texas.

101. Kenneth P. O'Donnell, Interview (telephone) conducted in Boston, Massachusetts, February 1975.

102 Arthur M. Schlesinger, Jr., <u>A Thousand Days</u> (Boston: Houghton Mifflin, 1973), p. 705.

103. Johnson, <u>The Vantage Point</u>, p. 52ff.

104. See Roy Wilkins, Oral History Interview, Lyndon B. Johnson Library, Austin, Texas, p. 5ff., for more on Johnson and civil rights.

105. Christian, <u>The President Steps Down</u>, p. 148.

106. For more on this point, see Schlesinger, <u>A Thousand Days</u>, p. 693ff.; Norbert Schlei, Oral History Interview, John F. Kennedy Library, Columbia Point, Massachusetts, p. 22; Donald E. Larrabee, Oral History Interview, John F. Kennedy Library, Columbia Point, Massachusetts, p. 10; Emmanuel Celler, Oral History Interview, Lyndon B. Johnson Library, Austin, Texas, passim.

107. Schlesinger, <u>A Thousand Days</u>, p. 693ff.; Charles Halleck, Oral History Interview, John F. Kennedy Library, Columbia Point, Massachusetts, p. 37; Theodore

Sorensen, Kennedy (New York, Harper & Row, 1965), p. 267; Celler, Oral History Interview, p. 7; Donald Wilson, Oral History Interview, John F. Kennedy Library, Columbia Point, Massachusetts, pp. 27-28, for more on the JFK-RFK relationship.

108. See also Wicker, JFK and LBJ, p. 157.

109. Jenkins, Interview, May 1973.

110. Schlesinger, A Thousand Days, p. 705; Johnson, The Vantage Point, p. 278ff.; see also Richard E. Neustadt to Bill Moyers, February 28, 1961, FG 440, John F. Kennedy Papers. John F. Kennedy Library, Columbia Point, Massachusetts, in which Neustadt expressed concern for the protection of the constitutional position of the Vice President. Nicholas DeB. Katzenbach to Lyndon B. Johnson, April 18, 1961, provides the constitutional basis for the Vice-President's ability to serve as chairman of the National Aeronautics and Space Council, National and Aeronautics Space Council Microfilm, Reel 6, Lyndon B. Johnson Library, Austin, Texas.

111. Theodore C. Sorensen, Oral History Interview, John F. Kennedy Library, Columbia Point, Massachusetts, p. 1ff.; Sorensen, Kennedy, p. 525; Johnson, The Vantage Point, p. 278.

112. Dean Rusk, Interview, May 1973.

113. Pierre Salinger, With Kennedy (Garden City, N.J.: Doubleday, 1966), p. 333ff. See also "Happy Understudy."

114. Robert J. Sickels, Presidential Transactions (Englewood Cliffs, N.J.: Prentice-Hall, 1974), p. 52ff.

115. Albright, <u>What Makes Spiro Run</u>, p. 260ff.

116. As contained in Robert Curran, <u>Spiro Agnew: Spokesman for America</u> (New York: Lancer Books, 1970), p. 69ff.

117. Ibid., pp. 72-75.

118. Ibid., p. 75.

119. Ibid., p. 78.

120. Ibid., pp. 78-79; see also Evans and Novak, <u>Nixon in the White House</u>, pp. 213-313.

121. Curran, <u>Spiro Agnew: Spokesman for America</u>, pp. 89-90.

122. Ibid., pp. 91-98.

123. For more on the effects of the "effete corps of impudent snobs" speech, see Evans and Novak, <u>Nixon in the White House</u>, p. 314ff.; Curran, <u>Spiro Agnew: Spokesman for America</u>, pp. 17ff.; 85ff.; "Spiro Speaks," *Economist* (November 1, 1969) 233-50.

124. Richard M. Scammon and Ben J. Watternberg, <u>The Real Majority</u> (New York: Coward, McCann & Geoghegan, 1970), p. 211.

125. Judson L. James, <u>American Political Parties in Transition</u> (New York: Harper & Row, 1974), pp. 65-66, provides more on the potential Wallace candidacy in 1972; see also "Happy Warrior," *Economist* 233 (November 29, 1969): 51-52, Scammon and Wattenberg, <u>The Real Majority</u>, p. 208ff.

126. Curran, <u>Spiro Agnew: Spokesman for America</u>, pp. 107-20.

127. Ibid.

128. For further commentary on the Harrisburg speech, see Evans and Novak, Nixon in the White House, p. 314ff.

129. "Will the Press Be Out to Get Nixon?"

130. Curran, Spiro Agnew: Spokesman for America, pp. 121-30. For further commentary on the Des Moines speech, see Evans and Novak, Nixon in the White House, pp. 315-16, who claim that Pat Buchanan, a Nixon speechwriter, had focused on the idea and that Nixon knew about it from Buchanan. See also Voorhis, The Strange Case of Richard Milhous Nixon, pp. 254-56; and Albright, What Makes Spiro Run, p. 207ff.

131. Curran, Spiro Agnew: Spokesman for America, pp. 135-36.

132. Hubert H. Humphrey, Interview, March 1974.

133. Evans and Novak, Nixon in the White House, p. 315ff.

134. Barber, The Presidential Character, p. 429.

135. Kevin Phillips, The Emerging Republican Majority (Garden City, N.Y.: Doubleday, 1969), p. 23.

136. Evans and Novak, Nixon in the White House, p. 332.

137. James, pp. 202-203; Evans and Novak, Nixon in the White House, p. 332.

138. Evans and Novak, Nixon in the White House, pp. 333-34.

139. Albright, What Makes Spiro Run, p. 246.

140. New York Times Magazine, June 24, 1973.

141. Albright, <u>What Makes Spiro Run</u>, p. 232ff.; see *Time*, April 23, 1973, for a sense of Nixon's reduction of Agnew's role; "The Nixon Watch -- How It Works," *New Republic* (February 24, 1973); David Keene, Interview held at his Washington, D.C., office, March 1974.

142. *New York Times Magazine*, June 24, 1973; Albright, <u>What Makes Spiro Run</u>, p. 232ff.

143. Richard M. Cohen and Jules Witcover, <u>A Heartbeat Away</u> (New York: Viking Press, 1974), provides a good, thorough account of the Agnew investigation and scandal.

144. See also "A New Kind of Vice President?"; "The Bright Spirit"; White House File 192 FG440, Vice-President of the U.S., John F. Kennedy Papers, John F. Kennedy Library, Columbia Point, Massachusetts; DeToledano, <u>One Man Alone</u>, p. 160ff.; Evans and Novak, <u>Nixon in the White House</u>, p. 312; Louis W. Koenig, <u>The Chief Executive</u> (New York: Harcourt, Brace & World, 1964, 1968), p. 162ff.; Truman, <u>Years of Decisions</u>, p. 197ff.

145. Kenneth P. O'Donnell, Telephone Interview, February 1975.

146. For additional material on the Moscow trip, see OF 982. 225-D, Folder: Trip to Moscow, Nixon's Remarks in Poland, August 5, 1959, Dwight D. Eisenhower Papers, Dwight D. Eisenhower Library, Abilene, Kansas; OF 892. 225-D, Folder: Trip to Moscow, Nixon's remarks upon return from Moscow, August 5, 1959, Dwight D. Eisenhower Papers, Dwight D. Eisenhower Library, Abilene, Kansas; Hughes, The Ordeal of Power, p. 286ff.; Parmet, <u>Eisenhower and the American Crusades</u>,

pp. 547-48; OF 99B, Box 399, Dwight D. Eisenhower Papers, Dwight D. Eisenhower Library, Abilene, Kansas.

147. Howard K. Smith, Oral History Interview, Eisenhower Administration Oral History Collection, Columbia University, New York, New York, p. 28ff.

148. DeToledano, One Man Alone, p. 170ff.

149. Parmet, Eisenhower and the American Crusades, pp. 359-60.

150. DeToledano, One Man Alone, p. 170ff.

151. Confidential observer. See also Person to Willis, December 12, 1953, OF 116-I-A, Box 584, Dwight D. Eisenhower Papers, Dwight D. Eisenhower Library, Abilene, Kansas.

152. Mazo and Hess, Nixon, p. 280ff.; "Nixon's Own Story."

153. DeToledano, One Man Alone, p. 173.

154. Robert Finch, Oral History Interview, Eisenhower Administration Oral History Collection, Columbia University, New York, New York, p. 65ff. See also OF 586. 116-J-7. Remarks re: S. A. Trip, Dwight D. Eisenhower Papers, Dwight D. Eisenhower Library, Abilene, Kansas; OF 586. 111-J-5. Nixon's Trip to Middle American Countries, Dwight D. Eisenhower Papers, Dwight D. Eisenhower Library, Abilene, Kansas; GF 52. ZZ. 3-A-2. 1956 (3): "The Vice Presidency in 1956" -- Report by the Committee for Young Men in Government. Dwight D. Eisenhower Papers, Dwight D. Eisenhower Library, Abilene, Kansas; OF 853. 161-B. Vice-President's Trip to Austria. WH Press Release, December 12, 1956, Dwight D. Eisenhower Papers, Dwight D. Eisenhower

Library, Abilene, Kansas; OF 594. 116-NN. VP Report to Eisenhower on African Trip, April 8, 1957, Dwight D. Eisenhower Papers, Dwight D. Eisenhower Library, Abilene, Kansas; Mazo and Hess, Nixon, pp. 305-306; Parmet, Eisenhower and the American Crusades, pp. 273-74; Hughes, The Ordeal of Power; Prescott Bush, Oral History Interview, pp. 335-36; Milton S. Eisenhower, Oral History Interview, Eisenhower Administration Oral History Collection, Columbia University, New York, New York, p. 94; New York Times, May 15, 18, 1958; "Nixon's Own Story."

155. Albright, What Makes Spiro Run, p. 247; *New York Times Magazine*, June 24, 1973; *Time*, November 1, 1971, p. 20ff.; "A Look Inside the Nixon Administration," U.S. News 67 (October 6, 1969): 32-38.

156. Elie Abel, Oral History Interview, p. 48; Rovere, The Eisenhower Years, p. 56ff.; Roscoe Drummond, Oral History Interview, Eisenhower Administration Oral History Collection, Columbia University, New York, New York, p. 18; James R. Shepley, Oral History Interview, p. 29; "Nixon's Own Story."

157. Schlesinger, A Thousand Days, pp. 396-97; Jack Bell, Oral History Interview, John F. Kennedy Library, Columbia Point, Massachusetts, p. 5ff., who accompanied Johnson on the trip; Salinger, With Kennedy, passim; Sorensen, Kennedy, pp. 557; 594.

158. Sorensen, Kennedy, p. 653; Schlesinger, A Thousand Days, pp. 540-44; Wicker, JFK and LBJ, p. 199ff.; The Vantage Point, pp. 52ff.; 222ff; FG 440 August 22, 1962, Johnson's Mideast Trip, Lyndon B. Johnson Papers,

Lyndon B. Johnson Library, Austin, Texas; Bundy to LBJ, May 8, 1961, FG 440, Lyndon B. Johnson Papers, Lyndon B. Johnson Library, Austin, Texas.

159. Dean Rusk, Interview, May 1973. For more on the Johnson trips, see White House File 192, FG 440, VP of U.S., January 18, 1961-March 31, 1961, Lyndon B. Johnson Papers, Lyndon B. Johnson Library, Austin, Texas, for a sense of Johnson's early role as a replacement for Kennedy on ceremonial trips abroad. See Clarence Mitchell, Oral History Interview, Lyndon B. Johnson Library, Austin, Texas, p. 22f., and Roy Wilkins, Oral History Interview, p. 6ff., for the possible effects of Johnson's foreign travels on his domestic views.

160. Wicker, JFK and LBJ, p. 157.

161. Schlesinger, A Thousand Days, p. 705.

162. Eisele, Almost to the Presidency, p. 240; Johnson, The Vantage Point, p. 246; "Happy Understudy."

163. Eisele, Almost to the Presidency, p. 241; see also "The Bright Spirit."

164. *New York Times*, March 8, 1981.

165. Ibid., August, 1980.

166. Ibid.

167. Ibid.

168. Ibid.

169. *Christian Science Monitor*, March 3, 1981.

170. *New York Times*, March 29, 1981.

171. *New York Times*, March 25, 1981.

172. "Determined Second Fiddle," *Time* 116: (November 17, 1980) 38-39.

173. Ibid.

174. *Christian Science Monitor*, May 4, 1982.

175. Ibid.

176. Ibid., November 9, 1982.

177. *New York Times*, November 16, 1982.

178. Paul Kengor, "The Vice President, Secretary of State, and Foreign Policy," *Political Science Quarterly*, Vol. 115, n.2, 2000.

179. Vice President Richard ("Dick") Cheney, Speech delivered at the VFW 103rd National Convention, August 26, 2002.

180. Ibid.

181. White House Correspondent David Sanger, as quoted by Ron Brynaerl, "Vice President Cheney's Major Rhetorical Reversal on Iraq," *The Raw Story*, Sept. 2, 2006.

182. Ibid. Both Dick Cheney and former Secretary of State Condoleeza Rice disagree.

183. Joe Biden, Promise Me, Dad: A Year of Hope, Hardship, and Purpose (New York: Flatiron Books/Macmillan, 2017), p. 4.

184. Ibid., p. 63.

185. Ibid., p. 64.

186. Ibid.

187. Ibid., p. 4.

188. Barack Obama, as cited by Mark Liebovitch, *New York Times*, March, 2009.

189. Ibid.

190. McKay Coppins, "Trump Isn't Crazy to Question Mike Pence's Loyalty," *The Atlantic*, November 21, 2018.

191. Jane Mayer, "The Danger of President Pence," *The New Yorker*, October 23, 2017.

192. Address by Mike Pence, Indiana Republican, U. S. House of Representatives.   Delivered at Hillsdale College, Hillsdale Michigan, September 20, 2010. *Vital Speeches of the Day*, p. 504ff.

193. "Pence Is Trying to Control Republican Politics: Trump Aides Aren't Happy," *New York Times*, May 14, 2018.

194. "Vice President Mike Pence and the Government Shutdown," *The Atlantic*, Jan. 8, 2019.

195. Massoud Hayoun, "A Court Might Block Trump's Wall As Vice President Pence Argues Judges Should Not Have the Power To,; *Pacific Standard*, May 15, 2019.

196. Harriet Sinclair, "Pence Compares Trump to Roosevelt," *Newsweek*, August 18, 2017.

197. *Huffington Post*, October 8, 2016.

198. Brian Beutler, "Is Mike Pence the 'Deep State' That Trump Fears?" *The New Republic*, August 10, 2017.

199. Ron Klain, as cited by Beutler.

200. Chris Cillizza, "Mike Pence to Donald Trump: I Love You, Man," CNNPolitics, December 20, 2017.

201. Hubert H. Humphrey, Interview, March 1974.

202. Jane Mayer, "The Danger of President Pence, *The New Yorker*, October 23, 2017.

203. Ed Kilgore, "Mike Pence, First Toady," *New York Magazine,* December 6, 2017.

204. Ibid.

205. Josh Rogan, "Mike Pence Is Quietly Becoming a Foreign Policy Player," *The Washington Post,* March 6, 2017.

206. Ibid.

207. Ibid.

208. *New York Times,* May 14, 2018.

209. Josh Rogan, "Mike Pence Is Quietly Becoming a Foreign Policy Player, *The Washington Post, March 6, 2017.*

210. Ibid.

211. Jane Mayer, "The Danger of President Pence," *The New Yorker*, October 23, 2017.

212. Marie D. Natoli, "Perspectives on the Vice Presidency," *Presidential Studies Quarterly, Fall,* 1982.

213. Ibid., <u>American Prince, American Pauper: The Contemporary Vice Presidency in Perspective</u> (Greenwood/ Praeger, 1975); <u>American Prince, American Pauper:</u>

the Contemporary Vice Presidency and Presidential Relations, 2d. ed. (Trafford Publishers, 2010).

214. Vice President George H. W. Bush to Marie D. Natoli, November 26, 1982.

215. Conversation with Frances Humphrey Howard, Minneapolis, Minnesota, November, 1982.

216. Paul Kengor,"The Vice President, Secretary of State, and Foreign Policy," *Political Science Quarterly*, Volume 115,n. 2, 2000, p. 183.

217. Ibid., pp. 185-186.

218. As cited by Kengor, Ibid.

Chapter 6.

1. Time, November 19, 1975. Following Rockefeller's 1975 withdrawal from the nomination race, *Time* proclaimed that Rockefeller was even "overqualified" for the Presidency.

2. Michael Turner, "Finding a Policy Role for the Vice President: The Case of Nelson A. Rockefeller," unpublished Ph.D. dissertation, State University of New York at Binghamton, 1978, p. 320.

3. Ibid.

4. Ibid., p. 325.

5. Newsweek later reported the interaction between Ford and a "close associate" on this matter. Reportedly, the confidante had told Ford: "I have an idea that Nixon picked Spiro Agnew because he was insecure and didn't want anyone who would overshadow him. Don't you do anything like that! When you're President, you don't have to worry about being overshadowed by anyone." *Newsweek*, September 2, 1976; Turner, "Finding a Policy Role," identifies this "close associate" as Melvin Laird.

6. Turner, "Finding a Policy Role," pp. 314-15.

7. *Boston Globe*, July 10, 1975.

8. Ibid.

9. Ibid.

10. As Hubert Humphrey had termed it.

11. Carter news conference, New York City, July 15, 1976, quoted in the U.S. Congress, House of Representatives Committee on House Administration, *The Presidential Campaign, 1976, Vol. 1, Jimmy Carter,* 95th Congress, 2d Session, 1978, p. 317.

12. Transcription of 1976 Mondale-Carter Memo," Minnesota Historical Association.

13. Ryan Lizza, "The Mondale Memo," *The New Yorker,* October 13, 2008.

14. John Osborne, "Mondale at Work," *The New Republic* (April 23, 1977): 11-12.

15. "Walter Mondale," The MacNeil/Lehrer Report, WNET/ WETA, February 22, 1977, p. 5.

16. Osborne, "Mondale at Work," p. 10.

17. "Walter Mondale," p. 5.

18. Osborne, "Mondale at Work," p. 12.

19. *Los Angeles Times*, September 5, 1978.

20. Ibid.

21. *New York Times*, May 18, 1978.

22. Ibid., March 31, 1978.

23. Ibid.

24. Ibid., May 19, 1978.

25. *Chicago Tribune*, April 5, 1978.

26. Ibid.

27. *Los Angeles Times*, April 4, 1978.

28. *The Sun*, September 2, 1978.

29. *The Detroit News*, September 6, 1978.

30. In stark contrast to the role as administration spokesman which his mentor, Hubert Humphrey, had been forced to assume on Vietnam, even though Humphrey had not participated in policymaking in that area.

31. "Walter Mondale," MacNeil/Lehrer Report.

32. *Christian Science Monitor*, March 3, 1981.

33. Ibid.

34. Ibid.

35. Ibid.

36. Ibid.

37. Ibid.

38. *New York Times*, October 6, 1982.

39. Joel K. Goldstein, *The Modern American Vice Presidency* (Princeton, New Jersey: Princeton University Press, 1982), chapter 4 provides a useful discussion of the vice-presidential role in campaigns.

40. *New York Times*, August 24, 1984.

41. Bruce P. Montgomery, Richard B. Cheney and the Rise of the Imperial Vice Presidency (Westport, Ct., 2009), p. x.

42. Shirley Anne Warshaw, The Co-Presidency of Bush and Cheney (Stanford, CA: Stanford University Press, 2009), passim.

43. Ibid., pp. 58 – 59.

44. Robert Draper, Dead Certain: The Presidency of George W. Bush (New York: Free Press), p. 90.

45. Dana Millbank, "Cheney Authorized Shooting Down Planes," The Washington Post, June 18, 2004.

46. Peter Baker, Days of Fire (New York: Doubleday, 2013), p. 79.

47. Draper, pp. 177ff.

48. Warshaw, p. 6.

49. Jules Witcover, Joe Biden: A Life of Trial and Redemption (New York: HarperCollins, 2010), pp. 438ff.

50. Ibid., p. 40; also see Steven Levingston, Barack and Joe (Hatchett Books, 2019).

51. Ibid., p. 40

52. Mark Leibovitch, *The New York Times*, March 2009.

53. Brian Beutler, "Is Mike Pence the 'Deep State' That Trump Fears?" *The New Republic*, August 10, 2017.

54. *The New York Times*, August 6, 2017.

55. Gerald Ford, Interview, March, 1974.

56. Hubert H. Humphrey, Interview, March, 1974.

CPSIA information can be obtained
at www.ICGtesting.com
Printed in the USA
BVHW040555170922
647093BV00001B/16